D1222531

THE WORD OF GOD

ACCORDING TO ST. AUGUSTINE

THE WORD OF GOD

ACCORDING TO ST. AUGUSTINE

by

DR. A. D. R. POLMAN

Professor at the John Calvin Academy

Kampen, Holland

★

WM. B. EERDMANS PUBLISHING COMPANY

GRAND RAPIDS - MICHIGAN

DE THEOLOGIE VAN AUGUSTINUS
HET WOORD GODS BIJ AUGUSTINUS
PUBLISHED IN 1955 BY J. H. KOK N.V. KAMPEN

TRANSLATED BY A. J. POMERANS

PRINTED IN HOLLAND (1961)
BY DRUKKERIJ MEIJER N.V. WORMERVEER

CONTENTS

AUTHOR'S PREFACE TO THE ENGLISH EDITION

The publication of the English translation of my book has enabled me to enter into some of the criticisms which were voiced on the appearance of the original Dutch version, and quite particularly into the valuable comments by T. van Bavel (Revue d'Histoire Ecclésiastique 1956, pp. 945–47); W. F. Dankbaar (Nederlands Theologisch Tijdschrift 1957, pp. 37–59, and 62–63); R. Lorenz (Theologische Litteraturzeitung 1957, pp. 854–856); and E. Hendrikx (Studia Catholica 1958, pp. 232–236). As a result, I have completely revised part of the discussion of St. Augustine's views on the role of God's Word in the Church.

I am most indebted to Mr. Pomerans not only for the general excellence of his translation, but also for his agreement to consult the Oxford and Edinburgh editions of St. Augustine, whenever possible. Had he retranslated my Dutch quotations from St. Augustine, the inevitable distortion of the original would have been magnified even further.

A. D. R. POLMAN

GENERAL INTRODUCTION

One of the main reasons why it is not easy to write on the theology of St. Augustine is that his doctrine, far from being static, developed in the course of his life. St. Augustine may therefore be called the very antithesis of Calvin, who seized upon basic principles and then kept to them.

St. Augustine himself was sharply aware of this fact. Three years before his death, he wrote his remarkable *Retractationes* in which he tried to give an honest account of his development over the years, and in which he took stock of all his writings (with the exception of his Sermons and Letters). Still, it remains an open question whether or not St. Augustine did, in fact, appreciate his own development to the full and, after centuries of study, scholars continue to differ about the extent, date, and nature of these changes. Thus Etienne Gilson, in his well-known Introduction to the Study of St. Augustine, maintains that there were no changes at all in his fundamental belief, not even in the doctrine of grace. According to Gilson, therefore, St. Augustine changed his mind on minor points only[1]. On the other hand, Rottmanner, one of the greatest Roman Catholic authorities on St. Augustine, states quite frankly that St. Augustine's work will always remain a closed book to all those who ignore the radical changes in his thought. According to Rottmanner, no one who has not read all eleven folio volumes of the Benedictine edition has any right to pass an opinion on St. Augustine's theology. He makes his point by citing a number of striking errors of otherwise distinguished scholars[2].

Secondly, it must be remembered that St. Augustine never wrote systematic treatises in the manner of the later Scholastics. While he

[1] *Introduction à l'étude de Saint Augustin,* Paris 1949, 3rd ed., p. 310, note 1.
[2] *Geistesfrüchte aus der Klosterzelle,* München 1908 (passim).

had a keen logical mind, he was not a systematic writer, and though he rarely lost the thread of his argument, he liked to enliven it with all sorts of incidental points, puns included. His only attempt to write a systematic work *(Enchiridion ad Laurentium)*, was a hopeless failure, for though the book was instructive, brilliant, and penetrating, it was anything but what it set out to be. Closely related with this shortcoming, is the fact that important theological findings lie scattered throughout his writings—in a letter to a bereaved widow, in a keen controversy with one of the enemies of Christ's Church, in the exegesis of one of the books of the Old Testament, in a popular address, in confessions and soliloquies with God, or in the description of the battle between the City of God and the City of Devils. Thus a major point of St. Augustine's theology may be misinterpreted, simply because a subsequent change of outlook, hidden in a sermon or a letter, may have been overlooked. Or else a casual remark may be given too much weight, because it is not balanced against St. Augustine's theology as a whole.

In the third place, serious scholarship of St. Augustine's thought involves familiarity with the period in question, with its trends of thought, its social organisation, and its political, cultural, and religious problems. While there are many theologians whose doctrines can be expounded without reference to their personalities and times, St. Augustine's cannot. With him life and thought were closely related, and everything that impinged upon his Church and his world was reflected in his writings. He felt intensely responsible for the church and the world and gave himself wholeheartedly to any cause in countries near and far that could further the work of Christ's Body. Nor did he forget the individual Christian on whom he lavished all his pastoral love and care—as many of his moving letters bear out. While countless men had an effect upon his own work and thought, he, in turn, had as great an influence on as great a number of people. This very exchange of ideas lent his life much of its richness, but at the same time makes it difficult to do justice to his versatility. As Seeberg so rightly says: 'What normally breaks up into many, often opposed, schools and trends of thought, was in him (St. Augustine) an original creative whole, which, though not identical with any of its parts, yet gave its imprint to all. Such men have a prophetic view of what it will take later generations bitter struggles and fierce controversies to realise. Such minds may be compared with the flow of molten metal, which, while one stream now, will later become a means of peace or destruction'[3].

To give a systematic account of St. Augustine's theology, we must therefore do our utmost to gather, weigh, and collate the relevant material. The mere gleaning of the relevant facts is no light labour in the face of so much written material. Moreover, we must guard lest personal interests and prejudices cause us to neglect some aspects of St. Augustine's work and to overemphasise others. We cannot help being the products of our time, and, having problems of our own, we too often choose what suits our purposes—albeit unconsciously—and thus belittle St. Augustine's wide sweep of thought.

Giving correct weight to our findings presents another grave problem. Here the main danger is that we tend to apply standards which are the result of developments in Christian thought since St. Augustine's day. Thus certain ideas or terms may be explained in a sense which they assumed at a much later date. For instance, the word 'grace' is frequently interpreted in its later scholastic or Protestant sense. No wonder, then, that Roman Catholics, Anglicans, Lutherans, and Calvinists alike claim St. Augustine for their own.

Finally, the mere collation of the widely scattered material threatens to debase St. Augustine's thought into a system that he would have been the first to disown.

Even the greatest of scholars have not escaped all these pitfalls, as a mere comparison of Harnack's account with Seeberg's, or Mausbach's with Rottmanner's, will easily show. Hence we are under no illusion about our own studies in this field. True, forewarned is often forearmed, but there is no guarantee that we shall be able to avoid all the dangers. Still, even if we fail to be as objective as we sincerely hope we are, a Calvinist view of St. Augustine may rightly hope to receive a hearing. Roman Catholics, Anglicans, Lutherans and Neo-Protestants have all given their view of this great Father of the Church, and, after the great beginning made by Calvin himself, there is no reason why his work should not be continued.

We begin—and this, in itself, is a sign and proof of our Calvinist view—with an account of St. Augustine's doctrine of God's Word. Significantly enough, though the Word of God took so important a place in St. Augustine's life and thought, no comprehensive study on

[3] R. Seeberg, *Augustinus*, Stuttgart 1930, pp. 1 and 2.

this subject has been published—at least, not to our knowledge. We shall make a point of letting St. Augustine speak for himself, if sometimes in abbreviated form. Those who object to reading St. Augustine in translation, may take comfort in the fact that the original sources are always indicated; those, on the other hand, who complain about the wealth of quotations, may remember that they are, after all, the words of St. Augustine.

CHAPTER I

THE WORD OF GOD—CHRIST

No one familiar with the writings of St. Augustine will be surprised that we begin our discussion of his approach to, and his evaluation of, the Word of God with an account of his doctrine about the word Christ. After all, St. Augustine was always convinced that there was a very close connection between the two—each having an immediate influence on the other.

At first, St. Augustine, under the influence of Neo-platonism, saw Christ mainly as the eternal Word. The contemplation of this Word leads to knowledge of the truth and hence to salvation. Here, Christ's incarnation was no more than precept and example, just as, in the attainment of a blessed life of contemplation, the Scriptures are no more than a starting point. And the preaching of God's Word, is but a call to follow the glorious example of Christ.

Then this attitude of St. Augustine's gave way to one in which the philosophic interpretation of Christ as the Word still retained its value, but took its place side by side with a more scriptural interpretation, in which the Word was considered as the revelation of the Father, full of grace and truth. While St. Augustine always retained his longing for the contemplation of God's truth and wisdom, his deeper understanding of man's sinfulness and blindness caused him to shift the stress to the role of Christ as the Saviour and to His great acts of salvation. On the pilgrimage to the heavenly city, the Scriptures as the Word of Christ become a sure guide and a strong support, and in the preaching of His Word, we find the cause and the soil of the new life of the children of God.

This, by and large, was St. Augustine's development. Nowhere can we draw a sharp line between the first and second stages, for the entire process reflects the struggle in all spheres of St. Augustine's life and thought, between classical ideas and Christianity, between

Platonic idealism and prophetic realism[1], between Greek contemplative intellectualism and Biblical voluntarism[2]. Here as elsewhere, Christianity finally won the upper hand. St. Augustine likewise christianised and assimilated rather than rejected the noblest contributions of Greek philosophy, valuing them permanently as an anticipation of eternity. We shall now give a short sketch of both stages.

1. *The first stage.*

It would appear that, as a young man, St. Augustine, far from thirsting for forgiveness from sin and for God's grace, longed for the possession of truth and wisdom. At the age of nineteen, on reading Cicero's 'Hortensius' he was given 'an incredibly burning desire for an immortality of wisdom'[3]. Thus he was won over by the Manicheans simply because they claimed that the truth could only be attained by giving credence to reason[4], 'apart from all terror of authority and from the command to have faith before reason'[5]. 'Oh Truth, Truth! How inwardly did the marrow of my soul pant after thee!'[6] When this promise was not fulfilled, and the only way seemed to doubt all truth, St. Augustine came across some of the writings of Plotinus. 'Herein I read'—he wrote in his Confessions—'not indeed in the same words, but to the selfsame effect, enforced by many and divers reasons, that "In the beginning was the Word, and the Word was with God, and the Word was God. The same was in the beginning with God. All things were made by Him; and without Him was not any thing made that was made. That which was made is life in Him and the life was the light of man. And the light shineth in darkness and the darkness comprehended it not." And that the soul of man, though it "bears witness of the light", yet itself "is not that light" but the Word of God, being God, is that true light, that lighteth every man that comes in the world[7]. In like manner I read there,

[1] Johannes Hessen, *Augustins Metaphysik der Erkenntnis*, Berlin 1931, p. 15 ff.
[2] R. Seeberg, *Augustin und der Neuplatonismus.* In: *Moderne Irrtümer im Spiegel der Geschichte,* Leipzig 1912, p. 95–113; *Lehrbuch der Dogmengeschichte,* Leipzig 1923, II[3] p. 409 ff.; 511 ff.; *Augustinus,* Stuttgart 1930, p. 12 ff.
[3] Confess. III 7.
[4] De moribus Manichaeorum 55.
[5] De utilitate credendi 2.
[6] Confess. III 10.
[7] Confess. VII 13.

that God the Word was born not of flesh, nor of blood, nor of the will of man, nor of the will of the flesh, but of God. I discovered in those books that it was in many and divers ways said, that the Son was in the form of the Father, and "thought it not robbery to be equal with God", for that naturally He was the same substance. I read there, that before all times, Thy only-begotten Son remained unchangeably coeternal with Thee and that of His fullness souls receive, that they may be blessed; and that by participation of the wisdom remaining in them they are renewed, that they may be wise'[8].

This discovery was to become a revelation. He was dumbfounded to see how closely Plotinus' philosophy agreed with the beginning of the Gospel according to St. John. Never again was he to have any doubts on this question. Later, in one of his tractates on the Gospel of St. John, he declared that the Neoplatonic philosophers had clearly anticipated St. John's witness that all things were made by the Word of God. 'These things were also found in the books of the philosophers and also that God has an only begotten Son, by Whom are all things. These philosophers were able to see this, but they saw it from afar'[9]. In the *City of God* they are therefore praised above all other philosophers[10].

His opinion can no longer be upheld today, for all modern scholars know that there is no agreement between Plotinus and St. John[11]. A. Sizoo has pointed out which of Plotinus' words and phrases might have caused St. Augustine to discover this parallelism[12]. All of them occur in the first tractate of the Fifth Ennead, which St. Augustine had in fact been reading at that time. However, St. Augustine cannot

[8] Confess. VII 14; see also De vera religione 7.
[9] Tract. in Joannis evangelium II 4.
[10] De civitate Dei VIII 5–8; X 2.
[11] Cf. Eduard Zeller, *Die Philosophie der Griechen* III[2], 5th ed. Leipzig 1923: *Der Neuplatonismus*, pp. 468–735. See p. 495.
Joseph Wolf, *Der Gottesbegriff Plotins*, Leipzig 1927. See p. 19 ff.
Othmar Perler, *Der Nus bei Plotin und das Verbum bei Augustin als vorbildliche Ursache der Welt*, Freiburg in Sw. 1931. See p. 57 ff.; 106 ff.
Jakob Barion, *Plotin und Augustin, Unters. zum Gottesproblem*, Berlin 1935. See p. 40 ff.
Mary Patricia Garvey, *Saint Augustine: Christian or Neo-Platonist?* (diss.) Milwaukee 1939. See p. 52 ff.; 194 ff.; 236 ff.
Axel Dahl, *Augustin und Plotin. Philosophische Untersuchungen zum Trinitätsproblem und zur Nuslehre*, Lund 1945. See p. 30 ff.; 57 ff.; 84 ff. We hope to return to this subject in our discussion of the Trinity and Christology.
[12] A. Sizoo, *Toelichting op Augustinus' Belijdenissen*, Delft, p. 153.

have failed to notice a number of assertions in the same tractate which must have made it quite clear to him that even what appeared as parallel with the Gospel had been fused into a system radically different from Christianity. In particular, this is true of the clear gradation between the three archical[13] hypostases, of the difference between the *nous*[14] and the *logos*, and of the divinity of the soul.

How then could St. Augustine arrive at his firm convictions on this subject, particularly in the *Confessions* and subsequently in the *City of God?* The reason is, no doubt, that he read but a few of the Enneads, and even those only in translation. While Harder's claim that Plotinus' Greek is so difficult and full of grammatical pitfalls that no more than a score or so of people can claim to understand it nowadays, is surely somewhat exaggerated[15], it is nevertheless clear that all translations of Plotinus can be no more than approximations. If the claim of some scholars is correct, viz. that Victorinus Afer, after his conversion from Neoplatonism to Christianity, gave his translations of Plotinus an unconscious Christian twist[16] (a claim which is disputed by other scholars)[17], St. Augustine's concept of parallelism becomes a little more comprehensible. In any case, it is certain that, in his Milanese period, St. Augustine read no more Plotinus than the Treatise on Beauty and that he never read all the Enneads at any stage[18].

Moreover, in Milan he frequented Christian circles who generally assumed the affinity of Plotinus to St. John. When he told Simplicianus that he had read some of the books of the Platonists in Victorinus' Latin translation, Simplicianus testified his joy 'that he had not fallen upon the writings of other philosophers, which were full of fallacies and deceit "after the rudiments of the world", whereas the Platonists in many ways led to the belief in God and His Word'[19].

[13] Derived from arche, principle.

[14] The second of the hypostases. 'Mind', 'intellect', though really untranslatable. Perhaps thought about thought.

[15] *Plotins Schriften übersetzt*, Leipzig 1930, I, p. VII, quoted by Barion, p. 14.

[16] Ch. Boyer, *Christianisme et Néoplatonisme dans la formation de Saint Augustin*, Paris 1920, p. 83; R. Jolivet, *Saint Augustin et le Néoplatonisme chrétien*, Paris 1932, p, 123 ff.

[17] Barion, op. cit., p. 49 ff.

[18] Paul Henry (*Plotin et l'Occident*, Louvain 1934) thinks that St. Augustine read no more than I, 6; II, 2–3; IV, 3, 12, 17–25; V 1, 6. But cf. Pierre Courcelle, *Les lettres grecques en Occident*, Paris 1948, p. 159 ff.

[19] Confess. VIII, 3.

And in the *City of God* he narrates how Simplicianus used to tell him and his friends that a certain Platonist was in the habit of saying that this opening passage of the Holy Gospel according to St. John 'should be written in letters of gold, and hung up in all churches in the most conspicuous places'[20]. In Milan, St. Augustine also made contact with the Christian philosopher Manlius Theodorus who was a keen admirer of Plotinus[21]. St. Augustine was familiar with at least some of his books, and discussed God and the soul with him on a number of occasions. As a result, St. Augustine must clearly have been initiated into a form of Christian Neoplatonism[22]. It is even possible—although many pieces of this puzzle are still missing—that St. Ambrose, particularly in those of his sermons at which St. Augustine was present, had gone a long way towards 'christianizing' Neoplatonism[23].

In this way, we can understand how St. Augustine, by reading no more than a few of Plotinus' tractates and by adopting the christianized Neoplatonism of his day, could transpose Plotinus' philosophic speculations on the *nous* into Christian thought. Even in Cassiciacum, immediately after his conversion, he made it his maxim never to deviate one tittle from the authority of Christ, while expressing the hope that the Platonic philosophers might help him towards a real understanding of Divine truth[24]. Thus Plotinus was called in to help him to plumb the meaning of the Scriptural explanation that 'in the beginning was the Word and the Word was God'. Hence, it was in a purely Platonic sense that, in all his writings before 400 A.D., the Word was defined as 'the form of all forms', 'the most perfect of all forms'[25], 'the first species' (ontological form)[26], 'the rule, the form, the prototype or call it what you will of all that strives towards unity'[27], 'the exemplary cause of all things'[28], 'the seat of ideas, of all prin-

[20] De civitate Dei X, 29, 2.
[21] De beata vita 4.
[22] P. Courcelle, op. cit., p. 119 ff.; *Recherches sur les Confessions de Saint Augustin*, Paris 1950, p. 153 ff.
[23] Cf. P. Courcelle, *Plotin et Saint Ambroise. Revue de Philologie de littérature et d'histoire anciennes*, Paris 1950, pp. 29–56; *Recherches*, p. 93 ff.
[24] Contra Academicos III, 43.
[25] De vera religione 21.
[26] De divers. quaest. 83, 23.
[27] De vera religione 58.
[28] Epistula 11, 3.

cipal forms, of the fixed and immutable ideas of things'[29], 'the immutable force and eternal wisdom'[30], 'the Son through whom we exist, the form in which we are cast, the image of God by which we are formed and the Word by which everything is fashioned, by which we are re-formed to live wisely'[31]. This Word, which was with God and which was God Himself, this Word which contains all ideas[32], is not only the exemplary cause of all things[33], it is also the light which lighteth every man that cometh into the world[34]. Human instruction never goes further than admonition, awakening and stimulating thought. Christ as the Word is the inner teacher of all intelligible things grasped, not with the senses but with the spirit[35].

But what is the effect of his teaching?

The masses shut their eyes and ears to God's Word. They are caught in a lustful mesh[36]. Bogged down in the visible world, their souls are deceived by the senses, and they abandon the search for intelligible things[37]. Thus the masses deem themselves fortunate, indeed, when they can embrace the beautiful bodies of their wives or even of their whores with flaming lust, when they soothe their parched throats with clear spring water, when they still their hunger with lavish meals, when they can linger among flowers, and when they can savour the fragrance of delightful scents. Many entrust their happiness to song and string music, and bemoan their fates in the absence of these delights. They glory in the glitter of gold, silver, precious stones, colours, in the light of the sun, moon and stars, but they close their hearts to the beauty of wisdom and truth[38].

But even those devoted to the liberal arts can *never* be led to the contemplation of the intelligible world by reason alone, since their souls have become so blinded by the darkness of error and by the

[29] De divers. quaest. 83, 46, 2.
[30] De magistro 38–40.
[31] De vera religione 113.
[32] This idea was not rejected even after A.D. 400. Cf. De civitate Dei XI, 10, 3; De Gen. ad litt. V, 28; De Trinitate IV, 3.
[33] Epist. 11, 3; De vera religione 66; De divers. quaest. 83, 23. Cf. Perler, op. cit., *passim.*
[34] De vera religione 73.
[35] De magistro 38, 40; De Genesi contra Manichaeos II, 30; Epistula 7.
[36] De ordine I, 3, 24; II, 44.
[37] Contra Acad. III, 42; Solil. I, 24, II, 1; De ordine II, 24.
[38] De libero arbitrio II, 35, 36.

pollution of their bodies that they have forgotten that world[39]. Before the Fall, God spoke directly to man's soul but this privilege has been forfeited[40]. All knowledge of truth is thus derived from the Word as the inner teacher, but the fruit of this knowledge has been changed into pride and arrogance in those devoted to the liberal arts, so that they stray from the path and fall into darkness where God's light does not shine[41].

But then the Word became flesh!

Where someone has fallen, we must kneel down to help him[42]. The Word, which is the food of all righteous creatures, became visible the better to recall those who follow visible things to Himself, the Invisible. Thus the soul recovers the Word, from which it has turned away in pride, in visible humility. Only by humbling itself likewise can it return to God's invisible exaltation[43]. By His incarnation, He has shown carnal men who fail to seize the truth with their spirit, and who have become slaves to their senses, how high a place is assigned to man among all the creatures. Thus He appeared, not as an ethereal spirit but as man. He did nothing by force, but all by precept and example[44]. St. Augustine then contrasts the life of Christ with that of mortal man[45]. Christ came only to teach, and it is by following His example, that we can turn our soul inwards and receive back our fatherland.

Many are those who refuse to obey the call. They cannot submit to their Physician and refuse to abandon their lives of lust[46]. Others again, while open to persuasion, are too lazy or too stupid to use the exercise of the liberal arts as a ladder towards blessed contemplation. Their faith, by which they bend to Christ's authority, makes them blessed in the life to come, rather than in life on earth[47].

[39] Contra Academicos III, 42. It may be asked how the Neoplatonists could have invented these ideas, but St. Augustine fails to tell us. Cf. Jens Nörregaard, *Augustins Bekehrung*, Tübingen 1923, p. 131.

[40] De Genesi contra Manichaeos II, 5.

[41] Confess. V, 3, 4.

[42] De vera religione 45. This thought was fully retained later, as appears clearly from De Trinitate IV, 24.

[43] De libero arbitrio III, 30.

[44] De vera religione 30.

[45] De vera religione 31, 32. See also Contra Acad. III, 42; De ordine II, 27. Cf. Otto Scheel, *Die Anschauung Augustins über Christi Person und Werk*, Leipzig 1901, p. 26 ff., 80 ff.

[46] De ordine I, 24.

[47] De ordine II, 15, 26.

Things are quite different with those whose souls have been enriched with knowledge and who have been fashioned by virtue[48]. They follow the strait path, once Christ's authority has touched them. They are not satisfied with faith alone, but thirst for understanding, as well. For that reason, education in the liberal arts is a necessary means towards an unclouded vision of the sublime truth[49]. The world with its symbols and education awakens us and counsels us to turn inwards[50], not in order to make us feel sinful and force us to throw ourselves penitently upon God's mercy, but rather for the sake of immortality and the majesty of the intellect and the number by which alone man can advance to the contemplation of the truth and wisdom of the eternal Word, and hence to salvation[51]. In the rational soul, i.e. in the inward man, Christ dwells as in His temple. In him He appears as the Word. In him He is a source of inspiration and purification, feeding all those who adhere to Him[52]. Though St. Augustine had come to pay less heed to erudition than to love and moral purification[53], he had not changed his basic approach. Once the soul is purified, it appreciates its own grandeur to step out boldly towards God, that is towards the contemplation of truth[54]. United with Christ, Wisdom, and Truth, in sanctity the soul is awakened to an all-embracing love that eradicates all vices[55]. Even when St. Augustine subsequently went back on his belief in complete purification on earth[56], his purpose and direction remained unchanged.

This is doubtless connected with the fact that the Scriptures as the Word of God are only allotted a place in the forecourt of the temple. Without them, we cannot enter, but once we are admitted they have no further part to play. The stupid and lazy mass of mankind on earth probably never advances beyond this forecourt[57], but

[48] De ordine I, 24.
[49] De ordine II, 30 ff.
[50] De ordine II, 51; De magistro, *passim*; De Gen. contra Manich. II, 43; De Musicis VI, 29, 44; De libero arbitrio II, 13, 14.
[51] De ordine II, 48 ff.; De libero arbitrio II, 35 ff.
[52] De magistro 38; De quantitate animae 55, 80.
[53] De Musicis VI, 1. Cf. F. Hoffmann, *Wandlungen in der Frömmigkeit und Theologie des hl. Augustins,* Theol. und Glaube, 1930, p. 411 ff.
[54] De quantitate animae 79.
[55] De moribus ecclesiae 22, 64.
[56] Cf. Hoffmann, l. c.
[57] De ordine II, 5 ff. De utilitate credendi 33 ff.

the wise—later the holy and the spiritual—no longer need the Scriptures as authority. On three occasions, St. Augustine described their development without once mentioning the Scriptures[58]. True, they do not despise the Church or the milk of which St. Paul spoke in 1 Corinthians 3:2. A child must take this kind of nourishment from its mother, but once it grows older, it will prefer more solid fare. Still, we deplore the ungrateful manners of the child who spits out milk while he still needs it, and the impiety of the adult who condemns or hates it[59]. By the time that St. Augustine reviewed the matter in his *Sermon on the Mount*, his attitude had begun to change: In the first stage, the soul submits itself to divine authority. Then, at the second stage, it comes to the knowledge of the divine Scriptures. After that the Word of God is no longer consulted. At the sixth stage, there is purity of heart which, with a good conscience springing from good works, can contemplate the highest good by pure intellect alone. Lastly there is, at the seventh, wisdom itself, i.e. the contemplation of the truth, tranquillizing the whole man and bearing the likeness of God. And these promises can indeed be fulfilled in this life as we believe them to have been fulfilled in the Apostles[60].

The change in attitude appears even more clearly—we are close to St. Augustine's later view —when, for the fifth time, he outlines the development of the Christian in his *De doctrina Christiana*. First of all, it is necessary, at the first and second stages, that our hearts be subdued by the *fear of God* and by *piety*, so that we crucify all the motions of pride and pedantry.

After these two steps of fear and piety, the Christian comes to the third step—knowledge, in which every earnest student of the holy Scriptures exercises himself to find simply that God is to be loved for His own sake, and our neighbour for God's sake. 'So awakes the true self-knowledge by the Scriptures and the piety which gives him no option but to believe in and submit to the authority of Scripture, compel him to bewail his condition. And in this frame of mind he implores with unremitting prayers the comfort of the Divine help and so he gradually comes to the fourth step—that is strength

[58] De quantitate animae 70–76; De vera religione 49; De Genesi contra Manichaeos I, 43.

[59] De quantitate animae 76. Cf. F. Hoffmann, *Der Kirchenbegriff des hl. Augustinus*, München 1933, p. 46, Note 71.

[60] De sermone in monte I, 10–12.

and resolution—in which he hungers and thirsts after righteousness. He extricates himself from every form of fatal joy in transitory things and fixes his affection on things eternal, to wit the unchangeable Trinity in unity. At the fifth step follows the purification and so he mounts to the sixth step, in which he purifies the eye itself which can see God, so far as God can be seen by those who as far as possible die to this world. Such a man ascends to wisdom, which is the seventh and last step and which he enjoys in peace and tranquillity'[61]. Clearly the Scriptures were already given an important place in the life of Christians, but still St. Augustine continued to hold that man can advance beyond the Scriptures towards contemplation and wisdom. True, he has to make a temporary halt at the third stage of knowledge. After all, the entire book was written to introduce us to the knowledge of the Divine writings. Still, that stage is not the final one—albeit reached by few—where this help is no longer needed. And so St. Augustine declares in the first book of his *Doctrina* that any man who rests upon faith, hope, and charity, and who keeps a firm hold on these, does not need the Scriptures except for the purpose of instructing others. Accordingly, he says, many live without copies of the Scriptures even in solitude on the strength of these three graces, so that in their case the saying: 'whether there be prophecies they shall fail, whether there be tongues they shall cease; whether there be knowledge, it shall vanish away' (1 Cor. 13:8)[62] is already fulfilled.

We have reached the turning-point. During the same year (397 A.D.) there came a decisive change in approach which, slowly, led to a new orientation.

Not that Neoplatonism had lost its influence overnight, or was ever completely repudiated. This is particularly true of two of St. Augustine's ideas:

1. His notion of the immanent relations of the Holy Trinity. St. Augustine never relinquished his Neoplatonic idea of the Word which was in God and which was God Himself. This becomes very apparent in his sermons on the Gospel according to St. John, and in his work on the Trinity. In fact, it was a clear sign of his change of

[61] De doctrina Christiana II, 9–11.

[62] De doctrina Christiana I, 43. Romeis has tried to justify this attitude, but we cannot accept the reasons he has given. (P. Kapistran Romeis, *St. Augustins Bibelstudium und Stellung zur Bibellesung*, Fulda, Frauenberg 1911, p. 7 ff.)

attitude, that he so much as broached these involved questions during his sermons. He no longer developed an esoteric form of theological argument in front of a small group of intellectuals, but had begun to realise that God's people also, who had received salvation from the Holy Spirit, were in need of solid food. Thus this great preacher of the hidden truths of God, spoke movingly to God's congregation of God's profound mysteries. In the very first sermon, in which he preached on St. John I, 1–4 he compared Christ as the Word with our own words which are spoken only to disappear. 'What sort of a word, then, is that, which is both uttered and passes not away? There is a word in the man himself which remains within; for the sound proceeds from the mouth. There is a word which is spoken in a truly spiritual manner, that which you understand from the sound, not the sound itself. Mark, I speak a word, when I say "God". How short the word which I have spoken—four letters and two syllables (deus). Is this all that God is: four letters and two syllables? Or is that which is signified as costly as the word is paltry? What took place in thy heart, when thou heardest "God"? What took place in my heart when I said "God"? A certain great and perfect substance was in our thoughts transcending any changeable creature of flesh or of soul. What then is that in thy heart, when thou thinkest of a certain substance, living, eternal, all-powerful, infinite, everywhere present, everywhere whole, nowhere shut in? When thou thinkest of these qualities, this is the word concerning God in thy heart. But is this that sound which consists of four letters and two syllables? Therefore, whatever things are spoken and pass away, are sounds, are letters, are syllables. This word which sounds passes away, but that which the sound signified, and was in the speaker as he thought of it and in the hearer when he understood it, that remains while the sounds pass away[63]. Turn thy attention to that word. Thou canst have a word in thy heart, as it were a design born in thy mind, so that thy mind brings forth the design; and the design is, so to speak, the offspring of the mind, the child of thy heart. For first thy heart brings forth a design to construct some fabric, to set up something great on the earth; already the design is conceived and the work is not yet finished, thou seest what thou wilt make, but another does not admire, until thou hast made and constructed the pile, and brought that fabric into shape and to completion; then men regard

[63] Tractatus in Joannis evangelium I, 8.

the admirable fabric and admire the design of the architect; they are astonished at what they see and are pleased with what they do not see. Who is there who can see a design? If then on account of some great building a human design receives praise, do you wish to see what a design of God is the Lord Jesus Christ, that is, the Word of God? Mark this fabric of the world. View what was made by the Word and then thou wilt understand what is the nature of the Word. Mark these two bodies of the world: the heavens and the earth. Who will unfold in words the beauty of the heavens? Who will unfold in words the fruitfulness of the earth? From this fabric, then, judge the nature of the Word by which it was made and not it alone. By that Word angels also were made, powers, thrones, dominions, principalities; by that Word were made all things. Hence, judge, what a Word this is[64]! But how were all things made by Him? "That which was made, in Him is life"[65]. For He is the wisdom of God and it is said in the Psalm: In wisdom, i.e. in Christ, hast Thou made all things[66]. If then all things were made in Him and that which was made was life in Him, is then the earth life and wood life? The earth was made, but the very earth that was made is not life; but there exists spiritually in the wisdom itself a certain reason by which the earth was made: this is life[67]. A carpenter makes a box. First he has the box in design; for if he had it not in design, how could he produce it by workmanship? But the box in theory, is not as it appears to the eyes. It exists invisibly in design, it will be visible in the work; has it ceased to exist in design? The actual box is not life, to design the box is life; because the soul of the architect is living. So because the Wisdom of God, by which all things have been made, contains every thing according to design, before it is made, therefore those things which are made through this design itself are not forthwith life, but whatever has been made is life in Him[68]. The words that we speak are fleeting and transient; as soon as thy word has sounded from the mouth, it passed away; it makes the noise and passes away into silence. Thy thought, however, remains and of that thought that remains thou utterest many words that pass away. What say we, brethren? When God spake, did He give out a voice, or sounds, or

[64] ib. 9.
[65] St. Augustine's and other Church Fathers' rendering of verse 4.
[66] Ps. 104: 24.
[67] Tractatus in Joannis evangelium I, 16.
[68] ib. 17.

syllables? If He did in what tongue spake He? In Hebrew or in Greek, or in Latin? Tongues are necessary, where there is a distinction of nations. But there none can say that God spake in this tongue, or in that. Observe thy own heart. When thou conceivest a word to utter, thou meanest to utter a thing, and the very conception of the thing is already a word in the heart: it has not yet come forth, but it is already born in the heart, and is waiting to come forth. But thou considerest the person to whom it is to come forth, with whom thou art to speak: if he is a Latin, thou seekest a Latin expression; if a Greek, thou thinkest of Greek words; if a Punic thou considerest, whether thou knowest, the Punic language: for the diversity of hearers thou hast recourse in divers tongues to utter the word conceived; but the conception itself was bound by no tongue in particular. As in fact thou hast in thy heart the word that thou speakest, and as it is with thee, and is none other than the spiritual concept in itself (for just as thy soul is spirit, so also the word which thou hast conceived in spirit; for it has not received sound to be divided by syllables, but remains in the conception of thy heart and in the mirror of thy mind), so God gave out His Word, that is, begat the Son. And thou, indeed, begettest the word even in thy heart according in time; God without time begat the Son, by whom He created all times'[69].

St. Augustine developed the same thoughts in his work on the Trinity. In the fourth book he states that 'all things are together in the Word of God, by way of principle and unchangeable, not only those things which are now in this whole creation, but also those which have been and those which shall be, because the Word of God is One and the unchangeable truth. And therein they neither have been, nor shall be, but only are; and all things are life, and all things are one, or rather it is one being and one life'[70]. In the fifteenth book he points out at some length, that 'whoever is able to understand a word, not only before it is uttered in sound, but also before the images of its sounds are considered in thought—for this is which belongs to no tongue—whoever also is able to understand this, is able now to see through this glass and in this enigma some likeness of that Word of whom it is said: "In the beginning was the Word and the Word was with God and the Word was God". For of necessity, when we

[69] Tractatus in Joannis evangelium XIV, 7; cf. XXIII, 8 ff.

[70] De Trinitate IV, 3. Scheel (op. cit. p. 173) wrongly takes this as proof that St. Augustine had adopted Platonic Pantheism. Cf. the quotation on p. 20.

speak what is true i.e. speak what we know, there is born from the knowledge itself which the memory retains, a word that is altogether of the same kind with that knowledge from which it is born. For the thought which is formed by the thing which we know, is the word which we speak in the heart; which word is neither Greek, nor Latin, nor of any other tongue. But when it is needful to convey this to the knowledge of those to whom we speak, then some sign is assumed whereby to signify it. And generally a sound, sometimes a nod, is exhibited that the word which we bear in our mind may become known also by bodily signs to the bodily senses[71]. Accordingly, the word that sounds outwardly is the sign of the word that gives light inwardly; which latter has the greater claim to be called a word. For that which is uttered with the mouth of the flesh, is the articulate sound of a word, and is itself also called a word on account of that to make which outwardly apparent it is itself assumed. For our word is so made in some way into an articulate sound of the body, by assuming that articulate sound by which it may be manifested to men's senses. But we must not regard the word of ours that sounds in the ears, either when it is uttered in an articulate sound or when it is silently thought, if we are to arrive at any likeness of the Word of God. We must pass by this, in order to arrive at that word of man, by the likeness of which, be it of what sort it may, the Word of God may be somehow seen as in an enigma. We must go on, then, to that word of man, to the word of the rational soul, to the word of that image of God, that is not born of God, but made by God; which is neither utterable in sound nor capable of being thought under the likeness of sound, but which precedes all the signs by which it is signified, and is begotten from the knowledge that continues in the mind, when that same knowledge is spoken inwardly according as it really is. For the sight of thinking is exceedingly like the sight of knowledge. For when it is uttered by sound or by any bodily sign, it is not uttered according as it really is, but as it can be seen or heard by the body. When, therefore, that is in the word which is in the knowledge, then there is a true word. And so this likeness of the image that is made, approaches as nearly as is possible to that likeness of the image that is born, by which God the Son is declared to be in all things like in substance to the Father[72]. From the storehouse

[71] De Trinitate XV, 19.
[72] ib. 20.

of the memory is begotten a word that is true, when we speak what we know, but a word that is before all sound, before all thought of a sound. For the word is then most like to the thing known, from which also its image is begotten, since the sight of thinking arises from the sight of knowledge; when it is a word belonging to no tongue, but it is a true word concerning a true thing, having nothing of its own, but wholly derived from the knowledge from which it is born. But as our knowledge is unlike that knowledge of God, so is our word also, which is born from our knowledge, unlike that Word of God which is born from the essence of the Father. And this is as if I should say, born from the Father's knowledge, from the Father's wisdom, or still more exactly, from the Father who is knowledge, from the Father who is wisdom'[73].

One thing is plain from the above quotations: St. Augustine continued to use Platonic and Neoplatonic concepts and ideas to explain even such Scriptural facts as the immanent relationship of the Trinity. Plato already knew the distinction between 'voice' and 'word', between 'sound' and 'meaning', between unspoken and spoken words[74]. Plotinus distinguished between the spoken word and the word in the spirit, the former being an image, an imitation, of the latter, even in the definition of the three divine hypostases[75]. In the *nous*, he saw the archetypes of all being[76]. In this connection, Plotinus even brought in the simile of art and the box, which St. Augustine later used in his sermon. Since Plotinus looked upon ideas as the archetypal causes of all being, the visible world must derive its forms from an external source, much as fashioned wood receives its form from the art of the sculptor or carpenter[77]. Plotinus also considered the visible world with all its magnificence, beauty, order, visible and invisible gods, demons, plants, and animals, as pointing towards the archetype, its truest reality—the *nous*[78].

St. Augustine, on the other hand, tried to subordinate this use of Neoplatonic ideas to the authority of the Scriptures as the Word of God. In all conflicts between the Word and pagan philosophy, he

[73] ib. 22. See also 23.
[74] Cf. K. Kuypers, *Der Zeichen- und Wortbegriff im Denken Augustins*, Amsterdam 1934, p. 59 ff.
[75] Enneads I, 2, 3; V, 1, 3, 6.
[76] ib. V, 9, 5.
[77] ib.
[78] ib. V, 1, 4.

always and unerringly chose the former. Thus there was a complete denial of any subordination of the Word to the Father[79]. Moreover, St. Augustine declared, in flat contradiction with the doctrine of the *nous* in the Plotinic system, that the Word of God is so much in the form of God as not to have been formable before it was formed, or to have been capable at any time of being formless[80]. His differences from Neoplatonism emerge more clearly still when we appreciate that, on the basis of Scripture, he teaches that 'Christ is called the Word of God only relatively, but the power and wisdom of God that whereby He is essence'. Now, for years, he had been in danger of falling under the sway of Modalism. More than once he had identified wisdom with the word of God so as to express by these names two apparently unrelated attributes. Thus St. Augustine called the Son the Divine Intellect[81], the immutable power and the eternal wisdom of God[82], and, elsewhere, he wrote that, whenever God is called wise, He is not so called from participation in wisdom, but because He Himself begat wisdom, whence He is called wise[83]. All these ideas can be explained in the orthodox way, but the question remains whether, under the sway of Neoplatonism, St. Augustine did not in fact confuse the second hypostasis with Divine wisdom. Only in the seventh book of his *De Trinitate* did he finally resolve this question. Here, he gave a detailed answer to the question which he had posed in the preceding book[84] viz. whether the Father is wise and is Himself His own wisdom, or whether He is wise in the same way as He speaks. 'For He speaks by the Word which He begat and is equal to Himself, by whom He always and unchangeable utters Himself. For He is not Himself the Word, as He is not the Son

[79] He does this right from the start. As early as in *De vera religione*, the ontological unity of Son and Father is unequivocally propounded. Even Scheel (op cit., p. 38) who claimed elsewhere that St. Augustine's early christology was a complete replica of Neoplatonic ideas, had to recognise this fact. Bruining has stressed that this distinction is so essential, that a complete reproduction of Neoplatonic ideas is out of the question. St. Augustine used these ideas merely in order to serve his Christian faith (Collected Works, Groningen 1923, I, p. 298).

[80] De Trinitate XV, 25. Arnon has pointed out that this rejection can already be found in De beata vita 34 (*Dictionnaire de Théologie Catholique,* Paris 1935, XII, col. 2337).

[81] De ordine II, 16, 26; Contra Acad. III, 42.

[82] De magistro 38.

[83] De quaestionibus diversis 83, 23.

[84] De Trinitate VI, 1.

nor the image. But in speaking by that co-eternal Word, He is not understood singly, but with that Word itself, without which certainly He does not speak. This is the question: if He is in such way wise as He is one who speaks, so that both are relative concepts? This discussion has arisen from that which is written, that "Christ is the power of God and the wisdom of God"'[85]. Is the Father not singly powerful or wise, but together with the power and wisdom itself, which He begat, just as He is not singly one who speaks, but by that Word and together with that Word which He begat? To that question St. Augustine gave the clear answer, that, while all the attributes of God are identical with His essence, in the names Father, Son, Word, and Image, essence is not expressed, since they are spoken relatively. 'Therefore the Father and the Son are one essence and one greatness and one truth and one wisdom. But the Father and Son both together are not one Word, because both together are not one Son. For as the Son is referred to the Father, and is not so called in respect to Himself, so also the Word is referred to Him whose word it is, when it is called the Word. And therefore He is not the Word in that He is wisdom; since He is not called the Word in respect to Himself, but only relatively to Him whose Word He is, as He is called the Son in relation to the Father; but He is wisdom by that whereby He is essence. And therefore, because one essence, He is one wisdom'[86].

By now St. Augustine had moved a long way from Plotinus, who would have rejected all suggestions that the three hypostases could possibly be one being, one wisdom, and one power[87], as being opposed to Neoplatonic hierarchical ideas. As an implicit rather than explicit consequence of his new view, St. Augustine realised that the Divine Being rather than His Word must henceforth be considered the seat of all ideas, the better to attribute these qualities to the Son. This is borne out by his remarks in the *Retractiones*, viz. that he had been wrong to identify the intelligible world with the Kingdom of God[88].

[85] 1 Cor. 1 :24.
[86] De Trinitate VII, 1–3.
[87] Cf. Perler, op. cit., p. 106 ff.
[88] De Ordine I, 32. Constantin Ritter's suggestion (*Mundus intelligibilis*, Frankfurt 1937, p. 34 ff.) that the identification of the intelligible world with God's Kingdom already shows traces of the christianization of the Platonic ontology, cannot be verified from the sources. It is not that St. Augustine explained the intelligible world according to God's Kingdom, but rather that he explained that Kingdom by Platonic concepts.

Not that he wished to deny the existence of an intelligible world altogether, for he went on to say: 'Nor did Plato err in stating that there is an intelligible world, if we distinguish his terminology, which is not of the customary ecclesiastical usage in this connection, and attend only to the matter of what he says. For the world which he called by the name "intelligible" is that eternal and unchangeable reason by which God made the world'[89]. Thus Platonic ideas in their totality were taken to exist only as thoughts of God. Henceforth, in fact, Augustine expressly retracted his earlier point of view, propounded in *Quaest.* 83, 23, in favour of the new interpretation of the *De Trinitate*[90].

Hence it seems quite clear that St. Augustine looked upon Neoplatonic concepts as being no more than aids towards the interpretation of Biblical facts, which alone have complete Divine authority. However—and this is the crux of the matter under discussion—these concepts cannot be used for purely formal purposes; they always involve a measure of infiltration of Greek thought. His Neoplatonic and un-Biblical interpretation of the Word (Logos) in *On St. John* and the *Trinity* is proof positive of the justice of our claim, for that interpretation is suffused with Greek love for the contemplative life as man's highest goal. The identification of word and concept, and its use as an analogy for the immanent relation, within the Trinity, of the Father and the Word is deeply rooted in Greek intellectualism.

2. The very interpretation of the Logos as the inner teacher who shows us how to contemplate truth was never rejected by St. Augustine, and made its influence felt throughout his writings on the Word of God as Holy Writ and as proclamation. Just as the sensory world is only a symbol of the true, intelligible, world, simply awakening us to the contemplation of the latter, so St. Augustine continued to consider the Word as Holy Writ purely as a symbolic representation, and to ascribe to the word as proclamation the function of awakening us and of showing us the way. Fritz Hoffmann has perhaps exaggerated his otherwise excellent case when he says: 'Two basic truths were of

[89] Retract. I, 3, 2. Note in passing the radical reinterpretation of Plato's real doctrine. Only 'by means of the most fantastic and forced interpretation' (Verdenius: *Christianiserende en historische Plato-interpretatie*, Ned. Theol. Tijdschr. 1954, p. 129) can this meaning be read into Plato.

[90] ib. I 26.

lasting significance in all his subsequent thought, one ontological and the other epistemological, and both derived from Neoplatonism: the clear, dualistic, distinction between mind and matter, between lasting truth and transitory appearance, between inner and outer, and the concept of the "*magister intus*" according to which the *logos* is the only true teacher, in comparison with which all external words and material signs are mere "symbols" of the truth and "calls" to strive after it, which, short of inner illumination, fail to provide the truth by themselves'[91].

We shall now give a telling example. During his well-known sermons on the First Epistle of St. John, St. Augustine preached on the text: 'But the anointing which ye have received of him abideth in you, and ye need not that any man teach you' (1 John 2:27). He interpreted this text as follows: 'What, then, are we doing (in the pulpit), brethren? What can we teach you when His anointing teaches you all things? And why do we call out so loud? Why not leave you to His anointing so that you be taught by it? Yet I ask myself and indeed the apostle himself: Were they indeed anointed to whom you spoke? Truly, you have said, his anointing teaches you all things. Why therefore have you written your epistle? What were you teaching them? Why have you devoted yourself to their education? Lo, brethren, here lies the great mystery. The sound of our words meets the ears, but the teacher is within. Do not think that man can learn from man. We can but admonish with the sound of our voices, but if there is no one inside to teach, the sound of our voices is vain. Do you wish me to adduce proof of this contention? Have you not just heard this sermon of mine? How many of you will leave here without having learned anything at all? For my part, I have addressed you all, but those of you who are deaf to that inner anointing, who are not taught by the Holy Spirit within, will leave without any learning. External teaching is but a means of awakening you. In the Heavens, the pulpit is His who teaches man's hearts. Thus saith the Lord: Call no one your teacher on earth. Christ alone is your teacher. He Himself will be your inner voice, even when no man is about. Thus it is the inner teacher who will teach you. Christ teaches. His inspiration teaches. Where His inspiration and anointing are not, words from the outside will fall on deaf ears. Our outer words are alike to a grower and his tree. He works from

[91] op. cit., p. 48; cf. also pp. 259 ff., 275 ff., 292 ff.

the outside, he uses water, and tends the tree carefully. Does his outer application form the fruit? Does it cover the bare branches with shade-giving leaves? Or is this done from the inside? But who is inside? Listen to the husbandman, the Apostle Paul, and learn what you are; listen to the inner teacher: I have planted, Apollos watered, but God gave the increase (1 Cor. 3:6). God, that is His anointing, teaches you all things'[92]. All the characteristic traits of St. Augustine's epistemology, which was constructed under the influence of Neoplatonism, are found again in this assessment of the value of sermons. The antonyms outside–inside, the sound of the spoken word—the inner teacher, external education as a means of awakening and inspiring us through the inner Christ—all are of Neoplatonic origin. Accordingly, the sermon is used by His servants to call man's attention outwardly by the signs of things, while He Himself teaches men inwardly by the things themselves[93]. In a truly Neoplatonic way, words are here considered as mere signs of things[94]. Once again, we can see the fatal influence of this ancient philosophy, which was bound to interpret the Word in this way since it was ignorant of God's Word and work in history. Thus St. Augustine's adoption of its precepts often obscured his view of the full significance of God's Word as proclamation. In what we have called St. Augustine's second stage this attitude was certainly the exception rather than the rule. Here, the power of God's word generally breaks through the Neoplatonic system, to unmask its profound poverty. However, St. Augustine never openly renounced the system as such.

2. *The second stage.*

St. Augustine reached this stage purely through his deeper study of, and his dedicated reflections on, the Scriptures as the infallible Word of God. Against his own will, he had become a presbyter in Hippo in 391 A.D. Significantly enough, his first request to Bishop Valerius was to be granted Easter leave in order to study the Scriptures. Now that he had become second helmsman, he felt all the greater a need for learning to handle the oars[95]. From that moment on, he was to

[92] In epist. Joannis Tract, 3, 13; see also 4, 1.
[93] Epistula 144, 1 (412).
[94] See particularly the work of K. Kuypers, who discusses the subject in detail.
[95] Epistula 21.

devote his entire life to Scriptural study, all the while discovering new truths which wrought radical changes in his outlook—particularly during the years 391–397 A.D.[96]. His ideas on sin (original and actual), on the scope of human knowledge and ability, on man's need for God's grace, on faith, and the Church—all underwent far-reaching modifications, with direct repercussions on his soterology and soteriology.

This is shown in his ever more Biblical view of the Word which was with God and was God Himself. In his *De fide et symbolo* (391 A.D.) he wrote the following: 'We believe also in Jesus Christ the Son of God, the Only-begotten, that is, the only Son of the Father, our Lord. Of which Word, notwithstanding, we ought to conceive not as of our own words, which being put forth by the voice and mouth, strike upon the air, and pass away, nor exist any longer than they sound. For that Word abideth unchangeably. But therefore was He called the Word of the Father, because by Him the Father is made known. As therefore by our words this is our purpose, when we speak the truth, that our own mind may become known to him who hears us, and that whatsoever we hear secretly in our heart, may by means of signs of this sort be brought forth for another to understand: so that Wisdom which God the Father begat, seeing that by It there is made known unto worthy minds the most hidden Father, is most suitably called His Word. But there is a very great interval between our mind and our words, by which we endeavour to make known this our mind. That is, we do not beget audible words, but make them, and the body is the subject-matter for making them. But there is a very great difference between mind and body. But God, when He begat the Word, begat That which Himself is. For this we also endeavour, in speaking, if we diligently consider the aim of our will; not when we lie, but when we speak the truth. For what other thing do we attempt, than to carry our very mind, if practicable, into the mind of the hearer, that he may know and see it thoroughly; that we may indeed ourselves remain within ourselves, and not depart from ourselves and yet may put forth such a sign as that there be produced in the other a knowledge of us. This we do endeavouring both by words and by the very sound of the voice, by the countenance and

[96] See my: *De praedestinatieleer van Augustinus, Thomas van Aquino en Calvijn*, Franeker 1936, p. 37–57; Karl Adam, *Die geistige Entwicklung des heiligen Augustinus*, Darmstadt 1954, p. 24 ff.

by the gesture of the body, that is to say, by so many contrivances, desiring to shew that which is within. But God the Father, who both willed and was able to declare Himself most truly to minds about to know Him, This begat in order to declare Himself, which Himself is who begat; who also is called His Power and Wisdom, because by Him He wrought and set in order all things'[97]. Though the Neoplatonic influence can still be detected in this text, the Scriptural significance of the Word has clearly been pushed into the foreground. For the first time, St. Augustine stressed the importance of the Word as the adequate revelation of the Father speaking to us through the Son—a fundamentally Scriptural concept. The emphasis has been shifted from Neoplatonic seeing to Semitic hearing. This concept of the Word will often recur. Thus St. Augustine liked to stress that God's 'speaking' is without beginning and without end, and that yet the Word He utters from His heart, His very inmost, is but 'One'[98]. He also held up Christ's dictum that no man knoweth the Son but the Father, neither knoweth any man the Father save the Son, and he to whomsoever the Son will reveal Him[98]. 'Now, the Father reveals Himself by the Son, that is, by His Word. For if that word which we utter, and which is temporal and transitory, declares both itself, and that of which we speak, how much more the Word of God, by which all things are made? For this Word so declares the Father as He is the Father; because both itself so is and is that which the Father, in so far as it is wisdom and essence'[99].

But if, under the influence of Scriptural revelation St. Augustine turned towards a more Biblical interpretation of God's Word, he nevertheless retained a philosophic explanation by its side. This is shown clearly when, in the 12th Book of his *De Trinitate*, he made a clear distinction between wisdom and knowledge, the former embracing intellectual cognizance of eternal things, and the latter rational cognizance of temporal things[100]. In Book XIII he asserts that wisdom must be given pride of place, as is shown in St. John 1:1–14: 'For the first four verses call for a contemplative life, and must be discerned by the intellectual mind; and the more anyone has profited in this, the wiser without doubt will he be-

[97] De fide et symbolo 3, 4.
[98] Matth. 11:27; Enarr. in Ps. 44, 5.
[99] De Trinitate VII, 3; see p. 24
[100] De Trinitate XII, 25.

come'[101]. Now the philosophic interpretation of the Word of God which we found in St. Augustine's sermons on the Gospel according St. John and in his work on the Trinity, is part and parcel of the exercise of this kind of wisdom, which is far exalted above the knowledge of temporal things.

What is entirely new in St. Augustine's second stage is the full appreciation of Christ as the only Redeemer Who saves His chosen people by reconciling them with God. Christ's divinity and humanity were recognised by St. Augustine ever since his conversion to Christianity, but the new factor, according to Karl Adam's just observation, lies 'in the question what special functions in building and extending Christian life must be attributed to Christ's divinity and what special functions to His humanity. This question really amounts to asking ourselves whether we are saved because Christ is the divine wisdom of all wisdom, or because Christ became our brother in the flesh. Are we redeemed from error through the Word of God, or from sin through God's Servant? In his early days, St. Augustine favoured the first, and in his later, riper days, the second approach, which thereafter lent his entire theology its special colour'[102]. Originally, St. Augustine laid the stress on the divine Word and considered Christ's humanity as having a purely exemplary function. Christ's humility destroys our spiritual pride and forces us to contemplate the Word, which, as eternal truth, redeems our souls. Then he shifted the emphasis to the great historical acts of redemption which form the basis for man's reconciliation with God. Christ's incarnation, crucifixion, resurrection, and ascension show those who admit our sinfulness before God, the priestly and royal glory and importance of Christ as the mediator between God and man[103].

Again and again, St. Augustine's writings now reflected God's love for us, poor sinners though we are, through Jesus Christ. 'How hast Thou loved us, good Father, who sparedst not Thine only Son but deliveredst Him up for us ungodly! How hast Thou loved us, for whom, He who thought it no robbery to be equal with Thee, was made subject even to the death of the cross, He free alone among the dead having power to lay down His life and power to take again: for

[101] ib. XIII, 1 ff., 24.
[102] op. cit., p. 25.
[103] These ideas were first developed in De diversis quaest. 83, 61.

us to Thee both Victor and Victim, and therefore Victor, because the Victim; for us to Thee Priest and Sacrifice, and therefore Priest because the Sacrifice; making us to Thee, of servants sons, by being born of Thee and serving us'[104].

Philosophic systems, which have always tried to work out their own salvation and which have always held that salvation had to be earned rather than received, had no conception of these miracles of Grace[105]. True, the Platonists discovered that 'in the beginning was the Word, and the Word was with God, and the Word was God, the Creator of all things', but they knew nothing of the miracle of the Word being made flesh. None of their writings bear witness to the fact that He would die for the godless in due time. 'For Thou hiddest these things from the wise, and revealedst them to babes'[106]. 'Therefore those pages (of the works of the Platonists) contain not the expression of this piety—the tears of confession, Thy sacrifice, a troubled spirit, a broken and a contrite heart, the salvation of the people, the espoused city, the earnest of the Holy Ghost, the cup of our redemption. No man sings there: Shall not my soul be subject unto God? For of Him cometh my salvation, for He is my God and my salvation, my defender, I shall not be further moved. No one there hears Him calling: Come unto Me all ye that labour. They scorn to learn of Him, because He is meek and lowly of heart, for Thou hast hid those things from the wise and prudent and has revealed them unto babes. For it is one thing from the mountain's wooden summit to see the land of peace and not to find the way thither—in vain to attempt impassable ways, opposed and waylaid by fugitives and deserters, under their captain the "lion" and the "dragon", and another to keep to the way that leads thither, guarded by the host of the heavenly general where they rob not who have deserted the heavenly army, which they shun as torture[107]. They (the Platonists) have been able to penetrate with the eye of the mind beyond the whole creature and to touch, though it be in ever so small a part, the light of the unchangeable truth; a thing which they deride many Christians for being not yet able to do, who, in the meantime, live by faith alone. But of what use is it for the proud man, who on that

[104] Confessiones X, 69.
[105] Epistula 156, 2.
[106] Confess. VII, 13, 14.
[107] ib. 27; cf. A. Sizoo op. cit., p. 164.

account is ashamed to embark upon the ship of wood (an allusion to the cross), to behold from afar this country beyond the sea? Or how can it hurt the humble man not to behold it from so great a distance, when he is actually coming to it by that wood upon which the other disdains to be borne?'[108]

In this connection, St. Augustine gives a detailed account of how Platonism could not have fitted great historical facts into its philosophy[109]. This was the great privilege of Israel's prophets who had proclaimed the great truth, centuries earlier[110]. Then Christ Himself came to fulfil His task of reconciliation and redemption. His great historical acts of salvation are made known to us by the Scriptures alone, which therefore must take pride of place. The Bible is the inspired Word of God. In the proclamation of the Word of Christ and His Gospel, God performed the miracle of salvation. In this Word, in which God sealed His promises by His own hand, and fulfilled them through Jesus Christ, all true believers will find succour and great spiritual strength. All these ideas, which we shall discuss in greater detail in subsequent chapters, were clarified by St. Augustine during his second stage. But even the Scriptures must one day be superseded, essential though they are for every Christian's pilgrimage, and though they alone hold the key to our knowledge of God and to the wisdom which contemplates God's eternal truths[111]. Both find their concentration in Christ Jesus, in Whom are hid the treasures of all wisdom and of all understanding[112]. 'Therefore Christ is our knowledge, and the same Christ is also our wisdom. He Himself implants in us faith concerning temporal things, He Himself shows forth the truth concerning eternal things. Through Him we reach on to Himself: we stretch through knowledge to wisdom; yet we do not withdraw from one and the same Christ, in whom are hidden all the treasures of wisdom and of knowledge'[113]. However, all Christians confidently look forward to that eternal life in which prophecies, tongues, and signs have done, in which the Scriptures will have fulfilled their task and the pure in heart will behold God

[108] De Trinitate IV, 20.
[109] ib. 21–23; cf. K. Kuypers, op. cit., p. 46 ff.
[110] ib. 23.
[111] For a fuller discussion of this distinction, see Henri-Irénée Marrou, *Saint Augustin et la fin de la culture antique*, Paris 1949, p. 368 ff., 561 ff.
[112] Coloss. 2 : 1–3.
[113] De Trinitate XIII, 24. See also ib. XIV, 3.

and His Word face to face[114]. Thus life on earth and life to come revolve about the Word Christ, Who, as God, is the fatherland to which God's people are hastening, and Who, as Man, is the way they pursue, so that they may walk safely and be preserved from all error[115].

[114] Enarr. in Ps. 119, 6.i.
[115] Sermo 123, 3.

CHAPTER II

THE WORD OF GOD AS HOLY SCRIPTURE

This part of St. Augustine's doctrine about the Word of God has been discussed more fully than any other, even though its study was begun of fairly recent date. Thus, in 1827, when Clausen published his work on St. Augustine as interpreter of Holy Scripture, he complained that he was the first to write on this subject[1]. Almost seventy years later, Douais published his somewhat long-winded articles on St. Augustine and the Bible, in which he particularly discussed St. Augustine as an exegetist and as an opponent of Manichean views on the Scriptures[2]. Dorsch[3] concentrated mainly on St. Augustine's attitude to the historical value of the Scriptures and on his allegorical exegesis, and more incidentally on his views on the perspicuity and infallibility of the Scriptures. Vogels, again, in his study of St. Augustine's *De Consensu Evangelistarum* argued about his doctrine of inspiration[4]. In the Grabmann–Mausbach commemorative volume, Vogels made a further short contribution on St. Augustine and the Scriptures[5]. C. Pesch, in his comprehensive work on Scriptural inspiration quite naturally referred to St. Augustine, as well[6]. In 1927 and 1928, Eulogius Nebreda published various articles in a Spanish journal, as a first part of a detailed introduction to St. Augustine's Scriptural doctrine[7]. In it, he discussed St. Augus-

[1] Henricus Nicolaus Clausen, *Aurelius Augustinus Hipponensis Sacrae Scripturae interpres Hauniae,* Copenhagen 1827, p. 8.

[2] C. Douais, *Saint Augustin et la Bible,* Revue Biblique, Paris 1893, pp. 62–82, 351–377; 1894, pp. 110–136, 410–433.

[3] C. Dorsch, *Sint Augustinus und Hieronymus über die Wahrheit der biblischen Geschichte,* Zeitschrift für katholische Theologie 1911, pp. 421–448, 601–629, 629–641.

[4] H. J. Vogels, *Sint Augustinus' Schrift De Consensu Evangelistarum,* Freiburg 1908.

[5] *id., Die Heilige Schrift bei Augustinus.* In Festschrift der Görresgesellschaft, Cologne 1930, pp. 411–421.

[6] C. Pesch, *De inspiratione sacrae scripturae,* Freiburg 1906, pp. 111–122.

[7] Eulogius Nebreda, *Introductio divi Augustini ad sacram Scripturam,* Revista Espanola de Estudios Biblicos, 1927 and 1928.

tine's attitude to the canon, the relationship between the two Testaments, the value of the Septuagint, and the inspiration and properties of Scripture. Here we must especially mention Costello's dissertation on St. Augustine's doctrine of the inspiration and canonicity of Scripture[8]. Sasse's contribution in the Franz Dorneif festive volume struck us as having little relevance to our discussion[9], and van Itterzon's paper on St. Augustine and the Scriptures as being no more than a short and popular account[10]. In what follows, we have thought best to subdivide our own remarks.

1. *The fact of inspiration.*

Together with the entire Church of his day, St. Augustine was firmly convinced that the Bible was divinely inspired, and he was greatly heartened in his belief by the unanimous witness of the Church from Apostolic times onwards. 'It is not without good reason, that not merely a few people prating in the schools and gymnasia in captious disputations, but so many and great people, both learned and unlearned, in countries and cities, have believed that God spoke to them or by them, i.e. the canonical writers, when they wrote these books'[11]. From ancient times it has been agreed that the Holy Ghost spoke through the Scriptural writers so that everything found in the Bible must be exalted and divine[12]. St. Augustine would often gainsay opponents of his doctrine on divine inspiration by pointing out this strange unanimity of the Universal Church. For him it was a holy tradition, a holy patrimony, that must be preserved

[8] Charles Joseph Costello, *St. Augustine's Doctrine on the inspiration and canonicity of Scripture*, Washington 1930; see also his *St. Augustine's Canon of Scripture and his criterion of Canonicity*, University of Ottawa Review 1932, pp. 125*–138*; id., *St. Augustine's Concept of Inspiration*, ib. 1934, pp. 81*–99*. G. Strausz's dissertation *Schriftgebrauch, Schriftauslegung und Schriftbeweis bei Augustin*, Göttingen 1952, of which only six copies were made, was unfortunately not available for reference. It has since been printed (Tübingen 1959), but not in time to treat it here with the seriousness it merits. However, a first reading has shown that Strausz has failed to take full account of those quotations from St. Augustine's writings which we have used to characterise what we have called St. Augustine's second stage.

[9] Hermann Sasse, *Sacra Scriptura – Bemerkungen zur Insprirationslehre Augustins*, Festschrift Franz Dorneif, Bibliographisches Institut. Leipzig 1953, pp. 262–273.

[10] G. P. van Itterzon, *Augustinus en de Heilige Schrift*, Den Haag 1955.

[11] De civitate Dei XVIII, 41.

[12] De utilitate credendi 13.

with deep respect and gratitude. Naturally he did not overlook the witness of the Scripture itself. The Bible is quite unequivocal—so he told an anonymous opponent of the authority of the Law and the Prophets—that God speaks whenever the Law or the Prophets are consulted. Thus it is written: 'Thou shalt not muzzle the mouth of the ox that treadeth out the corn'. Doth God take care for oxen, or saith He it altogether for our sakes?[13]. Surely St. Paul could only have meant that God speaks in the Scripture. And again: 'And the Scripture, foreseeing that God would justify the heathen through faith, preached before the Gospel unto Abraham, saying, In thee shall all nations be blessed'[14]. St. Paul has here substituted Scripture for God, since Scripture is God[15]. 'Some one may say, Why then is it written "The Lord said to Moses" and not rather the angel said to Moses? Because when the crier proclaims the words of the judge, it is not usually written in the record, so and so the crier said, but so and so the judge. In like manner also, when the holy prophet speaks, although we say, The prophet said, we mean nothing else to be understood than that the Lord said; and if we were to say, The Lord said, we should not put the prophet aside, but only intimate Who spake by him'[16]. St. Augustine then quotes various examples from Scripture[17]. Thus he argues with the Manichean Adimantus that the agreement between the Old and New Testaments clearly shows that the two have been written by One Holy Spirit, by One God[18].

However it remains a strange fact that St. Augustine very rarely proved the inspiration from Scripture itself. He simply took it for granted. To him, 'the Holy Scriptures were the work of God's fingers, because they have been completed by the operation of the Holy Ghost, who worketh in the holy authors'[19]. Hence he called Scripture 'the Word of God'[20], 'a kind of bond of God's, which all who pass by, might read'[21], 'the divine books'[22], 'the divine Scripture'[23], 'the

[13] 1 Cor. 9:9.
[14] Gal. 3:8.
[15] Contra adversarium Legis et Prophetarum II, 13.
[16] De Trinitate III, 23.
[17] ib. III, 22–27.
[18] Contra Adimantum 3, 3; 7, 5.
[19] Enarr. in Ps. 8, 7.
[20] De civitate Dei X, 1, 2.
[21] Enarr. in Ps. 144, 17.
[22] De civitate Dei IX, 20.
[23] ib. XV, 8.

holy Scripture'[24], 'the Scripture of God'[25], 'letters of that city, apart from which we are wandering'[26], 'the divine oracles'[27]. 'Christ, our Mediator, having spoken what He judged sufficient, first by the prophets, then by his own lips, and afterwards by the Apostles, has besides produced the Scripture, which is called canonical, which has paramount authority and to which we yield assent in all matters[28]. These books are the work of the good, supreme and very God'[29].

2. *The nature of inspiration.*

Luckily, there is one of St. Augustine's works in which he was forced to consider the nature of Scriptural inspiration. In order to refute all sorts of blasphemies against the Gospels by the Manicheans, Porphyrius, and others, he wrote his *De Consensu Evangelistarum* in about 399–400 A.D., in which he showed the complete agreement between the Gospels. In this work, he examined the problems posed by the synoptic question so completely and open-mindedly that later centuries have had little to add to his remarks. In any case, the work brought him up against all sorts of problems which forced him to think more closely about the nature of divine inspiration.

One is struck at once by two facts:

On the one hand he emphasises the divine factor of the inspiration. The Evangelists wrote the Gospels in the name of God[30], each according to how God inspired him[31]. 'Christ who sent the prophets before His own descent also despatched the Apostles after His ascension. Moreover, in virtue of the humanity which He assumed, He stands to all his disciples in the relation of the head to the members of his body. Therefore, when those disciples have written matters which He declared and spoke to them, it ought not by any means to be said that He has written nothing Himself[32]; since the truth is, that his members have accomplished only what they became

[24] De Trinitate I, 2.
[25] Epistula 78, 1.
[26] Enarr. in Ps. 90 II, 1.
[27] Epistula 55, 37; 147, 40.
[28] De civitate Dei XI, 3.
[29] De gestis Pel. 15.
[30] ib. I, 3.
[31] ib. 4.
[32] This was one of the blasphemies of his opponents, as appears from I, 24, 25.

acquainted with through the dictation of the Head[33]. For all that He was minded to give for our perusal on the subject of his own doings and sayings, He commanded to be written by those disciples, whom He used as if they were his own hands. Whoever apprehends this correspondance of unity and this concordant service of the members all in harmony in the discharge of diverse offices under the Head, will receive the account which he gets in the Gospel through the narratives constructed by the disciples, in the same kind of spirit in which he might look upon the actual hand of the Lord himself, which he bore in that body, which was made his own, were he to see it engaged in the act of writing'[34].

In Book II, St. Augustine observed that 'it is reasonable enough to suppose that each of the evangelists thought it his duty to relate what he had to relate in that order in which it has pleased God to suggest[35] to his recollection the matters he was engaged in recording. At least this might hold good in the case of those incidents with regard to which the question of order, whether it were this or that, detracted nothing from evangelical authority and truth[36]. But as to the reason why the Holy Spirit who divideth to every man severally as He will, and who therefore undoubtedly, with a view to the establishing of their books on so distinguished an eminence of authority, also governs and rules the minds of the holy men themselves in the matter of suggesting the things they were to commit to writing, has left one historian at liberty to construct his narrative in one way, and another in a different fashion, that is a question which anyone may look into with pious consideration, and for which by divine help the answer also may possibly be found'[37]. When he discussed the problem posed in Matthew 27:9, where the prophecy of the potter's field is attributed to Jeremiah rather than Zechariah, he suggested that it was so attributed because it pleased God, in his hidden wisdom, thus to charge the evangelist.

'What necessity was there for Matthew to correct his text when he read over what he had written, and found that the one name had occurred to him instead of the other? Was it not rather the proper course for him to bow to the authority of the Holy Spirit, under

[33] *quod dictante capite cognoverunt.*
[34] I, 54.
[35] St. Augustine uses the verb *suggerere.*
[36] II, 51.
[37] II, 51.

whose guidance[38] he certainly felt his mind to be placed in a more decided sense than is the case with us and consequently to leave untouched what he had thus written, in accordance with the Lord's counsel and appointment, with the intent to give us to understand that the prophets maintain so complete a harmony with each other in the matter of their utterances that it becomes nothing absurd to credit Jeremiah with a sentence originally spoken by Zechariah?' Some paragraphs further, he notes that 'Mark the evangelist has judged it right to insert a statement just at the point at which it was suggested to him by divine inspiration. For the recollections of those historians (the evangelists) have been ruled by the hand of Him who rules the waters, as it is written, according to his own good pleasure. For the human memory moves through a variety of thoughts, and it is not in any man's power to regulate either the subject which comes into his mind or the time of the suggestion. Seeing then that those holy and truthful men, in this matter of the order of their narrations, committed the casualties of their recollections to the direction of the power of God, to whom nothing is casual, it does not become any mere man, in his low estate, removed far from the vision of God and sojourning distantly from Him, to say "This ought to have been introduced here", for he is utterly ignorant of the reason which led God to will its being inserted in the place it occupies'[39].

A number of things strike one in these quotations:

1. Inspiration is attributed to God, to Christ, or to the Holy Ghost, as it is in his other writings[40]. Here, too, he upholds his consistent belief that all the external works of the Trinity are indivisible even when they can be attributed to a specific Divine Person[41]. It is only in that sense that St. Augustine ascribes the inspiration of Scripture to the Holy Spirit.

2. It must also be noted that St. Augustine used different words for these inspirational acts of the Holy Ghost, viz. *inspirare*, *dictare*, *suggerere* and *gubernare*. *Inspirare* occurs most frequently, and St. Augustine must have taken it from 2 Tim. 3:16, where this verb appears in

[38] III, 30; St. Augustine uses the verbs *gubernare* and *regere* for guidance, in this context.

[39] III, 48.

[40] Costello, in his dissertation (p. 6 ff.) gives various examples.

[41] Cf. De Trinitate II, 9; Enchiridion 38; Tract. in Joannem 18, 6; 20, 7. This was obviously a well-known thesis, since it was mentioned in Epist. XI, 2 as early as A. D. 389, when St. Augustine still knew little about theology.

the Latin translation of the New Testament which he was using[42]. Oddly enough, St. Augustine used the same verb to describe the various effects of the Holy Spirit on the faithful. Thus we meet it constantly, particularly in his writings against the Pelagians, whenever he discusses the Spirit's inspiration of faith, goodwill or love[43]. Thus he could write to Proba that it was the Holy Spirit who inspired her with 'that devout anxiety which makes her to think it necessary to ask him various questions'[44]. Often, when he had to interpret a difficult Biblical passage, he would say that he could only perform that task in so far as the Lord or the Holy Ghost would inspire him[45]. In his *De Consensu Evangilistarum*, he declared that he was refuting the blasphemers of the Holy Gospels solely under the inspiration and with the help of the Lord Our God[46]. Hence it seems certain that this term had not yet been given a precise dogmatic significance. And yet, St. Augustine clearly distinguished between the inspiration of the writers of Scripture and the inspiration of the faithful, since he assumed an essential difference in the effect of their inspiration. Hence he probably used the word in two senses: one broad and the other narrow. This is equally true of his use of *dictare*. We have seen that St. Augustine held that the evangelists and the members of Christ's Body wrote 'under the dictate of the Head'. And yet, he wrote to Jerome that he must investigate Scripture 'since the Holy Spirit not only gave it to you, but *dictated* it to you'[47]. Now, the verb can, in fact, be translated thus[48], though it may equally be rendered as: charge, direct, urge, incite[49]. In his letter to Jerome, however, St. Augustine must have meant *charge* since in the very next paragraph he makes a clear distinction between the canonical books of

[42] Cf. Coll. cum Maxim. c. 30.
[43] E.g. De gratia Christi 43; De gratia et libero arbitrio 3 and 9.
[44] Epist. 130, 2.
[45] E.g. Enarr. in Ps. 126, 1.
[46] I, 10.
[47] Ep. 82, 2 'non tantum donante, verum etiam dictante Spiritu'.
[48] Costello (Diss. p. 15) rightly points to Retract. II, 67.
[49] Thus Cunningham renders the above quotation as 'not only giving you but expressly charging you'. (Letters of St. Augustine, Edinburgh 1872, p. 318) and Kranzfelder translates it as: Denn der Heilige Geist hat es dir nicht nur verliehen, sondern er befehlt es dir (*Bibl. der Kirchenväter*, Kempten 1878, Part III, p. 314). Poujoulat, on the other hand, has translated it as: Ce ne sera pas seulement avec la science, ce sera sous l'inspiration même de l'Esprit Saint (Bar le Duc 1864, II, 107).

Scripture and all other writings[50]. The question, in what sense we must translate it in *De Consensu Evangelistarum* I, 54, cannot be answered satisfactorily.

For the meaning of *suggerere*, Vogels[51] and Costello[52] point to the translation of the Vulgate, where it is used in St. John 14:26 to refer to 'calling to memory' or 'calling to mind'. They are probably quite right, though St. Augustine never used this verb in connection with this text.[53]

The verbs *gubernare* and *regere* are used to refer to God's general guiding precepts, so that we can learn nothing from any distinction between them, except perhaps one of slight degree.

Now, since none of these verbs had a strict dogmatic significance, we cannot base any clear theory upon them.

3. By virtue of a single expression, St. Augustine is thought to have held that the inspiration of canonical writers differed in degree rather than in essence from the inspiration of the faithful. For instance, he said that 'St. Matthew's mind was placed under the guidance of the Holy Spirit in a more decided sense than is the case with us'. St. Augustine's use of the Biblical symbolism of the Head and the Members is adduced as further evidence. However, a closer investigation of these passages will show beyond doubt that he could not possibly have been thinking of a gradual distinction, and that there are no grounds for Vogels to have claimed that all these verbs were merely used to describe the complete unity and harmony between the disciples themselves and between them and Christ as their Head, so much so that what the disciples wrote was like the writing of Christ[54].

4. The initiative was entirely God's. The Evangelists were ordained by Him to write Scripture. Christ as their Head, ordered His apostles to record those of His acts he wished to have recorded. The Holy Ghost inspired, suggested, moved their spirit, and brought to mind what they had to write, and supervised their writings down to the chapters, the plan, the execution, and the order and the choice of words. This is thrown into high relief, when St. Augustine declared that the Holy Spirit not only determines the differences between the respective accounts of the Evangelists, but even pays heed

[50] Ep. 82, 3.
[51] op. cit., p. 66.
[52] Dissertation p. 13.
[53] He always uses: *commemorabit*.
[54] op. cit., p. 67, 68.

to the smallest details—the placing of a given event in a given text, the insertion of the name of Jeremiah where we might have expected that of Zechariah, etc.

Although St. Augustine emphasised the divine factor in the inspiration of God's work, he never lost sight of the human factor. In the very beginning of his *De Consensu Evangelistarum*, he wrote that the evangelists not only kept in remembrance the words heard from His (Christ's) lips and the deeds wrought by Him beneath their eyes, but they were also careful to make mankind acquainted with those divine and memorable occurrences which took place at a period antecedent to the formation of their own connection with Him, which belonged also to the time of His nativity, His infancy or His youth, and with regard to which they were able to institute exact inquiry and to obtain information, either at His own hand or at the hands of His parents or other parties, on the ground of the most reliable intimations and the most trustworthy testimonies[55]. In Book II he referred to the fact that each Evangelist constructed his own particular narrative on a kind of plan which gives it the appearance of being the complete and orderly record of successive events. 'Preserving a simple silence on the subject of those incidents of which he intends to give no account, he then connects those which he does wish to relate with what he has been saying, in such a manner as to make the recital seem continuous'[56]. More than once, he entered in to the fact that each Evangelist told of Christ's words and deeds in his own way, so that we may sometimes have four entirely different versions. 'On this question we ought not to suppose that anyone of the writers gave an unreliable account, if, when several persons recall some matter either heard or seen by them, they fail to follow the very same plan, or to use the very same words, while describing, nevertheless, the selfsame fact. This is absolutely impossible, since the truth of the Gospel, conveyed in that word of God which abides eternal and unchangeable above all that is created, but which at the same time has disseminated throughout the world by the instrumentality of temporal symbols, and by the tongues of men, has possessed itself of the most exalted height of authority'[57]. This is a basic article of St. Augustine's faith. 'Therefore there can be no

[55] De Consens. Evang. I, 1.
[56] II, 16.
[57] II, 28.

thought of a lie, although the order of the words may be varied; or although some words may be substituted in place of others, which nevertheless have the same meaning; or although something may be left unsaid, either because it has not occurred to the mind of the recorder, or because it becomes readily intelligible from other statements which are given; or, although, among other matters which (may not bear directly on his immediate purpose, but which) he decides on mentioning rather for the sake of the narrative, and in order to preserve the proper order of time, an Evangelist may introduce something which he does not feel called upon to expound as a whole at length, but only to touch in part; or although, with the view of illustrating his meaning and making it thoroughly clear, the person to whom authority is given to compose the narrative makes some additions of his own, not indeed in the subject-matter itself, but in the words by which it is expressed; or although, while retaining a prefectly reliable comprehension of the fact itself, he may not be entirely successful, however he may make that his aim, in calling to mind and reciting anew with the most literal accuracy the very words which he heard on the occasion'[58]. To the objection that the Evangelists must surely have been instructed by the Holy Spirit not to differ in the choice or number of their words, he replied in a way which makes it perfectly clear how firmly convinced he was of the divine authority of Scripture. He did not argue from the common experience that a number of people may tell the same story but not with precisely the same words, but rather used the differences between the Gospels to prove that different versions of common events must never be called lies. Moreover—and this he considered of the utmost importance in the reliable doctrine—we must seek and embrace the truth not so much from words as from matters of fact[59]. He then gave two clear examples, the first taken from Matthew 3:11, where John the Baptist says: 'I am not worthy to bear his shoes', which in Mark 1:7 is rendered as: 'whose shoes I am not worthy to stoop down and unloose'. There can be no lie in this distinction, since 'if it is pertinent to the matter to deduce one sense from the words *to bear the shoes*, and another sense from the words *to unloose the shoes*, what should one suppose the correct interpretation to be put on the facts, but that John did give utterance to both these

[58] ib.
[59] ib.

sentences, either on two different occasions or in one and the same connection? But further, if, when he spoke of the shoes of the Lord, John meant nothing more than to convey the idea of His supremacy and his own lowliness, then, whichever of the two sayings may have actually been uttered by him, the selfsame sense is still correctly preserved by any writer, who, while making mention of the shoes in words of his own, has expressed at the same time the same idea of lowliness, and thus has not made any departure from the real mind (of the person of whom he writes). It is therefore a useful principle, and one particularly worthy of being born in mind, when we are speaking of the concord of the Evangelists, that there is no divergence from truth, even when they introduce some saying different from what was actually uttered by the person concerning whom the narrative is given, provided that, notwithstanding this, they set forth as his mind precisely what is also so conveyed by that one among them who reproduces the words as they were literally spoken. For thus we learn the salutary lesson, that our aim should be nothing else than to ascertain what is the mind and intention of the person who speaks'[60]. The other example was taken from the Father's words at Christ's Baptism. In the Gospel according to St. Matthew this is rendered as: 'This is my beloved Son in whom I am well pleased'[61]; St. Mark renders it as: 'Thou art my beloved Son in whom I am well pleased'[62], and St. Luke as: 'Thou art my beloved Son; in thee I am well pleased'[63]. The words may differ slightly, but they only help us to a greater understanding[64]. Later, in the same book, he remarked: 'From these varied and yet not inconsistent modes of statement adopted by the Evangelists, we evidently learn a lesson of the utmost utility, and of great necessity—namely that in any man's words the thing which we ought narrowly to regard is only the writer's thought which was meant to be expressed, and to which the words ought to be subservient; and further that we should not suppose one to be giving an incorrect statement, if he happens to convey in different words what the person really meant whose words he fails to reproduce literally. And we ought not to let the wretched

[60] II, 29.
[61] Matth. 3:17.
[62] Mark 1:11.
[63] Luke 3:22.
[64] II, 31.

cavillers at words fancy that truth must be tied somehow or other to the jots and tittles of letters; whereas the fact is, that not in the matter of words only, but equally in all other methods by which sentiments are indicated, the sentiment itself, and nothing else, is what ought to be looked at'[65]. And again: 'From all this variety of statement which is found in connection with a genuine harmony in regard to the matters of fact and the ideas conveyed, it becomes sufficiently clear that we have the wholesome lesson inculcated upon us, that what we have to look to in studying a person's words is nothing else than the intention of the speakers'[66].

The work abounds with expressions emphasising the autonomy of the Evangelists. Thus St. Matthew is said to have told of the healing of Peter's mother-in-law simply because he remembered that he had previously omitted it[67]. So St. Luke, too, has written now and then without any explicit note of the order of time, but after the fashion of one only bethinking himself of the incident at that point. He, too, leaves us uncertain whether he introduces these points as something previously omitted, or as an anticipatory notice of something which in actual fact took place subsequently to those incidents by which it is followed in the history[68]. Similarly John's version of Christ's denial by Peter differs from Mark's and Luke's[69]. Moreover, among the multitude of sayings and replies which passed between Pilate and the people, these writers have made their own selections as far as their judgment allowed them to go and each of them has introduced into his narrative just what he considered sufficient[70]. The historians were at liberty to select for narration any particular incident[71]. Luke wrote a treatise of all these things, in so far as he made a selection out of the whole mass of materials for his narrative and introduced those facts which he judged fit and suitable for the satisfactory discharge of the responsible duty laid upon him'[72].

These quotations speak for themselves: St. Augustine clearly rejected the idea of a purely mechanical inspiration. The Evangelists

[65] II, 67.
[66] II, 97; see also II, 128.
[67] II, 53.
[68] II, 54.
[69] III, 23.
[70] III, 35.
[71] III, 57.
[72] IV, 9.

were no mere clerks, no passive tools of the Holy Ghost but assumed full responsibility for their work[73].

Not surprisingly, therefore, Schanz took the following view: 'While divine inspiration is often stressed so much that the human factor seems to have disappeared completely, the human factor is elsewhere given such prominence that there seems little room left for inspiration'[74]. St. Augustine obviously wished to maintain both attitudes at once. *The Bible was both the exclusive work of the Holy Spirit alone and at the same time the exclusive work of the Biblical writers*. Beyond that St. Augustine did not theorise[75]. On the one hand, he followed Scripture[76] in using the ablative for the work of the Holy Spirit and the preposition 'per' for that of Biblical authors (whence it appears clearly that he thought of the Holy Spirit as the *auctor primarius*, the actual author, and of the Biblical writers as the organs through whom God speaks). He put it thus in a sermon on Psalm 5: 'We read that the law was written with the finger (ablat.) of God and given through (per) Moses, his holy servant'[77]. And at the end of the same paragraph he said that 'the Scriptures, by the operation of the Holy Ghost[78], are written by the ministers'[79]. But on the other hand, he stressed the independence of the Biblical authors, fully admitting their personal idiosyncracies, ability, insight, inclinations, tendencies, and character. Thus the difference between the Gospels must be attributed both to what it pleased the Holy Ghost to put in them and also to the spiritual tendencies of the Evangelists. Accordingly St. John was considered to have been head and shoulders above the others, soaring to heights where we earth-bound mortals cannot hope to follow him[80]. Thus St. Augustine fully appreciated what Bavinck has called 'organic inspiration', at least in his total approach, though not perhaps in some of his more equivocal utterances.

[73] Various authors have claimed that St. Augustine also spoke of a mantic inspiration, according to which the authors of the Bible were used as unconscious tools. This has been refuted fully by Vogels (op. cit., p. 72 ff.), nor is there any support for this claim in St. Augustine's writings.

[74] Paul Schanz, *Apologie des Christentums*, Freiburg, 3rd edition 1906, II, 636.

[75] See Vogels, op. cit., p. 79; Costello, Diss. p. 28.

[76] See H. Bavinck, Geref. Dogmatiek I², p. 451.

[77] *Legimus digito Dei scriptum legem et datum per Moysen.*

[78] *Operante Spiritu sancto per ministros.*

[79] Enarr, in Ps. 8, 7; see also Enarr. in Ps. 104, 27.

[80] De cons. Ev. II, 52; IV, 11, 21.

3. *The extent of inspiration.*

St. Augustine was fully convinced that the Scriptures were entirely God's work[81]. Everything in the Old and New Testaments was written by one Spirit[82] and must hence be believed beyond all doubt[83]. Any suggestion of partial inspiration was rejected out of hand. Divine inspiration provided not only the religious and moral tone of the Scriptures, but contained quite literally everything that God has revealed to man. In the Scriptures, even historical events are related by divine authority, and must therefore be believed absolutely. What the Scriptures tell of history must be believed firmly and whatever disagrees with the Scriptural accounts must be rejected as utterly false[84]. This is true also of the account of the Creation. 'That God made the world we can believe from no one more safely than from God Himself. But where have we heard Him? Nowhere more distinctly than in the Holy Scriptures, where his prophet said: In the beginning God created the heavens and the earth. Was the prophet present? No, but the wisdom of God, by whom all things were made, was there and wisdom insinuates itself into holy souls and makes them the friends of God and his prophets and noiselessly informs them of his works'[85]. True, the Bible does not describe the Creation in detail, but merely tells us what the Holy Ghost in the Biblical author saw needful to report[86]. What the Scriptures say on this subject is completely reliable, and even when they tell us that a single source watered the whole earth we have no reason for disbelief. Our interpretation may be false, and we must do our utmost to look for an explanation which is in agreement with the Scriptures, for they are undoubtedly truthful even when their truth cannot be demonstrated[87]. When the Bible tells us that there were waters above the firmament, waters there must have been. In any case, the authority of the Scriptures surpasses the capacity of all our reason[88].

This is equally true of the purely historical accounts[89]. Whatever

[81] De civitate Dei XXI, 6, 7.
[82] Contra Adimantum 3, 3.
[83] De civitate Dei XI, 7.
[84] ib. XVIII, 40.
[85] ib. XI, 4; see also Confessiones XII, 24 ff.
[86] De Genesi ad litteram V, 23.
[87] ib. 24.
[88] ib. II, 9.
[89] Cf. C. Dorsch, op. cit.

the Scriptures tell of Enoch, Elijah and Moses is absolutely true[90]. Admittedly, St. Augustine believed—and Dorsch has discussed this point in detail—that the Scriptures contained different literary forms, which all interpreters must take into account. Thus he distinguished between prophetic and profane, and again between prophetic and historical accounts, while holding that these differences in no way detracted from the Bible's reliability. 'All that is given as history, is written with historical diligence[91] and with prophetic authority[92]. Therefore the chronology of the Holy Scripture is absolutely trustworthy'[93]. At first, St. Augustine generally subordinated the historical meaning to a spiritual meaning which he would derive by way of strange allegorical interpretations, but he later accepted the full historical truth of Biblical events[94] and defended them staunchly, particularly against the attacks of Faustus, the Manichean. Wherever the Bible states facts clearly, these facts are indisputable and put an end to all arguments. Hence he told Faustus, who denied the truth of the Biblical account of Christ's birth: 'The reason of our believing Christ to have been born of the Virgin Mary, is not that he could not otherwise have appeared among men in a true body, but because it is so written in the Scripture, which we must believe in order to be Christians or to be saved. We believe then, that Christ was born of the Virgin Mary, because it is so written in the Gospel; we believe that He died on the cross, because it is so written in the Gospel; we believe that both his birth and death were real, because the Gospel is no fiction'[95].

Divine inspiration extends not only to reports of divine and human acts but also into the spoken word. For has not God always spoken through His prophets? 'If it is said: "Honour thy father and thy mother", God has commanded it. If it is said, "Thou shalt not commit adultery, Thou shalt not kill, Thou shalt not steal" and other similar commandments, not human lips, but the divine oracles have enounced them'[96]. It was through divine inspiration that the prophet said: 'Grant me a pure heart, oh Lord'[97]. As for not marrying 'in the latter

[90] Contra Faustum XXVI, 3.
[91] De civitate Dei XVII, 1.
[92] ib. XI, 8.
[93] ib. XII, 10.
[94] See the detailed discussion by Dorsch, op. cit., and also Costello, *Diss.* p. 45 ff.
[95] Contra Faustum XXVI, 7.
[96] De civitate Dei XVIII, 41.
[97] De quantitate animae 75.

times'[98], St. Augustine stated expressly that this prohibition was a prediction of the Holy Spirit[99].

In a sermon, he claimed that the Psalms were dictated by the Holy Spirit[100]. His sermon on Psalm 33 began with the words: 'Let us then hear what the Holy Spirit by the mouth of his holy prophet says in the words of the Psalm'[101]. In his sermons on Psalm 118 he repeatedly referred to a given text as spoken by the Spirit or else as being a divine saying[102]. Psalm 105 gives a number of details from the life of Joseph and tells us, *inter alia*, that Joseph's feet were hurt with fetters and that he was placed in irons. St. Augustine then claims that we ought no ways to doubt that it was so. For some things might be passed over in that (Scriptural) history, which nevertheless would not escape the Holy Spirit, Who speaks in these Psalms[103]. When Psalm 96:5 tells us that all the gods of the nations are idols, this is a judgment of the Holy Spirit[104]. Clearly, then, St. Augustine held that all Scripture was divinely inspired.

4. *The effect of inspiration.*

The effect of divine inspiration is that Holy Scriptures, as the Word of God, are absolutely true and trustworthy. 'God's Scripture neither deceives nor is deceived'[105]. It must be whole and true simply because it was written under the inspiration of the one spirit of truth[106]. For this reason St. Augustine could say in his Confessions: 'Oh Lord, true indeed are Your Scriptures since You Yourself are the truth and since You have given them as the truth[107]. Thus he objected most strongly when St. Jerome, in his Commentary on Galatians, claimed that St. Paul had used a white lie[108]. 'It seems to me', St. Augustine

[98] I Tim. 4:3.
[99] De moribus Manichaeorum 64.
[100] Enarr. in Ps. 62, 1. St. Augustine used the Septuagint method of numbering the Psalms, which differs from the Hebrew numbers. The Greek translation combined Psalms 9 and 10, thus missing a number. Later, Psalm 147 was split into two, so that Ps. 147:16–20 became Ps. 147 in the Septuagint.
[101] ib. 33 II, 1.
[102] ib. 118 I, 2; II, 1.
[103] ib. 104, 13, 14.
[104] ib. 135, 3.
[105] De patientia XXVI, 22.
[106] De Genesi ad litteram IV, 53.
[107] ib. XIII, 44.
[108] Gal. 2:14.

wrote, 'that most disastrous consequences must follow upon our believing that anything false is found in the sacred books: that is to say that the men by whom the Scripture has been given to us and committed to writing, did put down in these books anything false. If you once admit into such a high sanctuary of authority one false statement, there will not be left a single sentence of those books, which, if appearing to any one difficult in practice or hard to believe, may not by the same fatal rule be explained away as a statement, in which, intentionally, the author declared what was not true[109]. The authority of the divine Scriptures becomes unsettled (so that everyone may believe what he wishes, and reject what he does not wish), if it be once admitted, that the men by whom these things have been delivered unto us, could in their writings state some things which were not true'[110]. In a subsequent letter he returned to this point: if statements untrue in themselves have been admitted into the Holy Scripture, what authority will be left to them?[111] 'Manifestly, therefore, Peter was truly corrected and Paul has given a true narrative of the event, unless, by the admission of a falsehood here, the authority of the Holy Scriptures given for the faith of all coming generations is to be made wholly uncertain and wavering'[112].

'I confess', he wrote in a further letter still, 'that I have learned to yield this respect and honour only to the canonical books of Scripture: of these alone do I most firmly believe that the authors were completely free from error. And if in these writings I am perplexed by anything which appears to me opposed to truth, I do not hesitate to suppose that either the manuscript is faulty, or the translator has not caught the meaning of what was said, or I myself have failed to understand it'[113]. 'This is most pertinent to the matter which I have in hand—the confirmation of the universal and unquestionable truth of the divine Scriptures, which have been delivered to us for our edification in the faith, not by unknown men, but by the apostles, and have on this account been received as the authoritative standard'[114]. 'It must most assuredly be believed that a way of lying is far

[109] Epistula 28, 3.
[110] ib. 5.
[111] Epistula 40, 3.
[112] ib. 5.
[113] Epistula 82, 3.
[114] ib. 7.

removed from the authors who were employed to write holy writings, especially the canonical Scriptures; because they are the stewards of Christ, of whom it is said, "It is required in stewards that a man be found faithful"'[115]. 'It is to the canonical Scriptures alone that I am bound to yield such implicit subjection as to follow their teaching, without admitting the slightest suspicion that in them any mistake or any statement intended to mislead could find a place. To the apostle Paul I betake myself and I hear him in reply proclaiming with a solemn oath in an early part of the epistle, when he began this narration, "The things that I write unto you, behold before God, I lie not"'[116]. All these quotations make it perfectly clear that St. Augustine based his belief in the infallibility of the Scriptures on religious and moral grounds and never on purely formal considerations.

St. Augustine made the same point time and again in his argument with the Manicheans and other blasphemers who claimed that the Bible was full of contradictions. Although he often failed to counter their arguments, and though he was often forced to call on his remarkable gift of producing allegories[117], he held fast to his firm belief in the Word of God as the unshakeable foundation of his faith. If the Scriptures, which are the Word of God, are uncertain, nothing else can be certain either. He thought it inconceivable that the Holy Spirit, the real author of Holy Scripture should have contradicted himself. Hence he told Faustus the Manichean, that it was not permissible to say, if we are perplexed by an apparent contradiction in Scripture, 'The author of this book is mistaken'; for either the manuscript is faulty, or the translation is wrong, or you have not understood. In the innumerable books that have been written latterly we may sometimes find the same truth as in the Scripture, but there is not the same authority. Scripture has a sacredness peculiar to itself. In consequence of this distinctive peculiarity of the sacred writings, we are bound to receive as true whatever the canon shows to have been said by even one prophet, or apostle, or Evangelist[118]. Thus Holy Scripture is holy, truthful, and pure. Scripture as a whole, inspired as it is by God Himself, is profitable for doctrine,

[115] 1 Cor. 4:2; Epistula 82, 22.
[116] Gal. 1:20; Epistula 82, 24.
[117] See Clausen, op. cit. p. 100 ff.; Maurice Pontet, *L'exégèse de St. Augustin*, Aubier 1944, p. 149 ff.; 195 ff.
[118] Contra Faustum XI, 5.

for reproof, for correction, and for instruction in righteousness[119].

While St. Augustine thus emphasized the truth and validity of Scripture, he also held that:

1. Holy Scripture, though fully reliable, does not give an *adequate* description of God and things divine. St. Augustine, no doubt, stressed this fact under the influence of Neoplatonism. God in His great Mercy humbled Himself to fit our measure. Scripture speaks in our own words and by them shows that nothing worth saying can be affirmed about God's essence. God's inexpressible Majesty always exceeds all our expectations[120]. 'The Holy Scripture, which suits itself to babes, has not avoided words drawn from any class of things really existing, through which, as by nourishment, our understanding might rise gradually to things divine and transcendent. For, in speaking of God, it has both used words taken from things corporeal, as when it says, "Hide me under the shadow of Thy wings", and it has borrowed many things of the spiritual creature, whereby to signify that which indeed is not so, but must needs so be said, as for instance, "I the Lord thy God am a jealous God" and "It repenteth Me that I have made man". But it has drawn no words whatever, whereby to frame, either figures of speech or enigmatic sayings, from things, which do not exist at all. For divine Scripture is wont to frame, as it were, allurements for children, from the things which are found in the creature; whereby, according to their measure, and as it were by steps, the affections of the weak may be moved to seek those things that are above, and to leave those things that are below. But the same Scripture rarely employs those which are spoken properly of God, and are not found in any creature; as for instance, that which was said to Moses, "I am that I am" and "I am has sent me to you". So too, that which the apostle says, "Who only has immortality". So also James says, "Every good gift and every perfect gift is from above and comes down from the Father of lights, with whom is no variableness, neither shadow of turning"[121].

God's Majesty is inexpressible and can, in any case, never be described by one man to another, unless he speak of places and times, though God Himself is above all places and times[122]. Divine Scrip-

[119] 2 Tim. 3:16; Sermo 23, 3.
[120] Contra Adimantum VII, 4.
[121] De Trinitate I, 2.
[122] De Genesi ad litteram V, 34.

ture expresses the inexpressible in words which may strike us as absurd, and we must learn that even what we can fully understand in Scripture must not be judged by human standards[123].

When the Manicheans object to Biblical references to God's jealousy and wrath, they simply fail to understand that there are no words to express God's inexpressible Majesty. The Holy Spirit has been forced to use words with which we normally describe human failings, the better to show us that even those things which we believe we may truthfully say of God, can never measure up to His Majesty, which is far better rendered by reverend silence than by human words[124]. When Scripture tells us that God is angry, we must not take it that God's emotions are upset, since nothing can validly be said about them. Scripture merely uses this and similar expressions to make us realise that all our sayings of God fall far short of His inexpressible Majesty. God's Wisdom, which shall descend on the human body, has already descended on human words. Even 'descend' must not be read in its literal sense, since God's Wisdom is all-pervasive and does not move from place to place. Thus some have objected when St. John said in the Gospel: 'He came unto his own and his own received him not'. How, they ask, could He have 'come' when He has always been with us? Simply because His inexpressible glory must be described in human terms, according to our lowly measure. Nothing valid can be said of God, for by the very saying of it we depreciate it[125]. 'I venture to say, perhaps not John himself spoke of the matter as it is, but even he only as he was able; for it was man, that spoke of God, inspired indeed by God, but still man. Because he was inspired he said something; if he had not been inspired, he would have said nothing, but because he was inspired, he spoke not the whole but only what a man could speak'[126].

Yet this very poverty of the Scriptures is also their greatest riches. It was not from the Neoplatonists but from the Holy Spirit that St. Augustine learned of these glad aspects. Thus he could say in one of the sermons on the Gospel according to St. John that 'God becomes all to thee; for He is to thee the whole of the things which thou lovest. If thou regardest things visible, neither is God bread,

[123] Contra advers. legis I, 40.
[124] Contra Adimantum 11; here, the Neoplatonic influence is quite unmistakable.
[125] Contra Adimantum 13, 2.
[126] Tract. in Joannis evangelium I, 1. Here, by the realisation of the presence of inspiration, the Neoplatonic spell is broken.

nor is God water, nor is God this light, nor is He garment nor house. For all these things are visible and single separate things. What bread is, water is not; and what a garment is, a house is not; and what these things are, God is not, for they are visible things. God is all this to thee: if thou hungerest, He is bread to thee; if thou thirst-test, He is water to thee; if thou art in darkness, He is light to thee, for He remains incorruptible. If thou art naked, He is a garment of immortality to thee, when this corruptible shall put on incorruption. All things can be said of God and nothing is worthy of God. Nothing is wider than this poverty of expression. Thou seekest a fitting name for Him, thou canst not find it; thou seekest to speak of Him in any way soever, thou findest that He is all'[127].

Moreover this poverty is riches, simply because, through it, Scripture calls to us all. 'If Scripture were not to use such expressions (the anger of God, the repentance of God), it would not familiarly insinuate itself into the minds of all classes of men, whom it seeks access to for their good, that it may alarm the proud, arouse the careless, exercise the inquisitive, and satisfy the intelligent; and this it could not do, did it not first stoop, and in a manner descend, to them where they lie'[128]. And thus we have lifted the lid to face a riddle, for while a lid withdraws what it hides from our gaze, a riddle makes us see through a glass, darkly[129], that is not fully, but at least to some extent[130].

2. Secondly, St. Augustine laid great stress on the religious, moral and soteriological aim of Scripture, which was given to us by God to acquaint us with Christ and His Gospel. St. Augustine knew—although he but too often ignored this knowledge—that Scripture, far from being a textbook of science, or an academic tract, was the Book of Life, written in the language of life. When Felix, the Manichean, claimed that the Paraclete had revealed to Manicheus the beginning, the middle, and the end, and also the orbits of the moon, the sun and the stars, St. Augustine replied that there is nothing in the Gospel about such matters, God having desired us to become Christians rather than astronomers[131]. In the same spirit, he also wrote: 'People often ask what Scripture has to

[127] ib. XIII, 5.
[128] De civitate Dei XV, 25.
[129] 1 Cor. 13:12.
[130] De diversis quaestionibus ad Simplicianum II, 1.
[131] De actis com Felice I, 10.

say of the shape of the heavens. Many have argued about this subject, but our authors (of the Scriptures) have omitted to tell us about it, and with great wisdom, seeing that such knowledge is of no advantage in eternal life. And what is worse, it takes up much of our valuable time and thus detracts our attention from more wholesome matters. Although our authors knew the truth about the shape of the heavens, the Spirit of God who spoke by them did not intend to teach men these things, in no way profitable for salvation[132]. When the Bible calls heaven a taut skin or a vault, only the part directly above us is referred to[133]. People will also ask whether the sun, the moon and the stars are equally bright. But for us it is sufficient to know that God has created the stars, even though we are told on apostolic authority that they differ in glory[134]. We can, indeed, agree with the apostles that they differ in glory, but to our eyes alone[135]. Similarly with the great lights mentioned in Genesis 1:16. We must certainly agree that, to our eyes, these two lights shine more brightly on the earth than all the others'[136].

St. Augustine was fully convinced that there can be no discrepancy between the revelations of Scripture and the manifest evidence of reason: 'For if reason be found contradicting the authority of the Divine Scriptures, it only deceives by a semblance of truth, however acute it be, for its deductions cannot in that case be true. On the other hand, if, against the most manifest and reliable testimony of reason, anything be set up claiming to have the authority of the Holy Scriptures, he who does this does it through a misapprehension of what he has read, and is setting up against the truth not the real meaning of Scripture, which he has failed to discover, but an opinion of his own; he alleges not what he has found in the Scriptures but what he has found in himself as their interpreter'[137]. Whenever, therefore, the nature of things is discovered by reliable investigation, these discoveries will always be capable of being reconciled with the Scripture. Quotations from profane authors that are apparently opposed to the Scriptures must, according to our Catholic faith, be

[132] De Genesi ad litteram II, 20.
[133] ib. 21.
[134] 1 Cor, 15:41.
[135] De Genesi ad litteram II, 33.
[136] ib. 34.
[137] Epistula 143, 7.

utterly refuted[138]. St. Augustine remembered vividly how many telling blows he himself had delivered during his Manichean days, against those Christians who lacking thorough instruction yet tried to defend their faith with all their might[139]. Hence he warned the pious not to try to cover up their ignorance of matters of fact by discussing scientific questions with an easy appeal to Scriptures. Many non-Christians happen to be well-versed in knowledge of the earth, the heaven, of all the other elements of the world, of the motion, the revolutions, the size and distance of the stars, of eclipses of the sun and the moon, of such periodic events as the years and the tides, of the nature of animals, plants, stones and of other things which can all be understood by keen reasoning or experience. It is therefore deplorable that Christians, even though they ostensibly base their dicta on the Bible, should utter so much nonsense that they expose themselves to ridicule. While ridicule is all they deserve, they also give the impression that the Biblical authors are responsible for their mutterings, thus discrediting Christianity before the world, which is led to assume that the authors of the Scriptures were ignorant fools also. Whenever any Christian is confounded and shown to be an idle chatterer, his chatter is attributed to our Holy Books. No wonder, that the critics refuse to believe what Scripture has to say on the resurrection, on life eternal and the kingdom of heaven, when they can point out that the Bible is ostensibly wrong about facts which they can see or determine for themselves. Hence these idle boasters cause untold grief to our more thoughtful brethren[140].

3. Thirdly, St. Augustine believed firmly that the historical descriptions in Scripture were unlike all other histories, since they are mainly concerned with Christ and His Church or with the City of God of which Christ is the Head, and of which His chosen people are the members. This is discussed at length, particularly in his *City of God:* 'From the blessing of the two sons of Noah, and the cursing of the middle son, down to Abraham, or for more than a thousand years, there is no mention of any righteous persons who worshipped God. I do not therefore conclude that there were none; but it had been tedious to mention everyone and would have displayed histori-

[138] De Genesi ad litteram I, 41.
[139] De duabus animis 11.
[140] De Genesi ad litteram I, 39.

cal accuracy rather than prophetic foresight. The object of the writer of these sacred books, or rather of the Spirit of God in him, is not only to record the past, but to depict the future, so far as it regards the city of God; for whatever is said of those who are not its citizens, is given either for her instruction, or as a foil to enhance her glory. Yet we are not to suppose that all that is recorded, has some signification; but those things which have no signification of their own are interwoven for the sake of the things which are significant. It is only the ploughshare that cleaves the soil; but to effect this, other parts of the plough are requisite. It is only the strings in harps and other musical intruments which produce melodious sounds; but that they may do so, there are other parts of the instrument, which are not indeed struck by those who sing, but are connected with the strings which are struck, and produce musical notes. So in this prophetic history some things are narrated which have no significance, but are, as it were, the framework to which the significant things are attached'[141]. And elsewhere, he wrote with even greater incisiveness: 'The writer of the sacred history (of Genesis) does not necessarily mention all the men who might be alive at that time, but those only whom the scope of his work required him to name. The design of that writer (who in this matter was the instrument of the Holy Ghost) was to descend to Abraham through the successions of ascertained generations propagated of one man, and then to pass from Abraham's seed to the people of God, in whom was prefigured and predicted all that relates to the city whose reign is eternal, and to its king and founder Christ, which things were foreseen in the Spirit as destined to come; yet neither is this object so effected as that nothing is said of the other society of men which we call the earthly city, but mention is made of it so far as seemed needful to enhance the glory of the heavenly city by contrast to its opposite'[142]. Clearly, therefore, when discussing the Bible's historical accuracy, we must always bear in mind these Scriptural aims and objects.

4. Finally, St. Augustine was fully aware that many Biblical data were not necessarily true by themselves. Thus he told Orosius who had put all manner of questions to him: 'I have said indeed, let us but read the divine books and we shall believe them. However, on reading the utterances of one of Job's comforters, we must not take

[141] De civitate Dei XVI, 2, 3.
[142] De civitate Dei XV, 8.

his words as having divine authority, for he spoke falsely of God. Similarly, while everything in the Gospel is perfectly true as far as the telling of it, not everything that is told must be believed to be true. The Gospel makes it quite clear that the Jews spoke many false and godless things. Thus in this book (Job) which reports the sayings of many people, we must not only consider what was said but also by whom it was said. While we must accept without distinction everything that is written in a Holy Book, we need not hold that everything reported was true and correct. For in that case we should have to believe what Job's wife in her delusion told her husband, viz. that it was right to speak out against God and thus to rid oneself of an unbearable burden through death. I have said this, not because I believe that those friends of Job, reproved as they were by the Lord, and justly rebuked by that same holy servant of the Lord, could not have said anything true, but for the reason that not everything that they said is to be regarded as true. Thus it is true that the Jews said to Christ: "Say we not well that thou art a Samaritan and hast a devil", though we know Christ for our dearly beloved. We, who hold the Gospel to be absolutely true, must nevertheless admit that the Jews rejected Him in this way. The sayings, not only of godless and sinful human beings, but even of the poor, the meek, and the unlearned (faithful) whose words are often mentioned, must therefore not be considered to have canonical authority. Even the apostle Peter was rebuked and justly called a Satan because of some of the things he said'[143].

5. *The divine authority of Scripture.*

We have discussed St. Augustine's approach to the divine authority of Scripture more than once, and we shall now try to summarise his views briefly. From his first writings onwards, St. Augustine was clearly and fully convinced of the divine authority of Holy Writ,[144] and recognised no authority above it[145]. In his famous discussion with Jerome he observed that Scripture must be placed on the highest pinnacle of authority[146]. 'The universal and unquestionable

[143] Ad Orosium 12.
[144] De beata vita 34; De libero arbitrio I. 7; De Musica VI, 43; cf. Clausen, op. cit., p. 91 ff.; Hoffmann, *Kirchenbegriff*, p. 289 ff.
[145] De Musica VI, 52.
[146] Epistula 82, 5.

truth of the Divine Scriptures has been delivered to us by the apostles and has on this account been received as the authoritative canonical standard'[147]. 'What is written by divine inspiration has the authority of religion'[148]. 'Whatever the canon shows to have been said by even one prophet, or apostle, or evangelist, we are bound to receive as true, in consequence of the distinctive peculiarity of the sacred writings'[149]. For that reason, St. Augustine could openly state that a saying of St. Paul's has more authority by itself (i.e. not *a posteriori* from its content) than all the sayings of the philosophers[150].

Because of its divine authority, all of us must bow down unreservedly before Scripture. What is stated by the clear authority of the divine writings which the Church calls canonical, must be believed without any hesitation[151]. Although we cannot see it, we must nevertheless believe in the divine authority which is revealed in the Scriptures[152]. 'The evidence of the Scriptures determines our faith, and we unhesitatingly give credence to the divine Scriptures'[153]. 'Only to the canonical writings must I give agreement without hesitation'[154]. 'God's Word is always the rule of truth'[155]. 'Therefore everything written in Scripture must be believed absolutely'[156]. 'It is an error to doubt truth'[157]. 'In canonical authority, all things agree so well that we must surely believe with well-founded and wise piety that they were spoken as if with one mouth'[158]. 'Not without reason was the Church canon instituted under divine vigilance to contain certain books of the prophets and the apostles, which we dare not criticize'[159]. 'If the authority of the divine Scriptures is undermined, faith itself will become undermined, and once faith is shaken, love will abate'[160]. We have seen, that St. Augustine

[147] ib. 7.
[148] De civitate Dei XVIII, 38.
[149] Contra Faustum XI, 5.
[150] Epistula 167, 4.
[151] Epistula 147, 4.
[152] ib. 12.
[153] ib. 39, 40; De peccatorum meritis et remissione III, 7.
[154] De natura et gratia 71.
[155] Sermo 30, 2.
[156] De civitate Dei XXI, 6, 1.
[157] Contra Faustum XI, 5.
[158] ib. 6.
[159] Contra Cresconium II, 39.
[160] De doctrina Christiana I, 41.

dismissed the idea that Holy Writ could tell white lies out of hand[161]. Hence, the divine authority of the Scriptures must be distinguished from all other autority. St. Augustine kept stressing this fact to Manicheans, Donatists, and Pelagians alike, all of whom claimed the authority of all sorts of Fathers of the Church. Dorner has pointed to a contradiction in St. Augustine's attitude to them, the only psychological explanation for which he saw in the different fronts presented by his opponents[162]. We, for our part, have been unable to discover this contradiction, and have found that he proclaimed the same belief to all these heretics. Thus he told Faustus the Manichean: 'All our writings are read with the right of judgment and without any obligation to believe. In order to leave room for such profitable discussions of difficult questions, there is a distinct boundary line separating all productions subsequent to apostolic times, from the authoritative canonical books of the Old and New Testaments. The authority of these books has come down to us from the apostles through the successions of bishops and the extension of the Church, and, from a position of lofty supremacy, claims the submission of every faithful and pious mind'[163]. Similarly, he pointed out to the Donatists, who based their faith in rebaptism on the authority of Cyprian, that there was an essential difference between the canonical authority of the Scriptures and all other writings. 'We do no injustice to Cyprian', he wrote, 'when we make a distinction between his epistles and the canonical authority of the divine Scriptures. Apart from the Sacred canonical Scriptures, we may freely pass judgment on the writings of believers and disbelievers alike'[164]. For that reason Cyprian's epistles, which have no canonical authority must be judged according to their agreement with the authority of the divine writings. Thus we can accept from Cyprian only what agrees, and safely reject what does not agree, with Scripture[165]. So firmly convinced was he of this position, that he wrote in his well-known *De baptismo*: 'Who can fail to be aware that the sacred canon of Scripture both of the Old and New Testament, is confined within its own limits, and that it stands so absolutely in a superior position

[161] See p. 50 ff.
[162] A. Dorner, *Augustinus, Sein theologisches System und seine religions-philosophische Anschauung*, Berlin 1873, p. 237 ff.
[163] Contra Faustum XI, 5.
[164] Contra Cresconium II, 39.
[165] ib. 40.

to all later letters of bishops, that about it we can hold no manner of doubt or disputation whether what is confessedly contained in it is right and true; but that all the letters of bishops which had been written, or are being written, since the closing of the canon, are liable to be refuted, if there be anything contained in them which strays from the truth; and that even of the universal Councils, the earlier are often corrected by those which follow them, when things are brought to light which were before concealed?'[166] Hence not even the universal council of the Church is infallible, for infallibility is the exclusive prerogative of Holy Writ[167]. He put forward similar arguments against the Pelagians who claimed the authority of Hilary, Ambrose, and many other Fathers[168]. With perfect consistency, he also showed that the same criticism applied to his own works[169]. These have authority only in so far as they reflect the clear evidence of God's Word, for, in that case, they speak, not with human, but with divine authority, and can therefore be accepted by one and all[170]. Thus man's hard and proud necks are bent by the authority of the Holy Scriptures[171]. Whenever God speaks—this was St. Augustine's firm conviction—it behoves us to submit to Him and to obey His commands. Therein lies our freedom and our salvation[172].

6. *The perspicuity of Scripture.*

St. Augustine's thoughts on the perspicuity of Scripture may be summarised as follows: Scripture is clear and obscure, simple and

[166] De baptismo II, 4. Various authors (e.g. Karl Adam, *Gesammelte Aufsätze* 1936, p. 231; Hoffmann, op. cit. p. 313; Dankbaar op. cit. p. 42) have interpreted this text as referring to purely interpretative corrections, so that Augustine apparently foreshadowed Vincent of Lerinum's famous formula. Reuter's arguments (*Augustinische Studien*, Gotha 1887, particularly pp. 340 ff.) against this attractive but untenable hypothesis, were not refuted by these authors.

[167] Cf. De unitate ecclesiae 6, 28, 31; Epistula 93, 35, 36. The interesting question whether St. Augustine held the Church to be infallible, will be treated in our discussion of his ecclesiology.

[168] Cf. De gratia Christi I, 47; De natura et gratia 71.

[169] Epistula 193, 10.

[170] De peccatorum meritis et remissione I, 33; De gratia et libero arbitrio 41; De correptione et gratia 1.

[171] De sancta virginitate 17.

[172] Clearly, he did not consider this kind of submission a form of restriction, as Harnack suggests he did (*Lehrbuch der Dogmengeschichte* III^4, p. 96, Note 3).

profound, lucid and yet full of mysteries, sometimes so plain that one can grasp its meaning even in one's sleep[173], then again so deep that no man can fully plumb its depths[174]. 'Hasty and careless readers are led astray by many and manifold obscurities and ambiguities. And I do not doubt that all this was divinely arranged for the purpose of subduing pride by toil, and of preventing a feeling of satiety in the intellect, which generally holds in small esteem that which is discovered without difficulty. For those who seek but do not find, suffer from hunger. Those again, who do not seek at all because they have what they require just beside them, often grow languid from satiety. Now weakness from either of these causes is to be avoided. Accordingly the Holy Spirit has, with admirable wisdom and care for our welfare, so arranged the Holy Scriptures as by the plainer passages to satisfy our hunger, and by the most obscure to stimulate our appetite'[175]. In His medicine chest God keeps some medicines hidden the better to test the seekers after truth, while others are plainly displayed the better to fill those who thirst after righteousness[176]. Throughout Scripture, we are fed by the plain and tested by the obscure passages. The former still our hunger, the latter cast out our pride[177]. The profundity of God's Words does not exclude reason, for if all were obscure there would be nothing to break through the obscurity. Else, if everything were plain, whence would the soul obtain nourishment and strength to plumb the hidden depths?[178] 'There are in the Holy Scripture deep mysteries, which are for this cause hidden, lest they should be held cheap; for this cause sought, that they may employ us; for this cause opened, that they may feed us'[179]. 'If it were nowhere plain, it would not feed thee; if it were nowhere hidden, it would not exercise thee'[180].

Despite this combination of clarity and obscurity, Scripture is quite clear about all things needful for obtaining salvation and for living a godly life. 'The presumption of man ought to restrain itself, whenever a question arises on an unusual obscure subject, on which

[173] De civitate Dei XX, 23.
[174] Procemium in Ps. 118; cf. Clausen, op. 125 ff.; Pesch, op. cit. p. 573 ff.; Pontet, op. cit. p. 127 ff.; Marrou, op. cit. p. 478 ff.
[175] De doctrina Christiana II, 7, 8.
[176] Sermo 32, 1.
[177] ib. 71, 11.
[178] ib. 156, 1.
[179] Enarr. in Ps. 140, 1.
[180] ib. 2; Sermo 352, 6.

no assistance can be rendered by clear and certain proofs of the Holy Scripture'. At the same time, he confesses: 'In this, I believe that the Holy Scriptures possess a most clear authority, whenever a point arises, which no man can be ignorant of, without imperilling the salvation which has been promised him'[181]. Elsewhere, St. Augustine declared that the plain passages of the Scriptures contain everything needful to our faith and morals[182]. Thus faith finds its inner light in the Holy Scriptures, in the Prophets, in the Gospels and in the writings of the Apostles. They are as lights in dark places, dispelling the night. The Apostle Peter said: 'We have also a more sure word of prophecy; whereunto ye do well that ye take heed, as unto a light that shineth in a dark place until the day dawn and the day star arise in your hearts'[183]. Hence, 'the style, in which Sacred Scripture is composed, is accessible to all men, though its deeper mysteries are penetrable to very few. The plain truths which it contains, it declares in the artless language of familiar friendship to the hearts both of the unlearned and of the learned[184]. The Holy Scripture suits itself to babes and has not avoided words drawn from any class of things, through which as by nourishment, our understanding might rise gradually to things divine and transcendent[185]. It stoops to all in the great plainness of its language and lowliness of its style and yet exercises the application of such as are not light of heart; that it might receive all into its common bosom, and through narrow passages waft over some few towards God[186]. The waters of the Holy Scripture flow. Thence drinks the hare, thence the wild ass: the hare little, the wild ass great, the hare timid, the wild ass fierce, either sort drinks thence, but each for his thirst. The water does not say, "I am enough for the hare" and refuse the wild ass; nor does it say, "Let the wild ass come, the hare, if he comes, shall be swept away". So faithfully and gently doth it flow, as at once to satisfy the wild ass, and not to alarm the hare. The sound of Tully's voice rings out, Cicero is read, it is some book, it is a dialogue of his, whether his own, or Plato's or by whatever such writer; some hear that are unlearned, weak ones of less mind; who dareth to aspire to such a

[181] De peccatorum meritis et remissione II, 59.
[182] De doctrina Christiana II, 9.
[183] 2 Pet. 1 : 19; Sermo 126, 1.
[184] Epistula 137, 18.
[185] De Trinitate I, 2.
[186] Confessiones VI, 8.

thing? It is a sound of water, and that perchance turbid, but certainly flowing so violently, that a timid animal dare not draw near and drink. For whom has sounded, "In the beginning God has created the heavens and the earth" and he has not dared to drink? To whom sounded a Psalm and he saith, "It is too much for me?"[187]. There is no great difficulty in coming through the Scripture to know the things necessary to salvation, but when anyone has accepted these truths with the faith that is indispensable as a foundation of a life of piety and uprightness, many mysteries remain to be inquired into by those who are advancing in the study[188]. But even the truths which the Scripture veils in symbols it does not set forth in stiff and stately sentences, which a mind somewhat sluggish and uneducated might shrink from approaching, as the poor man shrinks from the presence of the rich; but, by the condescension of its style, it invites all not only to be fed with the truth which is plain, but also to be exercised by the truth which is concealed, having both in its simple and in its obscure portions the same truth. Lest what is easily understood should beget satiety in the reader, the same truth being in another place more obscurely expressed becomes again desired, and, being desired, is somehow invested with a new attractiveness, and thus is received with pleasure into the heart. By these means wayward minds are corrected, weak minds are nourished, and strong minds are filled with pleasure in such a way as is profitable for all[189]. Almost nothing is dug out of those obscure passages which may not be found set forth in the plainest language elsewhere'[190]. Hence, St. Augustine made it a rule to grasp the plain passages of Scripture the better to throw light on the dark passages[191].

Precisely because Scripture is clear, can it be consulted as a judge in disputes. In his controversy with the Donatists, St. Augustine therefore made a point of citing only the plain texts from which only unequivocal conclusions could be derived[192]. He did likewise in his struggle against the Pelagians, confounding them with absolutely clear texts, and repeatedly admonishing them to bow before these texts[193].

[187] Enarr. in Ps. 103, III, 4.
[188] Epistula 137, 3.
[189] ib. 18.
[190] De doctrina Christiana II, 8.
[191] De peccatorum meritis et remissione III, 7.
[192] De unitate ecclesiae 28, 31.
[193] De peccatorum meritis et remissione I, 29.

'What can be plainer than the many weighty testimonies of the inspired Scriptures, which afford to us the clearest proof possible that without union with Christ there is no man who can attain to eternal life and salvation; and that by the judgment of God no man can unjustly be damned'[194]. Firmly convinced, that in his struggle against them, he had argued not through himself but through the clear evidence of Scripture, he insisted on submission to its authority[195]. Scripture because of its clarity, must be accepted as the final judge and arbiter[196].

Yet Scripture is also full of shadowy depths and great mysteries[197], for it deals with God and things divine. Even so, St. Augustine would often deepen the mystery further still, by discovering shadows where none existed. He even went so far as to make it a rule that 'whatever there is in the Word of God that cannot, when taken literally, be referred either to purity of life or soundness of doctrine, may be set down as figurative'[198] Thus his extensively allegorical explanations took in numbers, names, headings, and particularly events in the Old Testament 'which is full of signs and symbols'[199]. Moreover, 'the Scriptures were written in a foreign language, and introduce us to a world greatly different to our own'[200].

'Therefore all men who fear God and are of a meek and pious disposition ought to seek the will of God in the Holy Scripture. And in pursuing this search, the first rule to observe is to know these books, if not yet with the understanding, still to read them so as to commit them to memory, or at least so as not to remain wholly ignorant of them. Next, those matters that are plainly laid down in them, whether rules of life, or rules of faith, are to be searched into more carefully and more diligently; and the more of these a man discovers, the more capacious does his understanding become. After this, when we have made ourselves to a certain extent familiar with the language of Scripture, we may proceed to open up and investigate the obscure passages, and in doing so draw examples from the

[194] ib. III, 7.
[195] De gratia et libero arbitrio 41; De correptione et gratia 1.
[196] See also: De peccatorum meritis et remissione I, 10, 33, 53, 56, III; 14; De natura et gratia 21, 22; De gratia Christi I, 27, 40; De praedestinatione sanctorum I, 3, 6, 16; 40–43; De dono perseverantiae 15, 27, 40, 47.
[197] Epistula 137, 3.
[198] De doctrina Christiana III, 14.
[199] See Marrou, op. cit. p. 478 ff.
[200] De doctrina Christiana II, 11 ff.

plainer expressions to throw light upon the more obscure, and use the evidence of passages about which there is no doubt to remove all hesitation in regard to the doubtful passages'[201]. A knowledge of languages, history, biology, astronomy, dialectics, is also of great benefit to our understanding[202]. 'But when the student of the Holy Scriptures, prepared in this way, shall enter upon his investigations, let him constantly meditate upon the saying of the apostle's "Knowledge puffeth up, but charity edifieth". For so he will feel that, whatever may be the riches he brings with him out of Egypt, yet unless he has kept the Passover, he cannot be safe. Alone when he is meek and lowly of heart, subject to the easy yoke of Christ and laden with his light burden, the knowledge of the Scripture cannot puff him up'[203]. We must hold fast to Christ with a firm and simple faith since it was to the faithful that he disclosed what treasures of wisdom and knowledge were hidden in Him. He did not conceal these treasures in order to keep them from us, but rather to cause us to thirst after them. Honour in Him what you do not understand, and honour Him the more, the greater is the number of veils you uncover. The more venerable a man, the thicker the curtains within his house[204]. 'Honour God's Word, honour God's Scripture, though it be not plain: in reverence wait for understanding. Be not wanton to accuse either the obscurity or seeming contradiction of Scripture. There is nothing in it contradictory: somewhat there is which is obscure, not in order that it may be denied thee, but that it may exercise him that shall afterward receive it. When it is obscure, that is the Physician's doing, that thou mayest knock. He willed that thou shouldest be exercised in knocking; He willed it, that he might open to thee when thou knockest. By knocking thou shalt be exercised, thou shalt be enlarged; enlarged, thou shalt contain what is given. Be not then indignant for that it is shut: be mild, be gentle. Kick not against what is dark, nor say, It were better said, if it were said thus. For how canst thou thus say, or judge how it is expedient it be said? It is said as it is expedient it be said. Let not the sick man seek to amend his remedies: the Physician knoweth how to temper them; believe Him who cared for thee'[205].

[201] ib. II, 9.
[202] ib. 16–60.
[203] ib. 61, 62.
[204] Sermo 51, 5.
[205] Enarr. in Ps. 146, 12.

The true understanding of the Scriptures—and St. Augustine was to stress this fact on many occasions—is often furthered even by heretics, who force the Church to look more closely into God's Word. The Church then uncovers what was previously hidden and God's Will is done. 'For was the Trinity perfectly treated of before the Arians snarled thereat? Was repentance perfectly treated of before the Novatians opposed it[206]? For many meanings of the Holy Scriptures are concealed and are known only to a few of singular intelligence, and are never vindicated so suitably and acceptably as when our diligence to make answer to heretics constraineth us. For then even they that neglect the pursuits of learning, shaking of their slumber, are stirred up to a diligent hearing, in order that their opponents may be refuted'[207]. For whenever the heretics blaspheme, those who are weak are thrown into confusion, and forced to look into things. In their investigations, they are like small children who beat their heads against their mothers' breasts to cause more milk to flow. The weak seek, and those who understand must explain[208].

'Whatever there is in the Scriptures, it is lofty and divine: there is in them altogether truth and a system of teaching most suited to refresh and to renew minds; and clearly so ordered in measure, as that there is no one but may draw thence, what is enough for himself, if only he approach to draw with devotion and piety, as true religion demands'[209].

7. *The sufficiency of the Scriptures.*

St. Augustine was convinced that the Scriptures sufficed for showing the road to eternal life, and he said so on many occasions. 'All that Christ was minded to give for our perusal on the subject of his own doings and sayings, He commanded to be written by his disciples[210]. Though the Lord Jesus did many acts, yet all of them are not recorded, just as St. John testifies, but such were chosen for record as seemed to suffice for the salvation of believers[211]. For among the

[206] Enarr. in Ps. 54, 22.
[207] ib. in Ps. 67, 39.
[208] Sermo 51, 11.
[209] De utilitate credendi 13.
[210] De Consensu Evangelistarum I, 54.
[211] Tractatus in Joannem XLIX, 1.

things that are plainly laid down in Scripture are to be found all matters that concern faith and the manner of life'[212]. Hence he told Petilian: 'Whether concerning Christ, or concerning his Church, or any other matter whatsoever which is connected with your faith and life, we must heed Paul's advice[213]. When he said, "Though an angel from heaven preach any other Gospel unto you than that which you have received in the lawful and evangelical Scriptures, let him be accursed"'[214]. For this reason, St. Augustine told his congregation in his sermon on the shepherds that they must disdain everything outside the Scriptures if they are not to be lost in the mists[215].

Quite apart from confessing the sufficiency of Scripture, St. Augustine also accepted a number of unwritten apostolic traditions. Thus he claimed that his rejection of rebaptism sprang from these traditions. Similarly, he held that many customs not mentioned in the Epistles nor by later Councils, and yet adopted by the Universal Church, must have been handed down from the apostles[216]. 'The apostles gave no injunctions on this point, but this custom may be supposed to have had its origin in apostolic tradition, just as there are many things which are observed by the whole Church and therefore are fairly held to have been enjoined by the apostles, which yet are not mentioned in their writings'[217]. Although the canonical writings cannot be cited for or against such traditons[218], we nevertheless adhere to these writings if we do what the Universal Church enjoins us to do, since the Church is established by divine athority[219]. Similarly, with the baptism of infants: 'If anyone seek for divine authority in this matter, though what is held by the whole Church, and that not so instituted by the Councils, but as a matter of invariable custom, is rightly held to have been handed down by apostolic authority, still we can form a true conjecture of the value of the sacrament of baptism in the case of infants, from the parallel of circumcision'[220].

[212] De doctrina Christiana II, 14.
[213] Gal. 1:8.
[214] Contra litteras Petiliani III, 7.
[215] Sermo 46, 24.
[216] De baptismo II, 12.
[217] ib. V. 31.
[218] Contra Cresconium I, 37.
[219] ib. 39.
[220] De baptismo IV, 31.

Thus St. Augustine covered a host of subjects, and particularly in his answers to Januarius' questions about all sorts of Church matters, he touched upon many traditional usages, not mentioned in Scripture, but presumably adopted by the apostles or by the Councils of the Church, for instance the yearly observance of Christ's Passion, Resurrection, and Ascension, the descent of the Holy Ghost, and many other customs that are observed by the Universal Church[221].

Remarkably enough, these unwritten traditions were said by St. Augustine to apply exclusively to certain customs and usages. The question whether this is accidental, and whether many Roman Catholic scholars are right in attributing a far wider role to St. Augustine's concept of tradition[222], can only be answered in our discussion of Church doctrine.

8. *The necessity of Scripture.*

St. Augustine has discussed the necessity of Scripture on many occasions, and his discussions are an excellent illustration of what we have called his first and second stages. In the first stage he held that Scripture is needed constantly by the uneducated masses, but temporarily by the spiritual elite. In the second stage, however, he emphasised the need for Scripture of *all* believers on their pilgrimage. God's Word has become a kind of bond with God, in which He has deliberately set down His promises to all generations, so that all mortals can read them and keep them[223]. This necessity is, however, restricted to mortal life. In the new heaven and on the new earth, God's people will no longer need any writings, for here faith will have become the direct contemplation of the Divine Countenance. This was another of St. Augustine's favourite topics, but since we shall discuss the necessity of Scripture more fully in Chapters VI and VII, we merely mention it in passing now.

[221] Epistula 54, 1.

[222] Schwane, *Dogmengeschichte der patristischen Zeit*, 1895, p. 703 ff.; E. Portalié, *Dict. de Théologie Catholique*, Paris 1937, I, col. 2340; F. Hoffmann, op. cit. pp. 295, 296. For the opposite point of view, see B.B. Warfield, *Studies in Tertullian and Augustine*, New York 1930, p. 182 ff.

[223] Enarr. in Ps. 144, 17.

CHAPTER III

THE WORD OF GOD AS THE WORD OF CHRIST

There are few topics that St. Augustine has treated as lovingly as the Christocentric character of the Scriptures[1]. This is borne out by the fact that, while he fully accepted the divine inspiration of the Scriptures as a sacred tradition, and defended it against all attacks, he only discussed it in detail on a few occasions, and never attempted to present a coherent theory. Not so with the acceptance of the Bible as the Word of Christ, on which subject he discoursed fervently on a vast number of occasions. Attacks by Manicheans, Jews, and Pelagians only served to consolidate St. Augustine's ideas on the subject.

1. *The opponents.*

In particular, the Manicheans, with their bitter attacks on the Old, and their highly selective attitude to the New Testament, forced St. Augustine to defend the former staunchly. Their main spokesman was Faustus, who raised four objections (antitheses) against the Biblical arguments of Catholic Christians. The first of these objections was that *the Old Testament contained no prophecies about the coming of Christ.* 'For my part', Faustus said, 'I have read the prophets with the most eager attention, and have found no such prophecies'[2]. And he told St. Augustine: 'You ask us why we do not believe Moses, when Christ says, "Moses wrote of me; and if ye believed Moses, ye would also believe me"?[3] I should be

[1] Little has been published on this subject, but the reader is referred to Pontet op. cit., pp. 149 ff., 305 ff.
[2] Contra Faustum XII, 1.
[3] Joh. 5:46.

glad if not only Moses, but all prophets, Jew and Gentile, had written of Christ. It would be no hindrance, but a help to our faith, if we could cull testimonies from all hands agreeing in favour of our God. You could extract the prophecies of Christ out of the superstition which we should hate as much as ever. I am quite willing to believe that Moses, though so much the opposite of Christ, may seem to have written of him. No one but would gladly find a flower in every thorn, and food in every plant, and honey in every insect, although we would not feed on insects or on grass, nor wear thorns as a crown. No one but would wish pearls to be found in every deep, and gems in every land, and fruit on every tree. We may eat fish from the sea without drinking the water. We may take the useful, and reject what is hurtful. And why may we not take the prophecies of Christ from a religion the rites of which we condemn as useless? If any similar testimony is found in Moses, I will accept it. But I will not on this account be brought into subjection to his law, which to my mind is pure Paganism. There is no reason for thinking that I can have any objections to receive prophecies of Christ from every spirit[4]. But I have searched the Scriptures, as we are told to do, and have found no prophecies of Christ[5]. Shall it be that passage which you often quote where the God of Moses says to him, "I will raise up unto them from among their brethren a prophet like unto thee"? But this does not refer to Christ. Christ was not a prophet, nor was he like Moses: for Moses was a man, and Christ was God. Or shall we take another favourite passage of yours: "They shall see their life hanging, and shall not believe their life" (Deut. 28:66)? You, Catholics, insert the words "on a tree", which are not in the original. Nothing can be easier than to show that this has no reference to Christ. Also I cannot admit that the words, "Cursed is every one that hangeth on a tree" (Deut. 21:23) refer to Christ[6]. So it is doubtful whether, on examination, it can be shown that the Hebrew prophets foretold our Christ. But were it so, what does it matter to us? We did not first become Jews, so as to reach Christianity through faith in their prophets; but were attracted solely by the fame, and the virtues, and the wisdom of our Saviour Jesus Christ. Again, I say, the Christian Church, which consists more of

[4] ib. XVI, 1.
[5] ib. XVI, 2, 3.
[6] ib. 4, 5.

Gentiles than of Jews, can owe nothing to Hebrew witnesses. If any prophecies of Christ are to be found in the Sybil, or in Hermes, called Trismegistus, or Orpheus, or any heathen poet, they might aid the faith of those who, like us, are converts from heathenism to Christianity. But the testimony of the Hebrews is useless to us before conversion, for then we cannot believe them; and superfluous after, for we believe without them[7]. And surely it shows a weak faith not to believe in Christ without proofs and testimonies. Indeed you yourself (Augustine) are accustomed to teach that Christian faith is so simple and absolute as not to admit of laborious investigations. Why then should you destroy the simplicity of faith by buttressing it with evidences, and Jewish evidences, too? Or if you are changing your opinion about evidences, what more trustworthy witness could you have than God Himself testifying to His own Son when He sent Him on earth,—not by a prophet or an interpreter—by a voice immediately from heaven: "This is my beloved Son, believe Him"?[8] And again He testifies of Himself, "I came forth from the Father and am come into the world"[9]. When the Jews quarrelled with this testimony, He replied, "Although I bear witness of myself, my witness is true, and the Father who sent me, beareth witness of me"[10]. He does not mention the prophets'[11].

Faustus' second objection was that *the Old Testament is of the flesh rather than of the spirit and hence can have nothing in common with Christ.* 'Remember that the promise of Canaan in the Old Testament is made to Jews, that is, to the circumcised, who offer sacrifice, and abstain from swine's flesh, and from the other animals which Moses pronounced unclean, and observe Sabbaths, and the feast of unleavened bread. Christians have not adopted these observances, and no one keeps them; so that if we will not take the inheritance, we should surrender the documents. This is my first reason for rejecting the Old Testament, unless you teach me better. My second reason is, that this inheritance is such a poor fleshly thing, without any spiritual blessings, that after the New Testament, and its glorious promise of the kingdom of heaven and eternal life, I think it not

[7] ib. XIII, 1.
[8] Matth. 3:17.
[9] Joh. 16:28.
[10] Joh. 8:13–18; 10:38.
[11] Contra Faustum XII, 1.

worth the taking[12]. The Old Testament promises riches, and plenty, and children, and children's children, and long life, and withal the land of Canaan; but only to the circumcised, the Sabbath observers, those offering sacrifices, and abstaining from swine's flesh. Now I, like any other Christian, pay no attention to these things, as being trifling and useless for the salvation of the soul. I conclude, therefore, that the promises do not belong to me[13]. We read in Matthew[14], that Christ said, "I came not to destroy the law, but to fulfil it". If these are Christ's words, they are as much against you as against me. Your Christianity as well as mine is based on the belief that Christ came to destroy the law and the prophets. Your actions prove this, even though in words you deny it. It is on this ground that you disregard the precepts of the law and the prophets. How, then, can you believe that Christ said these words without first confessing that hitherto we have been wholly in error and without showing our repentance by entering on a course of obedience to the law and the prophets, and of careful observance of their requirements? But grant that we have been in the wrong hitherto. What is to be done now? Shall we come under the law, since Christ has not destroyed, but fulfilled it? Shall we by circumcision add shame to shame, and believe that God is pleased with such sacraments? Shall we observe the rest of the Sabbath, and bind ourselves in the fetters of Saturn? Shall we glut the demon of the Jews, for he is not God, with the slaughter of bulls, rams and goats, not to say of men? Shall we call the flesh of some animals clean? Of course you will allow that as Christians we must not do any of these things, for you remember that Christ says that a man when circumcised becomes twofold a child of hell[15]. It is plain also that Christ never observed the Sabbath himself, nor commanded it to be observed. And regarding food, He says expressly that man is not defiled by anything that goes into his mouth, but rather by the things which come out of it[16]. Regarding sacrifices too, He often says, that God desires mercy, and not sacrifice[17]. What becomes then of the statement that He came not to destroy the law, but to fulfil it? If Christ said this, He must have

[12] ib. IV, 1; VI, 1.
[13] ib. X, 1.
[14] 5:17.
[15] Matth. 23:15.
[16] Matth. 15:11.
[17] Matth. 9:13; Contra Faustum XVIII, 1–3.

meant something else, or, what is not to be thought of, He told a lie, or He never said it. If He has said it, He means not the law of the Hebrews which the apostle calls the law of sin and death[18], nor that of the Gentiles[19], but the law of truth, the law of the spirit of life[20], the law of old promulgated by Enoch and Seth which dates from the earliest times: "Thou shalt not kill; thou shalt not commit adultery; thou shalt not bear false witness". Christ has fulfilled these commandments of the righteous men of antiquity in the Sermon on the Mount[21]. We do not blaspheme the law, promulgated throughout the world, that is, at the commencement of the present constitution of the world, but the Hebrew writers did violence, by infecting it with the pollution of their disgusting precepts about circumcision and sacrifice. We do not blaspheme your prophets and patriarchs, but the writers of the Old Testament. Their books contain shocking calumnies against God Himself. We are told that he exists from eternity in darkness, and admired the light when he saw it; that he was so ignorant of the future, that he gave Adam a command, not foreseeing that it would be broken; that his perception was so limited that he could not see Adam, when he hid himself in a corner of Paradise; that envy made him afraid lest his creature, man, should taste of the tree of life and live for ever; that afterwards he was greedy for blood and fat from all kinds of sacrifice, and jealous if they were offered to any one but himself; that he was enraged sometimes against his enemies, sometimes against his friends; that he destroyed thousands of men for a slight offence, or for nothing: that he threatened to come with a sword and spare nobody, righteous or wicked'[22]. Moreover, the Old Testament was full of tales of wickedness committed by patriarchs and prophets alike[23]. It is suffused with shameful examples and alien commandments, which no Christian holds or practises'[24].

Faustus' third objection was that *the acceptance of the New Testament is tantamount to the rejection of the Old*. 'The Scripture says that old and new do not agree. For "no one putteth a piece of new cloth unto an

[18] Rom. 8:2.
[19] Rom. 2:14, 15.
[20] Rom. 8:2.
[21] Matth. 5:21–44; Contra Faustum XIX, 1–3.
[22] Contra Faustum XXII, 4.
[23] ib. XXI, 5.
[24] ib. XXXII, 3–5.

old garment, otherwise the rent is made worse"[25]. To avoid making a worse rent, as you have done, I do not mix Christian newness with Hebrew oldness[26]. The apostles who were born under the Old Testament, have abandoned it, much more may I, who was not born under it, be excused for not thrusting myself into it. It is as if two trees, a sweet and a bitter, drew from one soil the sap which each assimilates to its own nature. The apostles passed from the bitter to the sweet; it would be madness in me to change from the sweet to the bitter[27]. When a vessel is full, what is poured on it is not received, but allowed to run over; and a full stomach rejects what it cannot hold. So the Jews, satisfied with the Old Testament, reject Christ; and we who have received the New Testament from Christ, reject the Old. You receive both because you are only half filled with each, and the one is not completed, but corrupted by the other. For vessels half filled should not be filled up with anything of a different nature from what they already contain. If it contains wine, it should be filled up with wine, honey with honey, vinegar with vinegar. For to pour gall on honey, or water on wine, or alkalies on vinegar, is not addition, but adulteration. This is why we do not receive the Old Testament. Our Church, the bride of Christ, the poor bride of a rich bridegroom, is content with the possession of her husband, and scorns the wealth of inferior lovers, and despises the gifts of the Old Testament and of its author, and from regard to her own character, receives only the letters of her husband. We leave the Old Testament to your Church, that, like a bride faithless to her spouse, delights in the letters and gifts of another. This lover who corrupts your chastity, the God of the Hebrews in his stone tablets, promises you gold and silver, and abundance of food, and the land of Canaan. Such low rewards have tempted you to be unfaithful to Christ, after all the rich dowry bestowed by him. By such attractions the God of the Hebrews gains over the bride of Christ. Go on, then, as you have begun, join the new cloth to the old garment, put the new wine in old bottles, serve two masters without pleasing either, make Christianity a monster, half horse and half man; but allow us to serve only Christ'[28].

[25] Matth. 9:16.
[26] Contra Faustum VIII, 1.
[27] ib. IX, 1.
[28] ib. XV, 1.

Fourthly, Faustus claimed that: *Just as Christ has taught the Catholic Church to reject much of the Old Testament in practice, so the Paraclete Manichaeus has taught men to sift the wheat from chaff in the New Testament.* 'Jesus teaches you, what you should receive of the Old Testament. So as Jesus after being predicted in the Old Testament, now subjects it to his sweeping criticism, and teaches you to receive a few things and to throw over many things, in the same way the Paraclete, who is promised in the New Testament teaches us what part of it to receive, and what to reject[29]. Hence, as you receive nothing in the Old Testament except the prophecies and the common precepts of practical morality and set aside the circumcision, and sacrifices and the Sabbath, why should not we receive nothing in the New Testament but what we find said in honour and praise of the majesty of the Son, either by Himself or by his apostles, with the proviso, in the case of the apostles, that it was said by them after reaching perfection, and take no notice of the rest which was the utterance of ignorance or inexperience, or, if not, was added by crafty opponents with a malicious intention, or was stated by the writers without due consideration, and so handed down as authentic? Take, as examples, the shameful birth of Jesus from a woman, His being circumcised like the Jews, His offering sacrifices like the Gentiles, His being baptised in a humiliating manner, His being led about by the devil in the wilderness, and His being tempted by him in the most distressing way. With these exceptions, besides whatever has been inserted under the pretence of being a quotation of the Old Testament, we believe the whole, especially the mystic nailing to the cross, emblematic of the wounds of the soul in its passion; and also the sound moral precepts of Jesus and his parables, and the whole of his immortal discourse[30]. As for the genealogy of Jesus, the evangelist himself does not venture to call it the gospel[31]. Luke and Matthew do not give the same genealogy. Mark and John have nothing of David, or Mary, or Joseph. This is my reason for not believing in the birth of Christ[32]. You ask me if I believe the gospel? The gospel is nothing else than the preaching and the precept of Christ. I have parted with all gold and silver, and left off carrying

[29] ib. XXXII, 6.
[30] ib. XXXII, 7.
[31] ib. II, 1.
[32] ib. III, 1.

money in my purse; content with daily food; without anxiety for tomorrow and without solicitude about how I shall be fed and do you ask if I believe the gospel? But according to you, to believe the gospel is not only to obey its commands, but also to believe in all that is written in it; and first of all, that God was born. But neither is believing the gospel only to believe that Jesus was born, but also to do what He commands. So, if you say that I do not believe the gospel because I disbelieve the incarnation, much more do you not believe because you disregard the commandments. At any rate, we are on a par till these questions are settled. If your disregard of the precepts does not prevent you from professing faith in the gospel, why should my rejection of the genealogy prevent me? And if to believe in the gospel includes both faith in the genealogies and obedience to the precepts, why do you condemn me, since we both are imperfect? What one wants the other has. But if, as there can be no doubt, belief in the gospel consists solely in obedience to the commands of God, then, as the proverb says, the deserter accuses the soldier. Christ says that who does the will of His Father, shall enter in His kingdom[33], and not, "He that confesses that I was born". And again He says to His disciples, "Go, teach all nations, teaching them to observe all things which I have commanded you"[34]. It is not "teaching them that I was born", but "to observe my commandments". Again, "You are my friends if you do what I command you"[35], and not, "if you believe that I was born". The kingdom, life, happiness, are everywhere promised to the part I have chosen[36]. Christ never declares with His own lips that He had an earthly father or descent'[37]. True, Paul seems to have thought that Christ was born from David's seed[38], but he afterwards corrected this erroneous belief[39]. And later, when he said: "When I was a child, I spoke as a child", he must have been thinking of what he had said in Rom. 1. We are thus justified in preferring the new and amended confession of Paul to his old and faulty one[40]. For my part, as a

[33] Matth. 7:21.
[34] Matth. 28:19.
[35] Joh. 15:14, 19.
[36] Contra Faustum V, 1–3.
[37] ib. VII, 1.
[38] Rom. 1:3.
[39] 2 Cor. 5:16.
[40] Contra Faustum XI, 1.

Manichean, I am taught that many things which pass in Scripture under the name of the Saviour are spurious, and that they must therefore be tested to find whether they are true, and sound, and genuine; for the enemy who comes by night has corrupted almost every passage by sowing tares among the wheat'[41].

St. Augustine also had to counter the arguments of the Jews, who were outraged by Christianity's usurpation of their Old Testament, and condemned it in terms which were to resound time and again during the internecine struggle between Church and Synagogue. They objected that Christians could not possibly claim the Old Testament as their own, since they had done away with the sacred rites of circumcision, offerings, the Passover and many other ceremonies[42]. They also insisted that there was no mention of Christ in the Old Testament, and that what prophecies there were referred not to Christ but to the Jewish people[43], viz. the prophecy of the righteous servant in Isaiah 53[44]. Hence they rebuked the Christians for turning the heroes of Israel's history, who had sacrificed their lives for God's chosen people, into Christian martyrs. In all their words and confessions they had never spoken of nor paid heed to Christ[45].

The Pelagians, again, had still another attitude to the Old Testament. According to them, there were three periods. Men first lived righteously by nature, then under the law, thirdly under grace. In the first period—from Adam to Moses— the Creator was known by the guidance of nature; and the rule of living rightly was carried in the hearts of men. In the second period men's manners became corrupt and 'when nature now tarnished began to be insufficient, the law was added to it, whereby as by a moon the original lustre was restored to nature after its blush was impaired. But after the habit of sin had become excessive by over-indulgence among men, and the law was unequal to the task of curing it, Christ came, and the Physician Himself brought relief to the malady at its most desperate development'[46]. Pelagius therefore considered that the three periods were interrelated. At the synod of Diospolis[47] he

[41] ib. XVIII, 3.
[42] Oratio adversus Judaeos (428), 3.
[43] ib. 9.
[44] ib. 10.
[45] Sermo 300, 3.
[46] De gratia Christi II, 30.
[47] Or Lydda, 415.

was confronted with his claim that 'the kingdom of heaven was promised even in the Old Testament'. Upon that, he replied in vindication; 'This can be readily proved by the Scriptures. The heretics, however, in order to disparage the Old Testament, deny this statement, but I simply followed the authority of the Scriptures when I said this, for in the prophet of Daniel it is written[48]: "The Saints of the Most High shall take the Kingdom" '[49].

2. *St. Augustine's own basic position.*

St. Augustine countered all these objections by stating the basic proposition that the entire Scriptures bear witness to Christ, to Christ entire, i.e. to the Head and His Body. Referring to Christ's converse with Moses and Elijah, he said in one of his sermons: 'What would be the worth of Moses and Elijah, that is of the Law and the Prophets, had they not held converse with Christ? Had they not given witness of Christ, who of us would read the Law and the Prophets? Thus Paul said[50]: "But now the righteousness of God without the law is manifested, being witnessed by the law and the prophets[51]. And lo, a voice from heaven affirmed: This is my beloved Son. Hearken unto Him!" For you hear Him both in the prophet and in the law. Indeed, where have you failed to hear Him? On hearing His voice, the disciples fell down to the ground. Here was the Lord, here was the Law, here were the Prophets, but the Lord was the Lord, and they were as His servants. Moses and the Prophets spoke and wrote, but He came to fulfil their witness'[52]. And in another sermon on the same text: 'Elijah speaks, but hearken unto Him; Moses speaks, but hearken to His Voice, the prophets and the law speak but hearken unto Him Who is the voice of the law and the tongue of the prophets. Through them He spoke, and appeared Himself when He thought the time had come. Hearken unto Him, one and all. During the reading of the Gospel, think of the cloud and the voice speaking out of it. Let us listen to that voice, do its bidding, and trust in His promises'[53]. Time and again, St. Augustine would

[48] Daniel 7:18.
[49] De gestis Pelagii, 13.
[50] Rom. 3:21.
[51] Sermo 78, 2.
[52] ib. 4.
[53] Sermo 79.

return to this subject in his sermons. Christ—and this was a point St. Augustine often stressed—not only spoke Himself but also through His apostles[54]. Thus Christ is not only in the Gospel but also in His apostles, speaking both with His own voice, and through his criers. For, the Acts tell us that whenever the crier speaks out before God's seat of justice, it is He who ordered the crier who addresses us to speak on His behalf[55]. The Scriptures are as the heart of Christ, as His wisdom[56]. All that we read in the Scriptures, serves for our edification and salvation. It was thus that Christ expounded the Scriptures before those who had gone to Emmaus, saying that all the things concerning His suffering written in the law of Moses and in the prophets must be fulfilled. The strength of our faith rests in Him, since all that was fulfilled in Him, had been foretold. Christ, and this you must observe and engrave upon your memory (for God desired to save us from dangerous error by giving as the Scriptures which no true Christian may doubt) when He allowed Himself to be touched by the eleven disciples, yet saw fit to strengthen their faith by quoting from Scripture, no doubt for the sake of later generations. For we have nothing that we can touch, but we always have that which we can read. Whence cometh our faith but from what He told those who wanted to touch Him? For He expounded the Scriptures to them, to show them that He had to suffer and that everything must be fulfilled that was written of Him in the Law, the Psalms and the Prophets. All these books speak of Christ. What then did the Lord tell of Christ in the Law, the Prophets, and the Psalms? The evangelist has put it all briefly so that we may learn what in so vast a treasure of words we must believe and understand. Many are indeed the pages, and many are the books. They contain everything the Lord told his disciples briefly. And what is that? That Christ must suffer and rise the third day[57].

In a famous sermon on the marriage in Cana, St. Augustine referred to the same text[58], and also to the removal of the veil of which St. Paul spoke[59]. 'When the veil is taken away, then the covering over of prophecy is taken away. We understand then the Scriptures

[54] 2 Cor. 13:4.
[55] Sermo 82, 8; cf. p. 37.
[56] Enarratio in Ps. 21 II, 14.
[57] In epistolam Joannis Tr. II, 1.
[58] Luke 24:25 ff., 44 ff.
[59] 2 Cor. 3:16

and what was water now becomes wine to us. Read all the prophetic books; and if Christ be not understood therein, what canst thou find so insipid and silly? Understand Christ in them, and what thou readest not only has a taste, but even inebriates thee[60]. When these words of the gospel[61] are understood, and they are certainly clear, all the mysteries which are latent in this miracle of the Lord will be laid open. Observe what He says, that it behoved the things to be fulfilled in Christ that were written of Him. Where were they written? "In the law," says He, "and in the prophets, and in the Psalms". He omitted no part of the Old Scriptures. These were water; and hence the disciples were called irrational by the Lord because as yet they tasted to them as water, not as wine. And how did He make of the water wine? When He opened their understanding, and expounded to them the Scriptures, beginning from Moses, through all the prophets; with which being now inebriated, they said, "Did not our hearts burn within us in the way, when He opened to us the Scriptures?" For they understood Christ in those books in which they knew Him not before. Thus our Lord Jesus Christ changed the water into wine, and that has now taste which before had not, that now inebriates which before did not. For if He had commanded the water to be poured out of the waterpots, and so Himself had put in the wine from the secret repositories of the creature, then He would appear to have rejected the Old Scriptures. When, however, He turns the water itself into wine, He shows us that the Old Scripture also is from Himself, for at His own command were the water-pots filled. It is from the Lord indeed, that the Old Scripture also is; but it has no taste unless Christ is understood therein[62]. Let us refer the whole of the Scriptures to Christ, if we wish to keep the road of a right understanding: let us not depart from the corner-stone, lest our understanding suffer a fall[63]: in Him let that become fixed, which wavered with unstable motion; let that rest upon Him, which before was waving to and fro in uncertainty. Whatever doubt a man has in his mind when he heareth the Scriptures of God, let him not depart from Christ; when Christ has been revealed to him in the words, let him then be assured that he has understood; but before he

[60] Tractatus in Joannis evangelium IX, 3.
[61] Luke 24:25 and 44.
[62] Tractatus in Joannis evangelium IX, 5.
[63] Eph. 2:20.

arriveth to the understanding of Christ, let him not presume that he had understood'[64]. But, as St. Augustine had already observed during his Christological explanation of the Psalms, in that case everything must be referred to the whole Christ, that is to Christ with this Body whereof He is the Head according to the word of St. Paul[65]: "Now ye are the body of Christ, and members in particular"[66]. Thence he told Faustus: 'All the passages of the Scripture speak of Christ. The head now ascended into heaven along with the body still suffering on earth is the full development of the whole purpose of the authors of Scripture, which is well called Sacred Scripture. Every part of the narrative in the prophetic books should be viewed as having a figurative meaning, except what serves merely as a framework for the literal or figurative predictions of this king and of his people. For as in harps and in other musical instruments the musical sound does not come from all parts of the instrument, but from the strings, and the rest is only for fastening and stretching the strings so as to tune them, that when they are struck by the musician they may give a pleasant sound; so in these prophetical narratives the circumstances selected by the prophetic spirit either predict some future event, or if they have no voice of their own, they serve to connect together other significant utterances'[67]. And in The City of God he stated: 'The object of the writer of these sacred books, or rather of the Spirit of God in him, is not only to record the past, but to depict the future, so far as it regard the city of God. Yet we are not to suppose that all that is recorded has some signification; but those things which have no signification of their own are interwoven for the sake of the things which are significant. It is only the ploughshare that cleaves the soil; but to effect this, other parts of the plough are requisite[68]. Therefore we will distinguish in the prophetic Scriptures three kinds of prophetic utterances; forasmuch as there are some relating to the earthly Jerusalem, some to the heavenly, and some to both'. He went on to give some examples. The prophet Nathan was sent to convict King David of heinous sin, and predict to him what future evils should be consequent of it. Who can question that this and the like pertain to the terrestrial city? But where we read of the

[64] Enarratio in Ps. 96, 2.
[65] 1 Cor. 12:27.
[66] Enarratio in Ps. 3,9.
[67] Contra Faustum XXII, 94.
[68] De civitate Dei XVI, 2, 3; cf. p. 62.

New Covenant in Jer. 31, without doubt this is prophesied to the Jerusalem above. When the king Solomon builds that most noble temple, all these things both happened in the earthly Jerusalem, as history shows, and yet were types of the heavenly Jerusalem'[69]. To those who wished to give a purely allegorical explanation and thus read a spiritual meaning into everything, St. Augustine said that, while he could not condemn them for that, he would above all have them hold fast to the historical veracity of Scripture[70].

3. *Christ in the Old Testament.*

Having outlined St. Augustine's basic position, as it is reflected by all his writings, we can now examine his reply to Faustus' four objections in greater detail. Faustus' first objection, viz. that the Old Testament contained no references to Christ, was gainsayed by the New Testament itself[71]. 'Paul said of himself and of his Gospel: "Paul, a servant of Jesus Christ, called to be an apostle, separated unto the Gospel of God, which He has promised before by His prophets in the Holy Scriptures, concerning His Son, who was made of the seed of David according to the flesh"[72]. It is plain that the apostle speaks of the Hebrew prophets[73]. The apostle also testified that to the Israelites pertains the adoption and the giving of the law and the promises; whose are the fathers, and of whom, as concerning the flesh, Christ came, who is over all, God blessed for ever[74]. And in the same epistle to the Romans he declared that unto the Jews were committed the oracles of God[75]. And if Christ had not been preached by the law, Christ Himself would not have said, "If ye believe Moses, ye would have believed me, for he wrote of me"[76]. And to the apostles He said, "All things behove to be fulfilled that were written in the law of Moses, and in the prophets, and in the psalms"[77].

[69] ib. XVII, 3.
[70] ib. see pp. 90 ff.
[71] His argument was justly adopted by the Church in her struggle against the synagogue. Cf. F.W.A. Korff, *Christologie*, Nijkerk 1941, Part II, p. 16ff.; and G.C. Berkouwer, *De persoon van Christus*, Kampen 1952, p. 89 ff.
[72] Rom. 1 : 1 1–3.
[73] Contra Faustum XII, 2.
[74] Rom. 9 : 1–5.
[75] Rom. 3 : 1–2.
[76] Joh. 5 : 46.
[77] Luke 24 : 44; Contra Faustum XII, 3.

Christ Himself has told us what Abraham said to a hard-hearted man, when he was in torment in hell: "They have Moses and the prophets, let them hear them"[78]. So we have a Christ true and truthful, foretold by the prophets, preached by the apostles, who in innumerable places refer to the testimonies of the law and the prophets in support of their preaching. Paul, in one short sentence, gives the right view of this subject. "Now", he says, "the righteousness of God without the law is manifested, being witnessed by the law and the prophets"[79]. Elsewhere, speaking of Christ, he says concisely: "All the promises of God are in Him yes"[80]. Christ is the end of the law[81]. We, then, are satisfied with the authority of the apostles, who declare that what we read in the writings of the Hebrew prophets was fulfilled in Christ, or with that of Christ Himself, who says that they wrote of Him[82]. What the New Testament testifies, is also found in the Old Testament. All the contents of the prophetic writings are either directly or indirectly about Christ. Often the reference is allegorical or hidden, perhaps in a verbal allusion, or in a historical narrative, requiring diligence in the student, and rewarding him with the pleasure of discovery. Other passages are plain; for, without the help of what is clear, we could not understand what is obscure'[83].

St. Augustine then gave a long list of clear passages that could serve for the interpretation of the more obscure. In particular, he mentioned God's promises to the Fathers[84] and the unequivocal sayings of the prophets and the psalmists[85], of which there exists a great number[86]. Faustus had failed to find these prophecies, simply because he could not understand them. 'And if anyone asks why he does not understand, the answer is that he reads with a hostile, unbelieving mind; he does not search in order to know, but thinks he knows when he is ignorant'[87]. St. Augustine then went on to discuss those passages of Deuteronomy in which Faustus had claimed there

[78] Luke 16:27–31; Contra Faustum XII, 4.
[79] Rom. 3:21.
[80] 2 Cor. 1:20.
[81] Rom. 10:4; Contra Faustum XII, 5.
[82] ib. 6.
[83] ib. 7.
[84] Gen. 22:18; 26:4; 28:14; 49:8–12.
[85] Isa. 53; Ps. 22; Ps. 2; Dan. 7:13–14 et al.
[86] Contra Faustum XII, 41–44.
[87] ib. XVI, 14.

was no reference to Christ. St Augustine pointed out at great length that there could be no doubt that Deut. 18:18 referred to none other[88], and, together with the other Fathers of the Church, he insisted that the same was true of Deut. 28:66[89].

In the same spirit, he replied to one of Marcion's adherents who claimed that no one before the apostles had prophesied of Christ. 'Who', St. Augustine asked him, 'was it that said "the stone which the builders refused has become the head stone of the corner?"[90]. And who was it that said: "Thy throne, O God, is for ever and ever: the sceptre of thy kingdom is a right sceptre. Thou lovest righteousness and hatest wickedness: therefore God, thy God, hath anointed thee with the oil of gladness above thy fellows"?[91] How can God, whose throne is for ever and ever be anointed by God Himself unless Christ Jesus (be meant) who by this anointing was given the name of Christ? And Who was it that said—of which Christ Himself bore witness that it was foretold of Him—The Lord said to my Lord, sit thou on my right hand?[92] Who, in Isaiah 11 and 53, spoke so powerfully of Christ and of the glorious future of Christ's Church[93]? All these and similar prophecies were clearly spoken of Christ and of His Church and were either fulfilled in complete agreement with the writings of the evangelists and the apostles, or else are the grounds of our future hopes'[94].

Next to these clear passages, Scripture was said to contain a host of allegorical or hidden allusions to Christ[95]. What precisely did St. Augustine understand by these? We have a number of unequivocal statements by him on that score. Thus, in his *De utilitate credendi*, he wrote that 'In the Old Testament all is handed down four-fold to

[88] ib. XVI, 15–21.

[89] St. Augustine read this text in the Septuagint where it is rendered as 'Thou shalt see thy life hanging, and shalt not believe thy life'. This clear curse over the people of Israel, was applied to Christ, quite arbitrarily, with the following argument: "Christ Himself says 'I am the life', and since there is no doubt that He was seen hanging by the unbelieving Jews, I see no reason for doubting that this was written of Christ, for, as Christ says, Moses wrote of Him". (XVI, 22). In XVI, 23, he even claimed, that Moses knew that he was speaking of Christ.

[90] Ps. 118:22.

[91] Ps. 45:6, 7. St. Augustine read this text as: Therefore God, Thou hast anointed Thee, O God, with the oil of gladness.

[92] Ps. 110:1; Mark 12:36.

[93] Is. 54:1–3.

[94] Contra adversarium legis et profetarum II, 12.

[95] Contra Faustum XII, 7.

them who desire to know it, according to history, according to aetiology, according to analogy, according to allegory. It is handed down according to allegory, when it is taught that certain things which have been written are not to be taken in the letter, but are to be understood in a figure'[96]. He went on to give three Biblical exemples: the sign of the prophet Jonas[97], Paul's description of the Exodus as an allegorical reference to God's future people[98], and Paul's parable in his Epistle to the Galatians[99]. During a sermon in Carthage, he called the wind an allegory of the soul. As the congregation reacted with apparent scepticism, he went on to say: 'Beware lest you suppose that when I named allegory, I spoke of anything like a pantomime. For some words, because they are words, and proceed from the tongue, are used by us in common with ridiculous and unworthy subjects, yet those words have their place in the Church, and their place on the stage. For I did not say any thing but what the apostle said when he spoke of the two sons of Abraham: which are, he says, in allegory. It is called allegory, when any thing appears to sound in words of one thing, and in meaning it signify another. As Christ is called a Lamb: is He cattle? Christ a lion: is He a wild beast? Christ a rock: is He hardness? Christ a mountain: is He a swelling of the earth? And so many things seem to have one sound and another meaning and that is called allegory. Therefore, we say a figure is an allegory in that a sacred meaning is figured'[100]. In his *De Trinitate* he said that 'there are some modes of speech, which the Greeks call tropes, which Greek word we also use in Latin, while it is a very difficult thing to express the names of the several modes or tropes in Latin. And hence some Latin translators, through unwillingness to employ a Greek word, where the apostle says, "which things are an allegory" have rendered it by a circumlocution—"which things signify one thing by another". But there are several species of this kind of trope that is called allegory, and one of them is that which is called enigma. Now the definition of the generic term must necessarily embrace also all its species; and hence as every horse is an animal, but not every animal is a horse, so every enigma is an allegory, but every allegory is not an enigma. What

[96] De utilitate credendi 5.
[97] Matth. 12:39.
[98] 1 Cor. 10:1–11.
[99] Gal. 4:24, 25; De utilitate credendi 8.
[100] Enarratio in Ps. 103 I, 13; cf. Gal. 4:24.

then is an allegory, but a trope wherein one thing is understood from another, as in the Epistle to the Thessalonians, "Let us not therefore sleep: for they who sleep, sleep in the night; and they who are drunken, are drunken in the night; but let us who are of the day, be sober"?[101]. But this allegory is not an enigma, for here is the meaning patent to all but the very dull; but an enigma is, to explain it briefly an obscure allegory, as e.g. "the horse-leech had two daughters"[102] and other like instances. But when the apostle spoke of an allegory, he does not find it in the words, but in the fact; since he has shown that the two Testaments are to be understood by the two sons of Abraham, one by a bond-maid, and the other by a free woman, which was a thing not said, but also done. And before this was explained, it was obscure; and accordingly such an allegory which is the generic name, could be specifically called an enigma'[103]. Hence it is clear why St. Augustine in his *De vera religione* could speak of 'the allegory of an history, of a fact, of a conversation and of a sacrament'[104]. And this rule, he explains, must be observed in every allegory, that what is expressed by the similitude should be considered agreeably to the meaning of the particular place: for this is the manner of the Lord's and the apostles" teaching[105]. Clearly, therefore, St. Augustine understood by the term 'allegory', every type of figurative speech. Symbolic language, simile, typology, allusion, and what we now understand by allegory, viz. a hidden emblem—all these were allegories to St. Augustine. And we cannot do justice to him, unless we remember this fact[106].

But to return to our main argument. St. Augustine considered the whole narrative of Genesis, in the most minute details, to be a prophecy of Christ and of the Church, with reference either to the good Christians or to the bad. 'There is a significance in the words of the apostle when he calls Adam "the figure of Him who was to come"[107], and when he says, "A man shall leave his father and mother, and shall cleave to his wife, and they two shall be one flesh. This is a

[101] I Thess. 5:6, 7.
[102] Prov. 30:15.
[103] De Trinitate XV, 15.
[104] De vera religione 99.
[105] Enarratio in Ps. 8, 13.
[106] Cf. *inter alia* Pontet, op, cit. p. 149 ff.
[107] Rom. 5:14.

great mystery– but I speak concerning Christ and the Church" '[108]. Similarly, Abel's sacrifice, the ark of Noah and many other histories were in fact predictions of Christ and His Church[109]. Faustus said that Christ was not foretold by the prophets of Israel, but St. Augustine was convinced that their Scriptures teem with such predictions. 'Who in Abraham leaves his country and kindred that he may become and prosperous among strangers, but He who, leaving the land and country of the Jews, of whom He was born in the flesh, is now extending his power among the Gentiles? Who in Isaac carried the wood for his own sacrifice, but He who carried his own cross? Who is the ram for sacrifice, caught by the horns in the bush, but He who was fastened to the cross as an offering for us? Who is the stone placed under Jacob's head, but Christ the head of man? And in its anointing, the very name of Christ is expressed: for, as all know, Christ means anointed. Christ refers to this in the gospel, and declares it to be a type of Himself[110]. In every page of these Scriptures, while I pursue my search as a son of Adam in the sweat of my brow, Christ either openly or covertly meets and refreshes me[111]. Christ appears to me in Joseph, who was persecuted and sold by his brethren, and after his troubles obtained honour in Egypt. Christ appears to me in the rod of Moses, which became a serpent when cast on the earth, as a figure of his death, which came from the serpent. Of the departure of Israel from Egypt, let us hear what the apostle himself says: "I would not, brethren, that ye should be ignorant that all our fathers were under the cloud, and all passed through the sea, and were all baptised into Moses in the cloud and in the sea, and did all eat the same spiritual meat, and did all drink of the same spiritual drink. For they drank of the spiritual rock which followed them, and that rock was Christ[112]. The explanation of one thing is the key to the rest. For if the rock is Christ from its stability, is not the manna Christ, the living bread which came down from heaven?[113] The Israelites died because they received the figure only in its carnal sense. The apostle, by calling it spiritual food, shows its reference to Christ, as the spiritual drink is explained by the words,

[108] Eph. 5:31, 32; Contra Faustum XII, 8.
[109] ib. XII, 9 ff.; 14 ff.
[110] Joh. 1:48, 52; Contra Faustum XII, 25, 26.
[111] ib. 27.
[112] 1 Cor. 10:1–4.
[113] Joh. 6:32, 33.

"That rock was Christ", which explain the whole. Then is not the cloud and the pillar Christ, who by his uprightness and strength supports our feebleness? In the Red Sea there is the baptism consecrated by the blood of Christ[114]. The Israelites are led through the wilderness, as those who are baptised are in the wilderness. The deadly bites of serpents are healed by the brazen serpent, which was lifted up that they might look at it. The Lord Himself gives the explanation of this: "As Moses lifted up the serpent in the wilderness, so must the Son of man be lifted up, that whosoever believeth in Him may not perish, but have everlasting life"[115]. In the Passover a lamb is killed, representing Christ, of whom it is said, "Behold the Lamb of God"[116]. In the Passover the bones of the lamb were not to be broken; and on the cross the bones of the Lord were not broken[117]. It is impossible to refer, however briefly, to all the figurative predictions of Christ which are to be found in the law and the prophets. Will it be said that these things happened in the regular course of things, and that it is a mere ingenious fancy to make them typical of Christ? Such an objection might come from Jews and Pagans; but those who wish to be considered Christians must yield to the authority of the apostle when he says, "All these things happened to them for an example"[118], and again, "These things are our examples"[119]. For if two men, Ishmael and Isaac, are types of the two covenants, can it be supposed that there is no significance in the vast number of particulars which have no historical or natural value? Suppose we were to see some Hebrew characters written on the wall of a noble building, should we be so foolish as to conclude that, because we cannot understand the characters, they are not intended to be read, and are mere painting, without meaning? Who, however with a candid mind reads all these things that are contained in the Old Testament Scriptures, must feel constrained to acknowledge that they have a meaning[120]. Examples of those which can have no meaning at all apart from a symbolical one: Granting that it was necessary that woman should be made as an help meet for man, what natural

[114] Contra Faustum XII, 28, 29.
[115] Joh. 3:14.
[116] Joh. 1:29.
[117] Joh. 19:36; Contra Faustum XII, 28–30.
[118] 1 Cor. 10:11.
[119] 1 Cor. 10:6.
[120] Contra Faustum XII, 37.

reason can be assigned for her being taken from his side while he slept? Granting that an ark was required in order to escape from the flood, why should it have precisely these dimensions, and why should they be recorded for the devoted study of future generations? The human mind is led by the consideration of the way in which these apparently superfluous things are blended with what is necessary, first to acknowledge their significance, and then to try to discover it[121]. The Jews themselves have seen this. This led Philo, a Jew of great learning, to interpret Noah's ark as a type of the human body[122]. Even the Pagans try to find in their own fables figures of natural and religious truth. Sometimes they give clear explanations, while at other times they disguise their meaning, and what is sacred in the temples becomes a jest in the theatres. They unite a disgraceful licentiousness to a degrading superstition'[123].

These quotations make it quite clear that St. Augustine's belief in, and search for, spiritual allegories had a sound Biblical foundation. The vision of Christ and His apostles in the Old Testament persuaded St. Augustine that Israel's history, too, had an allegorical meaning. A Jew or a Pagan may look upon this allegorical interpretation as contrived, but any Christian who bows down to the authority of God's Word will try to see the prophetic history of Israel through the eyes of Christ and His apostles. This point requires emphasising, for many theologians continue to think that St. Augustine's preoccupation with allegories was merely a sign of the decadent days in which he lived. Thus Marrou claims that allegorization was a cultural activity, a sort of poetic game, of the times, and was applied not only to the Bible but also to the works of Homer and Virgil. St. Augustine must therefore simply have followed custom in this respect, the more so since this custom is said to have agreed with his spiritual predisposition. It is for this reason that he failed to base his concept of allegories on a sound Scriptural foundation like that of St. Thomas. All he was interested in was in the poetic game with words[124]. Now, there is no doubt that there is an element of truth in Marrou's claim, for St. Augustine did in fact play on words on more than one occasion. However, this was by no means the crux of his

[121] ib. 38.
[122] ib. 39.
[123] ib. 40.
[124] Henri-Irénée Marrou, op. cit. p. 474 ff.; in his *Retractio*, Paris 1949, this point of view is developed further. See p. 646 ff.

approach. In his search for spiritual meanings, St. Augustine was the avowed disciple of Scripture itself, although, when it came to practical applications, he was swayed by the thought of his times. Thus he showed clearly what positive Biblical grounds there were in favour of his spiritual explanations. Nor did he err in this respect[125]. However, he often went too far, almost to the point of panallegorism. Pontet was therefore quite right to note that St. Augustine often lost sight of the real content of any part of Scripture, treating alike a Psalm, the parable of the strong woman in Proverbs, or that of the prodigal son[126].

To be fair, however, we must bear two things in mind. Zarb has shown[127] that from 415 A.D. onwards, when a letter from Orosius brought him into contact with the Priscillian heresy, St. Augustine fully realised the dangers of panallegorism. Henceforth, he would make a point of stressing that by no means everything could be spiritualised[128]. Secondly, we must bear in mind that St. Augustine's belief in the allegorical significance of all sorts of historical events underwent considerable changes in the course of his development. At first he was greatly influenced by St. Ambrose who treated historical material by means of the allegorical methods of Philo and Origines[129]. Added to this, St. Augustine's Neoplatonism caused him to neglect history as a whole, and to transform every historical event into a symbolic idea[130]. Hans Leisegang even claims that St. Augustine read all the Hebrew records in the Old Testament through Platonic eyes[131]. Now all this is undoubtedly true of the beginning of St. Augustine's work[132], but later, under the influence of Paul, he came to accept history as the fulfilment of God's counsel. Then the Platonic view of isolated facts was completely replaced by the vision of the prophets, and by Paul's picture of salvation in Rom.

[125] Cf. particularly the article by J. Ridderbos in *Bijbelsch Handboek*, Kampen 1935, Part I, *On the Interpretation of Holy Writ*, p. 390 ff.

[126] Maurice Pontet, op. cit. p. 233 ff.; see also p. 166 ff.

[127] S. M. Zarb, *Augustinus' leer over de verschillende betekenissen der H. Schrift*. Thomistisch Tijdschrift, Antwerp 1930, p. 618 ff.

[128] See pp. 83, 112 ff.

[129] P. de Labriolle, *St. Ambroise*, Paris 1908, p. 8 ff.

[130] Marie Comeau, *Saint Augustin Exégète du quatrième évangile*, Paris 1930, p. 110 ff.

[131] Hans Leisegang, *Denkformen*, Berlin 1928, p. 368.

[132] Cf. De Genesi contra Manichaeos (passim); De moribus ecclesiae I, 1; De catechizandis rudibus 50; De doctrina christiana I, 40; see also C. Dorsch op. cit.

9–11[133]. True, he continued to look for spiritual meanings, but he no longer built on thin air[134], searching for the real course of history rather than for its allegorical significance.

St. Augustine finally countered Faustus' argument that it was a poor faith which would not believe in Christ without the clearest evidence of prophecy. He, for his part, could quite understand why the Christians of his time, none of whom had, after all, heard the voice from the cloud during Christ's baptism, should have asked for this evidence. 'Whatever we know of Christ, we know through the witness of the apostles and the prophets'[135]. All simple faith must, in fact, embrace prophetic witness[136].

4. *The differences between, and the similarity of, the two Testaments.*

Faced with the total rejection of the Old Testament by the Manicheans and its over-estimation by the Pelagians, St. Augustine was forced to define the difference between, and the similarity of, the Old and New Testaments. 'The fact is that the term "Old Testament" is constantly employed in two different ways—the one following the authority of the Holy Scriptures; the other following the most common mode of speech'. According to St. Augustine, the apostle Paul applied this name in Gal. 4 exclusively to the dispensation of the law of Moses. 'We are, however, accustomed, in our ordinary use of words to designate all those Scriptures of the law and the prophets which were given previous to the Lord's incarnation under the name and title of the Old Testament'[137]. St. Augustine preferred to call the latter the "Old Instrument"[138]. It might be objected that Paul also used the name "Old Testament" in the common sense[139], but St. Augustine chose to attribute 2 Cor. 3:14 solely to the ministry of Moses[140]. While he tried to adapt himself to customary usage, he continued to speak of the "Old Instrument"[141].

[133] See my dissertation, pp. 109 ff., 173 ff.
[134] Sermo 8, 1.
[135] Rom. 10:14, 15.
[136] Contra Faustum XII, 45, 46.
[137] De gestis Pelagii 14.
[138] Contra duas epistolas Pelagii III, 12.
[139] 2 Cor. 3:14.
[140] Contra duas epistolas Pelagii III, 12.
[141] E.g. in De civitate Dei XX, 4; see also Nebreda, op. cit., I, I, 5 (page references indistinct in the copy used).

How then would St. Augustine have us understand the terms Old and New Testaments in the first sense of the word? The answer, according to him, is found in Gal. 3 and 4. 'The apostle makes a clear distinction between two Testaments[142]. The one is gendering from the mount Sinai to bondage, which was given to Moses[143]. Therefore God established the old covenant (Testament), because it pleased God to veil the heavenly promises in earthly promises, as if established in reward, until the fullness of time; and to give to a people which longed for earthly blessings, and therefore had a hard heart, a law, which, although spiritual, was yet written on tables of stone[144]. Those also belong to the Old Testament, who, when they have received a law which is holy and just and good, think that the letter can suffice them for life; and that they may become doers of the law, do not seek the mercy of God, but, being ignorant of the righteousness of God, and wishing to establish their own righteousness, are not subject to the righteousness of God[145]. Therefore are the children of the flesh and not the children of the promise the heirs of the Old Testament[146]. They belong to the earthly Jerusalem, which is in bondage with her children[147]. They are the natural men who do not receive the things of the Spirit of God[148]. At whatever time men have begun to be, if they yet savour of carnal things, and hope for and desire carnal things from God, whether in this life or afterwards, they belong to the Old Testament[149]. They look upon all things as carnal and live under the yoke of slavish servitude[150]. Slavery always goes with fear, freedom with love[151]. They who are established under the law, whom the letter killeth, do those things either with the desire of gaining, or with the fear of losing earthly happiness and thus they do it not truly, since fleshly desire, by which sin is rather changed or increased, is not healed by desire of another kind. These pertain to the Old Testament, which genders to bond-

[142] Gal. 4: 24.
[143] Contra duas epistulas Pelagii III, 8.
[144] ib. 10.
[145] ib. 9.
[146] Rom. 9:8.
[147] De gestis Pelagii 14.
[148] I Cor. 2:14; De baptismo I, 23.
[149] ib. 24.
[150] De catechizandis rudibus 8.
[151] Rom. 8:15; Sermo 33, 1.

age; because carnal fear and desire make them servants, gospel, faith, and hope and love do not make them children'[152].

'The New Testament on the contrary was not instituted, but revealed by the incarnation of Christ, "who is made unto us wisdom from God, and righteousness, and sanctification, and redemption"[153]. When He was manifested in the flesh, the righteousness of God appeared, that is, which is to men from God[154]. The children of this, worship God for the sake of Himself. It is a liberal service pertaining to the children of the freewoman, who is our mother eternal in the heavens who first appeared barren, when she had not any children manifest; but now we see what was prophesied concerning her, "Rejoice, thou barrren, that bearest not; break forth and cry, thou that travailest not: for there are many children of the desolate more than of her who has a husband"[155]—that is, more than of that Jerusalem, who in a certain manner is married in the bond of law, and is in bondage with her children'[156].

'In Christ revealed, not instituted!'

'In the Old Testament, from the mount Sinai gendering to bondage, was prefigured the New Testament[157]. The promises of the Old Testament were indeed figures of the spiritual blessings of the New Testament[158]. To the carnal belongs the old covenant, to the spiritual the new. In the first days both were hidden, from Adam even to Moses. But by Moses the old covenant was made manifest, and in it was hidden the new covenant, because after a secret fashion it was typified'[159].

'Owing to a perfectly just dispensation of that period, in the Old Testament that was hidden which is now revealed in the New Testament[160]. For what does the term old covenant imply but the concealing of the new?[161] Paul says it clearly in 2 Cor. 3:14–15, where he speaks of a veil in the reading of the Old Testament, which veil is taken away in Christ. In Christ there is made void not the Old

[152] Contra duas epistulas Pelagii III, 11.
[153] 1 Cor. 1:30.
[154] Rom. 3:21.
[155] Gal. 4:26, 27.
[156] Contra duas epistulas Pelagii III, 13.
[157] ib. III, 6.
[158] De gestia Pelagii 14.
[159] De baptismo I, 24.
[160] De peccatorum meritis et remissione I, 13.
[161] De civitate Dei XVI, 26; Sermo 300, 3; De catechizandis rudibus, 8.

Testament, but its veil: that so through Christ that may be understood, and, as it were, laid bare, which without Christ is obscure and covered'[162]. So St. Augustine saw in Christ's miraculous feeding of the five thousand with the five loaves an allegorical reference to the five books of Moses. He even said that 'they were not wheaten but barley loaves, because barley is so formed that we get at its pith with difficulty; for the pith is covered in a coating of husk, and the husk itself tenacious and closely adhering, so as to be stripped off with labour. Such is also the letter of the Old Testament, invested in a covering of carnal sacraments: but yet, if we get at its pith, it feeds and satisfies us'. 'A certain lad', so he goes on to explain. 'brought five loaves and two fishes. If we inquire, who this lad was perhaps it was the people Israel, which, in a childish sense carried, not ate. For the things which they carried were a burden while shut up, but when opened afforded nourishment. In the breaking of the loaves they are multiplied. Nothing is more true. For when those five books of Moses are expounded, how many books have they made by being broken up; that is, by being opened and laid out? But in that barley was the ignorance of the first people veiled, of whom it is said, "While Moses is read, the veil is upon their hearts"; for the veil was not yet removed, because Christ had not yet come; not yet was the veil of the temple rent[163]. Moses, who foreshadowed Christ, placed a veil over his face, when he spoke to the people since as long as they gave themselves to carnal pleasures and enjoyments and laid up treasures on earth, a veil was placed over their heart, so as to hide the Christ in the Scriptures from them. But this veil was taken away for the Lord has suffered and the hidden treasures of the temple were laid bare. Therefore, the veil of the temple was rent in twain[164] when Christ was nailed to the Cross, and therefore Paul could say: "When it (the people's mind) will turn to the Lord, the veil shall be taken away, but else the veil remaineth untaken away in the reading of Moses"[165]. The veil was taken away by Christ, so that what was once obscure might be understood. For understanding was surely cut off, ere the key of the Cross was delivered to us'[166].

[162] De utilitate credendi, 9.
[163] Tractatus in Joannis evangelium XXIV, 5.
[164] Matth. 27:51.
[165] 2 Cor. 3:16, 15; Sermo 137, 6; cf. Enarratio in Ps. 70, II, 9; in Ps. 89, 17; in Ps. 118 XXVI, 8.
[166] Sermo 300, 3.

'Therefore Christ is the Sealer, the Mediator of the Testament, the Surety of the Testament, the Witness of the Testament, the Heritage of the Testament'[167]. Or even: 'The Scripture was closed, no one understood it; the Lord was crucified, and the Scripture was melted like wax, that all the weak ones should understand it'[168].

Such forceful utterances gave the Pelagians cause to accuse St. Augustine of denying the presence of the Holy Spirit in the Old Testament[169]. Though this accusation was utterly unfair, since St. Augustine frequently corrected his outbursts of zeal, he took the opportunity to discuss the whole problem in detail. He defended his position fully, inasmuch as he had taken the Old Testament to mean, according to Gal. 4:24, 'the covenant from Mount Sinai which gendereth to bondage'. 'But because in it was prefigured the New Testament, the men of God who at that time understood this according to the ordering of the times, were indeed the stewards and bearers of the Old Testament, but are shown to be the heirs of the New. Shall we deny that he pertains to the New Testament who says, Create in me a new heart, O God; and renew a right spirit within me?[170] or he who says, He has set my feet upon a rock, and directed my goings; and He has put a new song in my mouth, even a hymn to our God[171]? or that father of the faithful before the Old Testament which is from the mount Sinai, of whom the apostle says, Brethren, I speak after the manner of men; yet when a man's convenant is confirmed, no man disannulleth or addeth thereto. To Abraham and to his seed were the promises made. He saith not, And to seeds, as of many, but as of one; and to thy seed, which is Christ. "And this I say", he said, "that the Testament confirmed by God, the law, which was made four hundred and thirty years after, does not weaken, so as to make the promise of none effect. For if the inheritance be of the law, it is no more of promise: but God gave it to Abraham by promise"[172]. Here, certainly, if we ask whether this Testament given to Abraham is to be understood as the New or the Old one, who can hesitate to answer the New, but it was hidden in the prophetic ciphers until the time should come wherein it should

[167] Enarratio in Ps. 88, 28.
[168] En. in Ps. 21 II, 15.
[169] Contra duas epistolas Pelagii III, 6.
[170] Ps. 51:10.
[171] Ps. 40:2, 3.
[172] Gal. 3:15–18; Contra duas epistolas Pelagii III, 6.

be revealed in Christ? For if we should say the Old, what will that be which genders from mount Sinai to bondage? For there was made the law four hundred and thirty years after, by which law he asserts that this Testament of the promise of Abraham could not be weakened. He will have this which was made by Abraham to pertain rather to us, whom he will have to be children of the freewoman, not of the bondwoman, heirs by the promise, not by the law[173]. Because the law was made four hundred and thirty years after, it might enter that the offence might abound and where sin abounded grace much more abounded[174], by the faith of the man now humble, failing in the law and taking refuge in God's mercy. Why then was the law made afterwards? "Because of transgression, until the seed should come to which the promise was made"[175]. "For if they who are of the law be heirs, faith is made void, and the promise is made of none effect, because the law worketh wrath"[176]. He therefore made it plain that our faith (which certainly is of the New Testament) contains what God gave to Abraham by promise'[177].

'Whether, then Abraham, or righteous men before him or after him, even to Moses himself, by whom was given the Testament gendering to bondage, or the rest of the prophets after him, and the holy men of God till John the Baptist, they are all children of the promise and of grace according to Isaac the son of the freewoman—not of the law, but of the promise, heirs of God and joint-heirs with Christ. Far be it from us to deny that righteous Noah and the righteous men of the earlier times, and whoever from that time till the time of Abraham could be righteous, either manifest or secret, belong to the Jerusalem which is above, who is our mother, although they are found to be earlier in time than Sarah, who bears the prophecy and figure of the free mother herself. How much more evidently, then, after Abraham, to whom that promise was declared, that he should be called the father of many nations, must all, whoever have pleased God, be esteemed the children of the promise!'[178].

On the other hand, Pelagius, with his three periods rigidly excluded the ancient saints of Christ's community from the grace of

[173] Gal. 3 : 18.
[174] Rom. 5 : 20.
[175] Gal. 3 : 19.
[176] Rom. 4 : 14.
[177] Contra duas epistolas Pelagii III, 7.
[178] ib. 8.

the Mediator[179]. Scripture tells quite a different story: 'Under the law which was unable to liberate any man from the dominion of death, there were even then men of God who were living under the delights and healing and liberating influence of grace. Some there were who said, "Take not thy Holy Spirit from me"[180] and, "I believed, therefore have I spoken"[181]. For they too were cleansed with the self-same faith with which we ourselves are. Whence the apostle also says, "We having the same spirit of faith, according as it is written, I believe, and therefore have I spoken; we also believe and therefore speak"[182]. Of very faith was it said, "Behold, a virgin shall conceive and bear a son, and they shall call his name Emmanuel"[183]. By the self-same Spirit of faith were all these things foreseen by them as about to happen, whereby they are believed by us as having happened. Therefore the apostle Peter says, "We believe that through the grace of the Lord Jesus Christ we shall be saved, even as they"[184]. Now on what principle does he make this statement, if it be not because even those (ancient saints) were saved through the grace of our Lord Jesus Christ, and not through the law of Moses, from which comes not the cure, but only the knowledge of sin. "Now, however, the righteousness of God without the law is manifested, being witnessed by the law and the prophets"[185]. If, therefore, it is now manifested, it even then existed, but it was hidden'[186].

'It is in this light also that we must view Pelagius' claim at the synod of Diospolis, that even the Old Testament contains the promise of the kingdom of heaven. If the Old Testament refers here to the Scriptures given before the Lord's incarnation. every Catholic, however moderately informed in ecclesiastical lore, must know fully well that the kingdom of heaven could be quite as well promised in those early Scriptures as in the New Testament itself, to which the kingdom of heaven belongs[187]. But Pelagius clearly referred to that Testament which was given on Mount Sinai, and promised only

[179] De gratia et peccato originali II, 31.
[180] Ps. 51 : 11.
[181] Ps. 116 : 10.
[182] 2 Cor. 4 : 13.
[183] Is. 7 : 14.
[184] Acts. 15 : 10, 11.
[185] Rom. 3 : 20.
[186] De peccato originali II, 29; Opus imperfectum contra Julianum I. 124.
[187] A reference to Jer. 31 : 31–32.

earthly happiness. In it, the New Testament lay indeed hidden and those who understood it in their time were children of the promise, the heirs to the New Testament according to God's secret purpose. Even so, they continued with perfect fitness to administer the Old Testament to the ancient people of God[188]. How then should there not be a feeling of just disquietude entertained by the children of promise, sons of the free Jerusalem, which is eternal in the heavens, when they see that by the words of Pelagius the distinction which has been drawn by Apostolic and Catholic authority is abolished, and Agar is supposed to be by some means on a par with Sarah? He therefore does injury to the Scripture of the Old Testament with the depravity of a heretic who denies that it was inspired by the good and supreme God, as Marcion does, as Manichaeus does, and other pests of similar opinions. But as much injury is done to the New Testament, when it is put on the same level with the Old Testament, as Pelagius does'[189].

Thus St. Augustine formulated a clear view of the stages of revelation. 'In the first days, the Old and the New Testament were hidden, from Adam even to Moses. But by Moses the old covenant was made manifest, and in it was hidden the new covenant, because after a secret fashion it was typified. But so soon as the Lord came in the flesh, the new covenant was revealed; yet, though the sacraments of the old covenant passed away, the dispositions peculiar to it did not pass away. For they still exist in those whom the apostle declares to be already born indeed by the sacrament of the new covenant, but yet incapable, as being natural, of receiving the things of the Spirit of God. For, as in the sacraments of the old covenant some persons were already spiritual belonging secretly to the new covenant, which was then concealed, so now also in the sacrament of the new covenant, which has been by this time revealed, many live who are natural. And if they will not advance to receive the things of the Spirit of God, to which the discourse of the apostle urges them, they will still belong to the old covenant'[190].

Beyond that, St. Augustine also reflected deeply on the significance and reason of these stages of revelation, and called them wise and just. God had chosen to give a people who longed for earthly bles-

[188] De gestis Pelagii, 14.
[189] ib. 15.
[190] De baptismo I, 24.

sings a law, which was written on a tablet of stone[191]. Moreover, Paul had said that "that which is spiritual came after that which is natural"[192]. 'To the image of the earthly man does belong the Old Testament, to the image of the heavenly man the New Testament. God is the Author of both Testaments. An earthly man bears in mind earthly things. When to a boy are given some boyish playthings, wherewith his boyish mind may be amused, are they not taken out of his hands when he groweth up in order that he now may take in hand something more useful, which becometh a grown person? For example, thou didst thyself give to thy son nuts when he was little, and a book when he was bigger. By no means therefore, because God through the New Testament hath taken out of the hands of his sons those things which are like the playthings of boys, in order that He might give something more useful to them growing up, on that account must He be supposed not to have given those former things Himself[193]. This is the mystery of the Old Testament that even earthly things are promised, because the people was still under the conduct of a very weak mind[194]. God knows to whom He should give, to whom not give, as a physician his medicines, knowing better the sick man's disease than the sick man himself'[195]. Therefore does the Old Testament start out with earthly promises made by God alone. Then came the New Testament, in which eternal blessings are bestowed upon the righteous by God in Christ'[196].

Many of St. Augustine's contemporaries failed to grasp that this distinction did not mean that God Himself was subject to change and had to correct what proved to be an error. St. Augustine attacked such views on many occasions. Thus, he wrote to Marcellinus, that 'many are the instances, in which the processes of nature itself and the works of men undergo changes according to the circumstances of the time, while, at the same time, there is nothing mutable in the plan or principle by which these changes are regulated. Does not summer follow winter, the temperature gradually increasing in warmth? Do not night and day in turn succeed each other? How often do our own lives experience changes? Boyhood departing,

[191] Contra duas epistolas Pelagii II, 10.
[192] 1 Cor. 15:46.
[193] Enarratio in Ps. 73, 2.
[194] De civitate Dei IV, 33.
[195] Enarratio in Ps. 34 I. 7,
[196] Epistula 140, 20; cf. also the whole letter.

never to return, gives place to youth; manhood, destined itself to continue only for a season, takes in turn the place of youth; and old age, closing the term of manhood, is itself closed by death. All these things are changed, but the plan of divine Providence which appoints these successive changes is not changed. I suppose, also, that the principles of agriculture are not changed when the farmer appoints a different work to be done in summer from that which he had ordered in winter. He who rises in the morning after resting by night, is not supposed to have changed the plan of his life. The schoolmaster gives to the adult different tasks from those which he was accustomed to prescribe to the scholar in his boyhood; his teaching, consistent throughout, changes the instruction when the lesson is changed, without itself being changed[197]. The eminent physician of our own times, Vindicianus, being consulted by an invalid, prescribed for his disease what seemed to him a suitable remedy at that time; health was restored by its use. Some years afterwards, finding himself troubled again with the same disorder, the patient supposed that the same remedy should be applied; but its application made his illness worse. In astonishment, he again returns to the physician, and tells him what has happened; whereupon he, being a man of very quick penetration, answered: "The reason of your having been harmed by this application is, that I did not order it". When he was afterwards questioned by some who were amazed at his words, he explained what they had not understood, namely, that he would not have prescribed the same remedy to the patient at the age which he had now attained. While, therefore, the principle and methods of art remain unchanged, the change which, in accordance with them, may be made necessary by the difference of times is very great[198]. To say, then, that what has once been done rightly must in no respect whatever be changed, is to affirm what is not true[199]. So God knows infinitely better than man what is fitting for every age, and who is, whether He give or add, abolish or curtail, increase or diminish, the unchangeable Governor as He is the unchangeable Creator of mutable things, ordering all events in his providence until the beauty of the complete course of time, the component parts of which are the dispensations adapted to

[197] Epistula 138, 2.
[198] ib. 3.
[199] ib. 4.

each successive age, shall be finished, like the grand melody of some ineffably wise master of song'[200].

Those who are blind to these things, are always ready to carp and to misjudge the purport of the Holy Scriptures. They are 'as if in an armoury, one knowing not what were adapted to the several members should put greaves on his head, or boot himself with a helmet, and then complain because they would not fit. Or as if, on some day when in the afternoon business was forbidden, one were to fume at not being allowed to sell as it was lawful to him in the forenoon. Or when in some house he sees a servant take something in his hand which the butler is not permitted to touch, or something done behind a stable which would be prohibited in the diningroom, and should be indignant that in one house, and in one family, the same thing is not distributed everywhere to all. They do not see, that the justice is not various and changeable, but the times over which she presides'[201].

It is on the basis of his view on the difference between, and the similarity of the two Testaments, that St. Augustine could counter Faustus' second antithesis. Since Faustus had reviled the Old Testament in three ways, by attacking its promises, commandments, and sacraments, St. Augustine's reply was threefold, as well[202].

Concerning the *promises*, he noted that 'no one doubts that promises of temporal things are contained in the Old Testament; or that the kingdom of heaven and the promise of eternal life belong to the New Testament. But that in these temporal things were figures of future things which should be fulfilled in us upon whom the ends of the world are come, is not my fancy, but the judgment of the apostle, when he says of such things, "These things were our examples". We receive the Old Testament therefore, not, as Faustus thinks, in order to obtain the fulfilment of these promises, but to see

[200] ib. 5; see also De vera religione, 34, where the same view was already propounded.
[201] Confessiones III, 13.
[202] He also used other categories. In *De civitate Dei* VII, 32 he spoke of prophecies in words, precepts, sacrifices, priesthood, etc. In the preface to his *Speculum*, he averred that Holy Scripture contained all that man was bound to know and believe, e.g. In the beginning God created the heaven and the earth; in the beginning was the Word; and other divine and human acts which need only be known. Then come the commandments, some of which are symbolically shrouded in the mystery of the sacraments.

in them predictions of the New Testament; for the Old bears witness to the New. So the Lord declares after His resurrection, "It was necessary that all things should be fulfilled which were written in the law of Moses, and in the Prophets and Psalms, concerning me"[203]. Our hope, therefore, rests not on the promise of temporal things. Nor do we believe that the holy and spiritual men of these times—the patriarchs and prophets—were taken up with temporal things. For they understood, by the revelation of the Spirit of God, what was suitable for that time, and how God appointed all these sayings and actions as types and predictions of the future. Their great desire was for the New Testament. The carnal people, however, thought only of present blessings'[204]. Thus there are two Testaments in the Law—the Old and the New. The Old contained temporal promises which, however, had a spiritual meaning. When the Jews were promised the Promised Land, the promise was one of a spiritual home. Those who took the promise as referring to earthly things alone, and who failed to seek future blessedness, who could not read a spiritual meaning into carnal happenings, belong to the Old Testament[205]. The Old Testament is the promise which foreshadows the spiritual promise of the New[206]. Thus all the saints before Christ's incarnation, who truly understood the Old Testament, and discerned the spiritual meaning of carnal promises, belong to the Church[207].

But St. Augustine did not leave it at that. He also showed how God fulfilled His earthly promises in the history of Israel: 'This people desired earthly goods: the kingdom of Jerusalem, the subjection of their enemies, abundance of fruits, their own health, their childrens' health. Such things they desired and such things they received. Under the Law they were kept. They desired from God goods which He gives even to beasts, because not yet had the Son of Man come to them[208]. Such were also those promises, which were not to endure, through which however were figured future promises which were to endure, so that all that course of temporal promises was a figure and a sort of prophecy of things future[209]. The

[203] Luke 24:44.
[204] Contra Faustum IV, 2.
[205] Sermo 4, 8.
[206] ib. 9.
[207] ib. 11.
[208] Enarratio in Ps. 35, 13.
[209] Enarratio in Ps. 72, 3.

people was led to a land of promise, but was that land always to remain? Nay; if this had been so, it would not have been a figure, but a substance. But because it was a figure, unto something temporal that people was led. If unto something temporal they were led, it must needs have failed, and by its failing they be compelled to seek that which never would fail[210]. It was the Synagogue therefore, that is, they that there worshipped God devoutly, but yet for the sake of earthly things. When therefore these godly men after the flesh were observing—that is that synagogue which was made up of good men, men for the time good, not spiritual men, such as were the prophets therein, such as were the few that understood the kingdom heavenly, eternal—that synagogue, I say, observed what things it received from God and they remarked and saw certain sinners, sons of the Devil, abounding in such things earthly, temporal, for which sort of things they were serving God themselves: and there sprang up a most evil thought in the heart. For what said that synagogue at that time? We serve God and are cut short, but those wicked men do abound in all the things for which we serve God: I think to no purpose God is served[211]. They were besieged, stormed, led captive; at the last there was overthrown even the city itself[212]. They desired but carnal things and temporal felicity. The same men's feet slipped away to make and to worship idols. For when God warned them and scourged them in those things in which they delighted, and took them away, they suffered famine, wars, pestilences, diseases, and so they turned themselves to idols. For they observed that those goods, which they sought, abounded to the ungodly and wicked and they thought that they worshipped God in vain, because He gave them not their hire on earth. If thy workman come up to thy house, wilt thou give him his hire, before he had finished his work? Thou wilt think him perverse if he say: First let me receive my hire, and then I will work. Thou wilt be angry, because he trusted not a deceitful man. How will not God be angry, when thou not trustest Truth, Itself?[213] There were others who were pricked in heart and they said, "O Lord, be Thou merciful to me a sinner. Have regard unto Thy Testament". Fulfil that which Thou hast promised. The tables

[210] ib. 5.
[211] ib. 6.
[212] ib. 3.
[213] Enarratio in Ps. 35, 13.

we have, for the inheritance we are looking. Have regard to Thy Testament, not that old one: not for the sake of the land of Canaan I ask, not for the sake of the temporal subduing of enemies, not for the sake of temporal welfare. Have regard to Thy Testament, wherein thou hast promised the kingdom of heaven. Now I acknowledge Thy Testament: now understanding is Asaph, no beast is Asaph, now he seeth that which was spoken of, "Behold, the days come and I will accomplish with the House of Israel and of Juda a new Testament"[214]. So there were under them clouds[215] declaring Christ and there were of them some who understood, and had hope of the future, to receive the mercy which is in the heavens[216]. This is also the mystery of the Old Testament, in which the New was hidden, that there even earthly gifts are promised: those who were of spiritual understanding even then, although not yet openly declaring both the eternity which was symbolised by these earthly things, and in what gifts of God true felicity could be found'[217].

Concerning the *precepts* of the Old Testament, St. Augustine said that 'Faustus displays ignorance of the difference between moral and symbolical precepts. For example, "Thou shalt not covet" is a moral precept; "Thou shalt circumcise every male on the eighth day" is a symbolical precept[218]. Only the precepts that prefigured Christ, are not observed by the Christians, because their fulfilment is in Christ, and what is fulfilled is no longer prefigured. But do not Christians observe the precept of Scripture, "Hear, O Israel; the Lord thy God is one God", "Thou shalt not make unto thee an image", and so on? Do Christians not observe the precept, "Thou shalt not take the name of the Lord thy God in vain"? Do Christians not observe the Sabbath, even in the sense of a true rest? Do Christians not honour their parents, according to the commandment? Do Christians not abstain from adultery, and murder, and theft, and false witness, from coveting their neighbour's wife, and from coveting his property—all of which things are written in the law? These moral precepts are distinct from typical sacraments: the former are fulfilled by the aid of divine grace, the latter by the accomplishment of what

[214] Enarratio in Ps. 73, 22, 23; in Ps. 84, 4.
[215] A frequently used image of the prophets who spread the Word of God among the people.
[216] Enarratio in Ps. 35, 13.
[217] De civitate Dei IV, 33.
[218] Contra Faustum VI, 2.

they promise. Both are fulfilled in Christ, who has ever been the bestower of this grace, which is also now revealed in Him, and who now makes manifest the accomplishment of what He in former times promised; for "the law was given by Moses, but grace and truth came by Jesus Christ"[219]. Again, these things which concern the keeping of a good conscience are fulfilled in the faith which worketh by love, while types of the future pass away when they are accomplished. But even the types are not destroyed, but fulfilled; for Christ, in bringing to light what the types signified, does not prove them vain or illusory[220]. So Christ took away from us that heaviest yoke of many observances. Shall we therefore say, that when it is written that whoever finds another man's property of any kind that has been lost, should return it to him who has lost it, it does not pertain to us; and many other like things whereby people learn to live piously and uprightly; and especially the Decalogue itself, which is contained in those two tables of stone, except the carnal observance of the Sabbath? For who can say that Christians ought not to observe to obey the one God with religious obedience, not to worship an idol, not to take the name of the Lord in vain, and so on? Who is so impious as to say that he does not keep those precepts of the law because he is a Christian, and is established not under the law, but under grace?[221] If we distinguish between the two Testaments, there are not the same sacraments nor the same promises; nevertheless, the same commandments for the most part. There are scarce in the Gospel which have not been spoken by the Prophets. The commandments are the same, because according to these we ought to serve God'[222].

But the symbolic precepts need no longer be kept by Christians. For what Christian would bore his servant's ear with an awl and fasten it to the doorpost, if the servant refuse to be released in the seventh year[223], or the like? But the other commandments must be kept by Christians[224], and in his *Speculum*, St. Augustine gave a list of all these contained in both the Old and the New Testaments.

[219] Joh. 1:17. Here, St. Augustine gave a truly Biblical interpretation, differing from his earlier one which was still under the influence of Neoplatonism.
[220] Contra Faustum XIX, 18.
[221] Contra duas epistulas Pelagii III, 10.
[222] Enarratio in Ps. 73, 2.
[223] Exod. 21:6.
[224] Speculum, Preface.

Now, while in his controversy with Faustus, St. Augustine was forced to stress the similarity between the Testaments as regards the commandments, he was forced to emphasise the difference between them, in his dispute with Pelagius. The Pelagians failed to realise that the Law without Christ's grace could only lead to Christ as a schoolmaster would[225]. St. Augustine dealt most severely with this kind of rationalist ethics. 'Without the grace of the Spirit, which is the grace of the New Testament[226], the law does none other than rouse desire for what is forbidden, just as a storm, checked by a windbreak, will throw itself upon it with redoubled force. This is why Paul said: "The letter, indeed, killeth, but the spirit giveth life"[227]. Where there is no law, there is no transgression[228], but sin, taking occasion by the commandment, wrought in me all manner of concupiscence[229]. Wherefore the law was our schoolmaster to bring us unto Christ[230]. It shows us our condition, but cures it not. It commandeth but helpeth not. It killeth[231], giveth not righteousness[232], but hath concluded all under sin[233] so "that every mouth may be stopped, and all the world may become guilty before God"[234]. Under the law, we are all dead in trespasses and sins[235], and are foolish, disobedient, deceived, serving divers lusts and pleasures, living in malice and envy, hateful, and hating one another[236]. All commandments and precepts in Scripture, which the Pelagians relied upon, therefore did no more than reveal our utter impotence, and thus aroused our longing for Christ, who alone, by the grace of the Spirit, can give us free will[237]. And it is through the Holy Ghost alone, who was present even in the children of promise of the Old Testament, that God's commandments were fulfilled by faith, which "worketh through love"'[238].

225 De gratia Christi I, 2, 8, 36.
226 Epistula 140, passim.
227 De spiritu et littera 6, 7, 25, 26.
228 Rom. 4 : 15.
229 Rom. 7 : 8.
230 Gal. 3 : 24.
231 2 Cor. 3 : 6.
232 Gal. 3 : 21.
233 Gal. 3 : 22.
234 Rom. 3 : 19; De gratia Christi, 9.
235 Eph. 2 : 1 ff.
236 Tutis 3 : 3; Contra duas epistulas Pelagii I, 13–15; (Opus imperfectum I, 99).
237 Opus imperfectum I, 45, 93; III, 116–119.
238 Contra duas epistulas Pelagii III, 11, 13.

Finally, St. Augustine discussed the *sacraments* of the Old Testament. We cannot here go into the manifold interpretations which St. Augustine gave of the word "sacraments"[239], but in his dispute with the Manicheans he used the word to cover everything that, in one way or another, prefigured Christ and the New Testament by way of symbols, ritual, or typology. His entire criticism of Faustus really amounted to the accusation that Faustus had failed to distinguish between moral and symbolic precepts[240]. True, Faustus spoke of a threefold law, but that argument really had little to do with Scripture itself. The New Testament leaves no doubt on the matter what law and what prophets Christ came not to destroy, but to fulfil[241]. The law given by Moses is that which by Jesus Christ became grace and truth. The law given by Moses is that of which Christ says, "He wrote of Me"[242]. Whatever was promised in the prophets, whether expressly or in figure, whether by words or by actions, was fulfilled in Him who came not to destroy the law and the prophets, but to fulfil them. 'You (Faustus) do not perceive that if Christians were to continue in the use of acts and observances by which things to come were prefigured, the only meaning would be that the things prefigured had not yet come. Either the thing prefigured has not come, or if it has, the figure becomes superfluous or misleading. Therefore, if Christians do not practise some things enjoined on the Hebrews by the prophets, this shows, that Christ did fulfil the prophets. So completely did Christ fulfil what these types prefigured, that it is no longer prefigured. So the Lord himself says, "The law and the prophets were until John"[243]. For the law which shut up transgressors in increased guilt, and to the faith, which was afterwards revealed, became grace through Jesus Christ, by whom grace superabounded'.

'Thus the law, which was not fulfilled in the requirement of the letter, was fulfilled in the liberty of grace. In the same way, everything in the law that was prophetic of the Saviour's advent, whether in words or in typical actions, became truth in Jesus Christ[244]. At

[239] See particularly C. Couturier, *Sacramentum et mysterium dans l'œuvre de St. Augustin.* In Etudes Augustiniennes, Paris 1953, pp. 161–332.
[240] Contra Faustum VI, 2.
[241] Joh. 1 : 17.
[242] Joh. 5 : 46; Contra Faustum XIX, 7.
[243] Luke 16 : 16.
[244] Joh. 1 : 17.

Christ's advent, the kingdom of God began to be preached, for the law and the prophets were until John'[245].

'Accordingly, when you ask why a Christian is not circumcised if Christ came not to destroy the law but to fulfil it, my reply is, that a Christian is not circumcised precisely for this reason, that what was prefigured by circumcision is fulfilled in Christ. Circumcision was the type of the removal of our fleshly nature, which was fulfilled in the resurrection of Christ. So, when you ask, why a Christian does not keep the Sabbath, if Christ came not to destroy the law but to fulfil it, my reply is that a Christian does not keep the Sabbath precisely because what was prefigured in the Sabbath was fulfilled in Christ. For we have our Sabbath in Him who said, "Come unto me, all ye that labour and are heavy laden, and I will give you rest"[246]. When you ask why a Christian does not observe the distinction in food, as enjoined in the law, I reply that a Christian does not observe this distinction precisely because what was thus prefigured is now fulfilled in Christ, who admits into his body, which in his saints He has predestined to eternal life, nothing which in human conduct corresponds to the characteristics of the forbidden animals. When you ask, again, why a Christian does not offer sacrifices to God of the flesh and blood of slain animals, I reply, that it would be improper for a Christian to offer such sacrifices, now that what was thus prefigured has been fulfilled in Christ's offering of his own body and blood. When you ask why a Christian does not keep the feast of unleavened bread as the Jews did, I reply, that a Christian does not keep this feast precisely because what was thus prefigured is fulfilled in Christ, who leads us to a new life by purging out the leaven of the old life. When you ask why a Christian does not keep the feast of the paschal lamb, my reply is, that he does not keep it precisely because what was thus prefigured has been fulfilled in the sufferings of Christ, the Lamb without spot. When you ask why a Christian does not keep the feasts of the new moon appointed in the law, I reply that he does not keep them precisely because what was thus prefigured is fulfilled in Christ. For the feast of the new moon prefigured the new creature, of which the apostle says, "If therefore there is any new creature in Christ Jesus, the old things have passed away; be-

[245] Contra Faustum XIX, 8.
[246] Matth. 11:28; Contra Faustum XIX, 9.

hold, all things are become new"[247]. When you ask why a Christian does not keep the feast of tabernacles, I reply that believers are God's tabernacle'[248].

'In the Old Testament the New lieth concealed, as though in the dregs of corporal Sacraments. The circumcision of the flesh is a thing of great mystery, and there is understood from thence the circumcision of the heart. The Temple of Jerusalem is a thing of great mystery, and there is understood from it the body of the Lord. The land of promise is understood to be the Kingdom of Heaven. The sacrifice of victims and of beasts is a great mystery: but in all those kinds of sacrifices is understood that one sacrifice and only victim of the cross, the Lord, instead of all which sacrifices we have one; because even those figured these, that is, with those these were figured. It is of pure wine, but full of mixed, that is, is together with the dregs of corporal Sacraments[249]. Thus, the slaying of the red heifer[250] was a clear symbol of Christ, and His passion was the great dividing line between the two Testaments[251]. When the King comes, his likenesses are removed. Only when he is absent, is his image displayed. Hence we had need of images ere our Lord, Jesus Christ, came to us. When the images are removed, the King himself shines by his presence[252]. In this change there is no difference in the doctrine, but in the time. There was a time when it was proper that these things should be figuratively predicted; and there is now a different time, when it is proper that they should be openly declared and fully accomplished[253]. Hence the Sacrament rather than faith has been changed. The signs have changed, which signify things, not the things themselves. In Christ's place we find a ram, a calf, a lamb, a deer—all these things (pointed to) Christ[254]. The men of old time—the true sacrifice, which is known to the faithful, was foreshewn in figures—used to celebrate rites that were figures of the reality that was to be hereafter; many of them understanding their meaning; but more of them in ignorance of it. For the

[247] 1 Cor. 5:7.
[248] Contra Faustum XIX, 10; see also VI, 2–5.
[249] Enarratio in Ps. 74, 12.
[250] Numeri 19.
[251] Quaestiones IV, 33; see also II, 42, 73; De Trinitate IV, 19; Tractatus in Johannem XVII, 15; L, 2.
[252] Sermo 74, 5.
[253] Contra Faustum XVI, 28.
[254] Sermo 19, 3.

prophets and the holy patriarchs understood what they were celebrating; but the rest of the "stiff-necked people" were too carnal[255]. Even after killing Christ the Jews continue to till the ground of an earthly circumcision, an earthly Sabbath, an earthly Passover, while the hidden strength or virtue of making known Christ, which this tilling contains, is not yielded to the Jews while they continue in impiety and unbelief, for it is revealed in the New Testament[256]. Faustus also does not understand it. Therefore he calls the institutions of the law disfigurements and excrescences. So he likes men displeased with things of which they do not know the use. As if a deaf man, seeing others move their lips in speaking, were to find fault with the motion of the mouth as needless and unsightly; or as a blind man, on hearing a house commended, were to test the truth of what he heard by passing his hand over the surface of the wall, and on coming to the windows were to cry out against them as flaws in the level, or were to suppose that the wall had fallen in[257]. And yet the Christians know that in these precepts and commands of the Law, which now it is not allowed to use, so great mysteries are contained, as that there is nothing more deadly than that whatever is there, be understood to the letter, and nothing more healthful than that it be unveiled in the Spirit[258]. The first sacraments are taken away, while Christ fulfilled them by His advent. And now that the righteousness of faith is revealed and the children of God are called into liberty, and the yoke of bondage is taken away, other sacraments are instituted, greater in efficacy, more beneficial in their use, easier in performance, and fewer in munber'[259].

St. Augustine also rebuked—and we mention this for the sake of completeness alone—the Manicheans for their claim that the Old Testament was full of blasphemies about God[260], and, in particular, that the Patriarchs and Prophets had lived shameful lives[261]. By allegorical interpretations, St. Augustine tried to show that many of their sinful deeds had a mystical or prophetic meaning. To judge him fairly, we must bear in mind two things: he insisted that no one

[255] Enarratio in Ps. 39, 12.
[256] Contra Faustum XII, 11; 2 Cor. 3:15, 16.
[257] Contra Faustum XXII, 7.
[258] De utilitate credendi, 9.
[259] Contra Faustum XIX, 13.
[260] ib. XXII, 8–22.
[261] ib. XXII, 24–97.

was bound to agree with his interpretation, and that all were at liberty to interpret the texts in a purely literal sense, according to their tastes[262]. Secondly, he stressed time and again that the Old Testament was history, in which God admonished us by precept warning. 'In fact, nothing could have been devised more likely and to instruct and benefit the pious reader of Sacred Scripture than that, besides describing praiseworthy characters as examples, and blameworthy characters as warnings, it should also narrate cases where good men have gone back and fallen into sin, whether they are restored to the right path or continue irreclaimable; and also where bad men have changed, and have attained to goodness, whether they persevere in it or relapse into evil; in order that the righteous may not be lifted up in the pride of security, nor the wicked hardened in despair of cure. If any one reading of the action of David, of which he repented when the Lord rebuked and threatened him, finds in the narrative an encouragement to sin, is Scripture to be blamed for this?'[263].

5. *The confirmation of true liberty.*

Faustus had claimed that whoever truly possessed the New Testament, would automatically reject the Old, and refuse henceforth to submit to its yoke. St. Augustine replied that 'a Catholic Christian maintains the authority of the Old Testament, not for the imitation of Jewish bondage, but for the confirmation of Christian liberty. So the apostle says, "All these things happened to them as an example, and they were written for our admonition, on whom the ends of the world are come"[264]. We do not therefore, as bondmen observe what was enjoined as predictive of us; but as free, we read what was written to confirm us. So any one may see that the apostle remonstrates with the Galatians not for devoutly reading what Scripture says of circumcision, but for superstitiously desiring to be circumcised[265]. We do not put a new cloth to an old garment, as Faustus says, but we are instructed in the kingdom of heaven, like the householder, whom the Lord describes as bringing out of his

[262] ib. XXII, 95. Note the word 'purely'.
[263] ib. XXII, 96–97.
[264] 1 Cor. 10:11.
[265] Gal. 5:2, 2.

treasure things new and old. He who puts a new cloth to an old garment is the man who attempts spiritual self-denial before he has renounced fleshly hope. Examine the passage, and you will see that, when the Lord was asked about fasting, He replied, "No man putteth a new cloth to an old garment"[266]. The Lord means not two Testaments, but two lives and two hopes, one of earthly felicity and the other of the kingdom of heaven'[267].

'Faustus says that the apostle, in leaving Judaism, passed from the bitter to the sweet. But the apostle himself says[268] that the Jews, who would not believe in Christ, were branches broken off, and that the Gentiles, a wild olive tree, were grafted into the good olive, that is, the holy stock of the Hebrews, that they might partake of the fatness of the olive. Paul himself had been by unbelief among the broken branches but when he made the happy transition from Judaism to Christianity, he has been grafted into the root of the olive tree and so was set free. For Christ was always preached in the olive tree and those who believed in Him were grafted in'[269]. It must be noted that St. Augustine equated the root of the good olive with Christ, who was thus once again prefigured to the Jews.

And it irked him all the more greatly, that the godless and impure Manicheans who rejected the Old Testament, should have the effrontery to call themselves the pure brides of Christ. 'All the effect of such a boast on the real chaste members of the holy Church is to remind them of the apostle's warning against deceivers, "I have joined you to one husband, to present you as a chaste virgin to Christ. But I fear lest, as the serpent deceived Eve by his guile, so your minds also should be corrupted from the purity which is in Christ"[270]. What do the preachers of another gospel do but condemn the laws of God as antiquated, while praising their own errors for the sake of their novelty? The apostle John, however, praises the old commandment[271], and the apostle Paul bids us avoid novelties in doctrine'[272].

As a prodigal son, who had once allowed himself to be misguided

[266] Contra Faustum VIII, 2; Matth. 9 : 16.
[267] ib. XV, 2.
[268] Rom. 11 : 16–20.
[269] Contra Faustum IX, 2.
[270] 2 Cor. 11 : 2, 3.
[271] 1 Joh. 2 : 7.
[272] 1 Tim. 6 : 4.

by the Manicheans, but had returned to the right path by Christ's merciful love, St. Augustine applied the title of Christ's bride to the Catholic Church, warning her against the Manichean heresy: 'It is a silly falsehood that thou hast been seduced to another God, who promises abundance of food and the land of Canaan. For thou canst perceive how the saints of old, who were also thy children, were enlightened by these figures which were prophecies of thee. Thou needest not to regard the poor jest against the stone tablets, for the stony heart of which they were in old times a figure is not in thee. For thou art an epistle of the apostles, "written not with ink, but with the Spirit of the living God; not on tables of stone, but on the fleshy tables of the heart"[273]. With a heart no longer stony, thou canst see in those stone tablets a suitableness to that hard-hearted people; and at the same time thou canst find even there the stone, thy Bridegroom, described by Peter as, "a living stone rejected by men, but chosen by God, and precious"[274]. Fear not, then, to read these tablets—they are from thy husband; to others the stone was a sign of insensibility, but to thee of strength and stability. Only be not under the law, but be under grace, that love, which is the fulfilling of the law, may be in thee. Love is the fulfilling of the law[275]. O chaste tablets, in which thy Lover and thy Beloved of old prefigured to thee the new song on a psaltery of ten strings'[276].

After this address to Christ's true bride, St. Augustine returned to the Manicheans who had brought shame on the bride by claiming her for their own. Few of his writings were as bitter and scathing as this. He called their 'bride' a slut, prostituted by devils, pregnant with godless vanities, and whoring after a multitude of false gods[277]. 'The true bride of Christ, on the contrary, knows the difference between the letter and the spirit, between law and grace, and serving God no longer in the oldness of the letter, but in newness of spirit, she is not under the law, but under grace. She knows that the law is always good: whether it hurts those who are destitute of grace, or benefits those who are filled with grace, itself is always good; as the sun is always good, for every creature of God is good, whether it

[273] Ezech. 11:19; 2 Cor. 3:2, 3.
[274] 1 Pet. 2:4–8.
[275] Rom. 13:9, 10.
[276] Contra Faustum XV, 3, 4.
[277] ib. 6, 7.

hurts weak eyes or gladdens the sight of the healthy[278]. And so she rejoices in true liberty under the New Testament in the hope of full salvation'[279].

6. *Acceptance of Scripture as a whole.*

Faustus, in his fourth antithesis, thought that he could see a correspondence between the Catholics' attitude towards the Old and the Manicheans' views of the New Testament, but St. Augustine would have none of it. To him, there was a fundamental difference between the two: 'We give to the whole Old Testament Scriptures their due praise as true and divine; you impugn the Scriptures of the New Testament as having been tampered with and corrupted. Those things in the Old Testament which we do not observe we hold to have been suitable appointments for the time and the people of that dispensation, besides being symbolical to us of truths in which they have still a spiritual use though the outward observance is abolished; and this opinion is proved to be the doctrine of the apostolic writings. The Manicheans, on the other hand, find fault with everything in the New Testament, which they do not receive, and assert that these passages were not spoken or written by Christ or His apostles. In these respects there is a manifest difference between the Catholics and the Manicheans[280]. If we are asked why we do not worship God as the Hebrew fathers of the Old Testament worshipped Him, we reply that God has taught us differently by the New Testament fathers, and yet in no opposition to the Old Testament, but as that Testament itself predicted. For it is thus foretold by the prophet Jeremiah, as we read in Chap. 31:3; 32. And to the objection that we do not belong to the house of Israel or to the house of Judah, we answer according to the teaching of the apostle, who calls Christ the seed of Abraham, and says to us, as belonging to Christ's body[281]. Again the same apostle teaches us[282] what we do not observe in the Old Testament, as a shadow of things to come which are now fulfilled[283]. And in reply to all objections whatsoever, we appeal to

[278] ib. 8.
[279] ib. 9.
[280] Contra Faustum XXXII, 8.
[281] Gal. 3:16, 29.
[282] Coloss. 2:16, 17; 1 Cor. 10:11.
[283] Contra Faustum XXXII, 9.

our established principles, on which we maintain the authority of sacred Scripture. The principle is this, that all things written in the books of the Old Testament are to be received with approval and admiration, as most true and most profitable to eternal life; and that those precepts which are no longer observed outwardly are to be understood as having been most suitable in those times, and are to be viewed as having been shadows of things to come, of which we may now perceive the fulfilments[284]. Hence the correspondence assumed by Faustus is utterly false. We accept the Old Testament without criticism[285], while Faustus is critical towards the New, and, without reason, questions the validity of many manuscripts, citing a Paraclete which is nowhere mentioned in the New Testament. The true Paraclete, the Holy Spirit, came immediately after the glorification of Christ, according to Christ's promise'[286].

Faustus had cited the Gospel which, he claimed, confessed Christ as God's Son, and not as the Son of Man, and demanded obedience to evangelical precepts. But this, St. Augustine said, was another gospel altogether, and one which Paul had accursed[287]. 'How could the incarnation not be part of the gospel when Paul had said: "Remember that Christ Jesus, of the seed of David, rose from the dead, according to my gospel"[288]? The Son of God became the Son of Man so that he could be delivered for our offences and be raised again for our justification[289]. Accordingly Christ calls Himself both Son of God and Son of man. To take only one instance out of many, in the Gospel of John it is written, "Verily verily, I say unto you, the hour cometh and now is, when the dead shall hear the voice of the Son of God; and they that hear shall live. For as the Father has life in Himself, so He has given to the Son to have life in Himself; and has given Him power to execute judgment also, because He is the Son of man"[290]. Since, then, He promises eternal life to those that believe in Him, and since to believe in Him is to believe in the true Christ, such as He declares Himself and His apostles declare Him to be, true Son of God and true Son of man;

[284] ib. 14.
[285] ib. 15.
[286] ib. 16 ff.; XI, 2, 3.
[287] Gal. 1:8.
[288] 2 Tim. 2:8.
[289] Rom. 4:25.
[290] Joh. 5:25, 26.

the Manicheans who believe in a false and spurious son of a false and spurious man, are plainly far from that eternal life which Christ promises to those who believe in Him. John even says, that he is Antichrist who denies that Christ has come in the flesh'[291].

Faustus' exclusive insistence on observing the evangelical precepts, which St. Augustine openly ridiculed, would never lead to salvation, for mere observance without faith is worthless. The end of the commandment, Paul said, is 'charity out of a pure heart, and of a good conscience, and of faith unfeigned'[292]. True love and feigned faith cannot go hand in hand[293]. 'The Catholic Christians have, on the contrary, the true love to God and man, for by the grace of Christ they keep this law, and on these two commandments hang all the law and the prophets. Besides, they see in Christ and the Church the fulfilment of all the prophecies of the Old Testament, whether in the form of actions, or of symbolic rites of figurative language[294]. Grace is the fulfilment of love and truth is the accomplishment of the prophecies. And as both grace and truth are by Christ, it follows that He came not to destroy the law, but to fulfil it'[295].

[291] 1 Joh. 4:3.
[292] 1 Tim. 1:5.
[293] Contra Faustum V, 4 ff.; see also II, 2; III, 2.
[294] ib. XVIII, 7.
[295] ib. XVII, 6.

CHAPTER IV

THE WORD OF GOD AS PROCLAMATION

For many centuries, the preaching of God's Word has lost its central place in Roman Catholic worship. True, there have been isolated attempts to change all that recently[1], but in practice the service continues to revolve exclusively about the altar. Thus the pulpit is not in the centre of the church, and the sermon plays no more than a marginal role during the Low Mass, attendance at which is not obligatory[2].

It is possibly due to this time-hallowed practice that St. Augustine's stress of the importance of the Word of God as proclamation has been so greatly neglected by Roman Catholic writers, to whom—and particularly to Zarb[3], Huyben[4], and Kunzelmann[5]—we are nevertheless much indebted for the accurate dating of his sermons. Moreover, the collection, publication, and full discussion of the number, style, etc. of the sermons was largely the work of Morin, Wilmart, Mohrmann, *et al.*[6].

But when it comes to St. Augustine's evaluation of the preaching of God's Word, we are made to believe that he never went beyond what we have called the first stage of his development. To all intents and purposes, there is no mention of the central place which he

[1] Cf. Th. Soiron, *Die Verkündigung des Wortes Gottes*, Freiburg 1943. August Schorn, *Das Wort Gottes bei den Vätern*. In: *Vom Hören des Wortes Gottes*, Freiburg (Herder) 1949, pp. 19–33; J. A. M. Waterman, *De verkondiging van het Woord Gods*. In: *Levende Zielzorg*, Utrecht 1954, pp. 174–205, Ernst Haemsli, *Verkündigung heute aus lebendigen theol. Einsichten* in: Fragen der Theologie heute, 1954.

[2] See K. Barth, *Kirchliche Dogmatik* I, I, p. 65–71.

[3] S. M. Zarb, various articles in Angelicum, from 1935 onw.

[4] J. Huyben, *De Sermoenen over het Johannesevangelie*. Miscellanea Augustiniana, Rotterdam 1930, pp. 256–274.

[5] A. Kunzelmann, *Die Chronologie der Sermone des hl. Augustinus*, Miscellanea Agostiniana, Rome 1931, pp. 417–520 (particularly pp. 512–520).

[6] See Christine Mohrmann's introduction to: *Sint Augustinus' preken voor het volk*, Utrecht 1948, pp. XIII–LXVIII.

assigned to God's Word, and by which he broke through the confining bounds of the Neoplatonic conceptual framework, to show it up for the poor thing it was. An example of this approach is found in Van der Meer's admirable work on St. Augustine, the spiritual mentor[7]. The author, while dealing with the subject of preaching at length[8], completely ignores the fact that St. Augustine, during his second stage, was firmly convinced of the efficacy of the Word of God in the preaching. Thus he refers quite unconsciously to Church custom, when he says that the aim of all St. Augustine's sermons was to open the senses (which St. Augustine himself would surely not have suggested in this context), or when he summarises the well-known passage from *De Doctrina Christiana* IV, 32, as follows: 'Pray before the sermon so that you may be granted understanding. Pray before you preach,' In his chapter on Church practice, he rightly quoted Paulinus of Nola as saying that the Lord's clarion sounded through St. Augustine's mouth, but he failed to give the reasons why Paulinus felt impelled to pass this judgment. True he alludes to this point[9] but on the same page, he remarks: 'What was and is decisive (for the almost exclusively Biblical approach) is the fact that Christianity believed in the divine character of the Holy Scriptures and, thanks to allegorical interpretations, was convinced, more fully than today, of the all-embracing character of Scripture. Furthermore, respect for the Word could be unconsciously associated with the ancients' respect for words in general; the Bible simply placed Homer and Virgil on a higher plane'[10]. No wonder therefore, that Van der Meer's treatment of the 'effects' of the sermon is so disappointing! 'What', he asks 'did St. Augustine think of the effects of his words, and of preaching in general? Very little, indeed[11]'. (He seems to forget that St. Augustine considered the effects of the sermon to be mainly the effects of God's Word!) Thereupon he cites the well-known passage from *In epist. Joannis Tract 3, 13* which we have quoted earlier[12] and which does anything but exhaust St. Augustine's thoughts on the effect of preaching. Van der Meer uses this quotation to point out that, according to St. Augustine's epistemology

[7] F. van der Meer, *Augustinus de zielzorger*, Utrecht 1947, pp. 358–412.
[8] pp. 342–355.
[9] Particularly pp. 388 and 389.
[10] p. 388.
[11] p. 397.
[12] See p. 28 of this book.

derived under the influence of Neoplatonism, no man can learn anything from the words of others, and hence that sermons play but a very modest role in the life of the Church. True, Van der Meer admits that St. Augustine occasionally saw the spiritual fruits of his words, but inasmuch as he enters into this problem at all, he fails to show that, according to St. Augustine, 'by the sword of the Word of God they (the people of God) fall that they may rise, are severed that they may be gathered, wounded that they may be made whole, die that they may live'[13].

And Van der Meer's approach, far from being the exception, is almost symptomatic of the Roman Catholic attitude, even though little on that subject has been published[14]. Thus Gustave Bardy, in a chapter of his well-known work on St. Augustine[15], devoted to St. Augustine's sermons, tells us simply that St. Augustine preached the Word of God, without entering into any analytic discussion. While all sorts of interesting questions are reviewed, St. Augustine's own doctrine of the preaching of the Word of God is not even touched upon. In a recent companion-work, Bernardin contributed an article on St. Augustine as Pastor[16], in which he discussed St. Augustine as the servant of the Sacraments at length, while devoting barely half a page to St. Augustine the preacher. One striking exception is once again the work of Pontet, of the Lyon-Fourvière school, who, while dwelling mainly on St. Augustine's exegesis, nevertheless devoted many pages to St. Augustine's sermons, and thus went beyond the traditional Roman Catholic approach[17]. It is regrettable that Pontet has not treated this subject *ex professo*.

From the Protestant side, the harvest is poorer still. It was Seeberg's great merit to have characterised St. Augustine as the draughtsman of the doctrine of God's Word, in which the Word serves not only as a lesson or as guide to the newly converted, but

[13] Enarratio in Ps. 149, 13.

[14] Nebreda in his *Bibliographia Augustiniana*, Rome 1928, mentions a very small number of publications (p. 88 f.). Neither in *Miscellanea Augustiniana*, Miscellanea Agostiniana, nor in the *Communications* in *Augustinus Magister* (Paris 1954) is there an article on this subject.

[15] *Saint Augustin, L'Homme—l'œuvre*, Paris 1948, pp. 213–263.

[16] Joseph B. Bernardin, *St. Augustine as Pastor*. In: *A Companion to the Study of St. Augustine*, New York 1955, pp. 57–89.

[17] Pontet was mainly concerned with St. Augustine's exegesis *as a preacher*—hence the title: *L'exégèse de St. Augustin prédicateur*.

inspires faith and works salvation as *vocatio*, as a call by God. But Seeberg left it at that[18]. Niebergall, in *Leiturgia*[19] gave a brief and extremely summary sketch of St. Augustine's work as a preacher, in which, despite a number of pertinent criticisms, he showed that St. Augustine preached in the conviction that God Himself was present in the faithful words of His preacher. Luiks was persuaded to investigate the place of God's Word in the service of the ancient church, after his reading of St. Augustine had shown him that God's Word held pride of place over the Sacrament[20]. At the conclusion of his important investigation, he was right to assert that, in the Church of North Africa, the pulpit (cathedra), from which the Word of God was preached, used to stand in the *presbyterium*, i.e. in the highest point of the church, thus overlooking the entire building[21]. Moreover, the church building, in which the regular service used to be conducted in North Africa, was meant first and foremost for preaching the Word, and only secondarily for the service of the Sacrament[22]. Still, Luiks could not, within the confines of his work, give a detailed discussion of St. Augustine's evaluation of the role in worship of the sermon as such.

In what follows, we shall try to show that St. Augustine was fully conscious of the central importance in worship of the Word of God as preaching, and that he can rightly be called the founder of the doctrine of God's Word.

1. *God Himself speaks when His Word is preached.*

More than once, St. Augustine expressed his firm conviction that, whenever God's Word is preached to the congregation, He Himself speaks through His Word. The word of the preacher who spreads God's Word is not only vouchsafed by divine authority, so that the authority of the Most High King pledges his every promise and admonition, but God Himself is present in it, turning it into a fire that singes, and into a hammer that crushes the rock. 'He makes it to the one a savour of life unto life, to the other a savour of death unto

[18] R. Seeberg, *Lehrbuch der Dogmengeschichte* II³, Leipzig 1923, pp. 452, 453.
[19] Leiturgia, *Handbuch des evangelischen Gottesdienstes*, Kassel 1954, pp. 230–232.
[20] A. G. Luiks, *Cathedra en Mensa*, Franeker 1955. Preface.
[21] ib. p. 138.
[22] ib. p. 156.

death'[23]. 'A fire blazes in God's Word. It is the fire of the Holy Ghost[24]. The gospel is the mouth of Christ. He is in heaven, but never ceases speaking on earth. Let us not be deaf, for He calls. Let us not be dead for He thunders[25]. Christ was silent when He was condemned. But as for those words which are needful for us, has He ever failed to speak? He was not silent in the Patriarchs. He did not keep silent with the mouth of His body, and if He kept silent now, the Sacred Scriptures would keep silent also. His Word is read out to us, and He does not keep silent. His Word is preached and inasmuch as the preacher speaks the truth, Christ speaks through him. Were Christ silent, I should not be telling you all this. Nor did he keep silent through your mouths, for when you sang it was He who spoke. Nay, He does not keep silent, and it is our duty to listen, but with the ears of our hearts'[26].

Precisely because God speaks through His preached Word, because He warns and consoles men, did St. Augustine refer to God's Word not only as *Verbum Dei* but also as *Sermo Dei* (literally: God's converse, whereby God's own speaking is stressed). St. Augustine took this term from Hebrews 4:12, of which the Latin translation which he used begins with *Sermo Dei*, the Word that is living and strong. And that is precisely how St. Augustine looked upon God's Word as proclamation. Whenever it came to preaching God's laws[27], or God's promises[28] or God's warnings and admonitions[29] he used the term *Sermo Dei* as an alternative to *Verbum Dei*, though the two might often be found together in one and the same paragraph[30]. It behoved all men to feel that the Word of God is inseparably bound up with the Triune Godhead and hence is living and strong, full of mercy and wrath, and thus the two-edged sword of Psalm 149: 'It is one sword, but therefore are they called many, because there are many mouths and many tongues of the saints. This Word of the Lord is a two-edged sword[31]. How is it two-edged? It speaks of things temporal. It speaks also of things eternal. In both

[23] Enarratio in Ps. 7, 15.
[24] Sermo 22, 7.
[25] Sermo 85, 1.
[26] Sermo 17, 1.
[27] Sermo 9, 3.
[28] Enarratio in Ps. 32 II, 9.
[29] Sermo 9, 10, 11.
[30] Sermo 4, 31; 5, 1.
[31] Hebr. 4:12.

cases it proveth what it saith, and him who it strikes, it severeth from the world. Is not this the sword whereof the Lord said, "I am not come to send peace upon earth but a sword"[32]? Observe how He came to divide, how He came to sever. He divideth the saints, He divideth the ungodly, He severeth from thee that which hindereth thee. The son willeth to serve God, the father willeth not: the sword cometh, the Word of God cometh, and severeth the son from the father. The daughter willeth, the mother willeth not: by the sword they are divided from another. The daughter-in-law willeth, the mother-in-law willeth not: let the sword sharpened on both sides come, let it bring the promise of the present and the future life, comfort in this life, enjoyment in eternity. Behold the sword sharpened on both sides promising things both temporal and eternal. Wherein hath it deceived us? Was there not a time when the Church of God was not spread throughout the whole world? Lo, now it is. Before it was read of, not seen: now, as it is read of, so also it is seen. Whatsoever is promised to us in this world belongeth to one side of the sword: whatever is promised for everlasting, belongeth to the other side. Thou hast hope for the future, comfort for the present; be not thou drawn back from Him who would draw thee to Him; be it father, mother, sister, friend, let him not draw thee back: so shall the sword sharpened on both sides profit thee. To thy profit does it sever thee, to thy harm dost thou bind thyself to them. Our Lord then came bearing the sword sharpened on both sides, promising things of eternity, fulfilling those of this life. For therefore also are they called two Testaments. In both is found the Word of God, as a sword twice sharpened[33]. Everywhere this sword is in the hands of the preachers, the people of God fall that they may rise, are severed that they may be gathered, wounded that they may be made whole, die that they may live'[34].

And this is how St. Augustine read Ps. 7:13, 14: "He hath bent his bow, and made it ready. And in it He hath prepared the instruments of death: He hath wrought his arrows for the burning". 'That bow', he declared in a sermon on this psalm, 'I would readily take to be the Holy Scripture, in which by the strength of the New Testament, as by a sort of string, the hardness of the Old has

[32] Matth. 10:34.
[33] Enarratio in Ps. 149, 11.
[34] ib. 13.

been bent and subdued. From thence the Apostles are sent forth like arrows, of divine preachings are shot. Which arrows He hath wrought for the burning, arrows, that is, whereby being stricken they might be inflamed with heavenly love. For by what other arrows was she stricken, who saith, "Bring me into house of wine, place me among perfumes, crowd me among honey, for I have been wounded by love[35]"? By what other arrows is he kindled, who, desirous of returning to God, and coming back from wandering, asketh for help against crafty tongues, and to whom it is said, "What shall be given thee, or what added to thee against the crafty tongue? Sharp arrows of the mighty, with devastating coals[36]", that is, coals, whereby, when thou art stricken and set on fire, thou mayest burn with so great love of the kingdom of heaven, as to despise the tongues of all that resist thee, and would recall thee from thy purpose, and to deride their persecutions, saying, "who shall separate me from the love of Christ?"[37] Thus for the burning hath He wrought his arrows'. St. Augustine went on to remark that there are apparently two different interpretations of this text. 'In the Greek copies it is found thus, He hath wrought his arrows for the burning. But most of the Latin copies have burning arrows. But whether the arrows themselves burn, or make others burn, which of course they cannot do unless they burn themselves, the sense is complete. In this psalm is also said that the Lord has prepared not arrows only, but instruments of death too, in the bow. He asks what are instruments of death? Are they peradventure heretics? For they too, out of the same bow, that is, out of the same Scriptures, light upon souls not to be inflamed with love, but destroyed with poison. Or has He haply ordained the same arrows to be at once instruments to death for the destruction of unbelievers, and wrought them burning, or for the burning, for the exercising of the faithful? For that is not false that the apostle says, "To the one we are the savour of life unto life, to the other the savour of death unto death"[38]. It is no wonder then if the same apostles be both instruments of death in those from whom they suffered persecution and fiery arrows to inflame the hearts of believers'[39].

[35] Song of Sol. 2:4, 5.
[36] Ps. 120:3, 4*M*.
[37] Rom. 8:35.
[38] 2 Cor. 2:16.
[39] Enarratio in Ps. 7, 14, 15.

St. Augustine treated this text in a sermon on Psalm 120 in much the same spirit. 'The sharp arrows of the Mighty One', he declared, 'are the Words of God. Lo, they are shot, and they transfix hearts: but when hearts have been transfixed by the arrows of God's word, love is roused, not destruction brought about. The Lord knows how to shoot arrows of love: and no one more graciously shooteth arrows of love, than He who shooteth with the Word; yea, He shooteth the heart of him that loveth, that He may aid the loving; He shooteth that He may make him loving'[40].

These are but a few gleanings from a wealth of material, in which St. Augustine stressed the presence of God in the faithful service of His Word. Where the preacher is faithful, his arrows are wrought by God Himself, to kindle our hearts in love. The forces of the kingdom of heaven begin to work in us. The dead arise, the wounds are struck whereby we may be healed, natural bonds are severed, so that love may rule supreme. The very fact that St. Augustine used the term *Sermo Dei* continually when discussing the preaching of God's Word, shows clearly that he had discarded Neoplatonic thoughts and concepts, in favour of new categories of which the ancient world was quite ignorant.

2. *God's Word alone must be preached and heard.*

Hence St. Augustine was emphatic that God's preachers must preach God's Word alone, while the congregation must heed the Word and not the preachers themselves. The pastors must simply proclaim the Gospel. In order to enlighten men, they need only cause the light of the Word to fall upon them, thus acting as lamps[41]. The divine content of the Scriptures is the substance of their sermons. In them lies the source of their knowledge, and from them they must sow what they have learned with the help of Him in Whose hands they and their sermons rest[42]. The Athenians mocked Paul by calling him a sower of words[43], but though they mocked him, the faithful must not despise his deeds. He was indeed a sower of words but also a reaper of morals. We (the preachers) sow God's

[40] Enarratio in Ps. 119, 5.
[41] Sermo 46, 5.
[42] Sermo 48, 1.
[43] Acts 17:18.

Word in God's acre, that is in your hearts, and count on the rich harvest of your morals[44]. The Athenians had no understanding, yet when they called Paul a sower of words, they did so rightly[45]. Thus did Apostles and the prophets sow the seed of the Gospel. Thus Christ, too, was a sower for He spoke in the Apostle. Hence Paul could say that he was sent to preach the Gospel 'where Christ was not named'[46]. St. Augustine himself strove to draw upon this treasure of the Lord[47], seeking in the Scriptures the salve which the preacher tries to apply to the wounds[48]. Hence, every preacher must be what Christ Himself has enjoined him to be: "a scribe which is instructed unto the kingdom of heaven being like unto an householder which bringeth forth out of his treasure things new and old"[49]. Why old? Because they have long been preached. Why new? Because they point to the kingdom of God[50].

Left to himself, the preacher has no light. God sends him his Word, the better to proclaim His heavenly mercy on earth, according to the saying of the Psalmist: "Thy mercy, O Lord, is in the heavens; and thy faithfulness reaches unto the clouds. Thy righteousness is like the great mountains"[51]. St. Augustine made this text a subject of one of his sermons: 'Thy mercy which Thou givest to Thy saints, is heavenly, not earthly; is eternal, not temporal. And how couldest Thou declare it unto men? Because Thy truth reacheth even unto the clouds. For who could know the heavenly mercy of God, unless God should declare it unto men? How did He declare it? By sending His truth even unto the clouds. What are the clouds? The preachers of the Word of God. Truth reached even to the clouds: therefore unto us could be declared the mercy of God which is in heaven and not in earth[52]. And truly, Brethren, the clouds are the preachers of the Word of God. When God threateneth through his preachers, He thunders through the clouds. When God worketh miracles through His preachers, He lighteneth through the clouds. He terrifieth through the clouds, and watereth by the rain. Those preachers

[44] Sermo 150, 1.
[45] Sermo 101, 1.
[46] ib. 3.
[47] Sermo 41, 1.
[48] Sermo 32, 1.
[49] Matth. 13:52.
[50] Sermo 74, 1, 5.
[51] Ps. 36:5, 6.
[52] Enarratio in Ps. 35, 8.

then, by whom is preached the gospel of God, are the clouds of God. But who are the mountains of God? Those who are called clouds, the same are also the mountains of God. The great preachers are the mountains of God. And as when the sun riseth, he first clothes the mountains with light, and thence the light descends to the lowest parts of the earth: so our Lord Jesus Christ, when He came, first irradiated the height of the apostles, first enlightened the mountains and so his light descended to the valleys of the world'[53]. St. Augustine hastened to add, that the congregation must not expect to gain this understanding from the preachers themselves, but only from their preaching of God's Word. As on many other occasions, he based this opinion on Psalm 121: "I will lift up mine eyes unto the hills, from whence cometh my help". 'Think not that the mountains themselves will give thee help: for they receive what they may give, give not of their own. And if thou remain in the mountains, thy hope will not be strong: but in Him, who enlighteneth the mountains, might be thy hope and presumption. Thy help indeed will come to thee through the mountains, because the Scriptures are administered to thee through the mountains, through the great preachers of the truth, but fix not thy hope in them. Hear what he says next following: I lifted up mine eyes unto the mountains, from whence cometh my help. What then? Do the mountains give thee help? No: hear what follows, my help is from the Lord. Through the mountains cometh help, but not from the mountains. From whom then? From the Lord. The preachers are as the friend of the Bridegroom[54]. And if the friend of the bridegroom is a mountain, yet hath not the mountain light from itself: but he heareth and rejoiceth greatly because of the Bridegroom's voice. So the apostle Paul says, "Let a man so account of us, as of the ministers of Christ, and stewards of the mysteries of God"[55]. But let thy hope again be fixed on God and not on the mountains[56]. God Himself has given the clouds as an ascent of heaven. What is this, brethren? I would the Lord may deign to number me among those clouds, such as they be; He will see how misty a cloud I am; yet all the preachers of the word of truth are clouds. Whosoever therefore of their own infirmity cannot ascend

[53] ib.
[54] Joh. 3:29.
[55] 1 Cor. 4:1.
[56] Enarratio in Ps. 35, 9.

into this heaven, that is, to the understanding of the Scriptures, let them ascend by the clouds[57]. Hence the preachers are said to impart understanding, much as anyone may be said to give light to a house, or to illuminate a house, for which he makes a window; when he doth not penetrate and light it by a light of his own, but merely opens an entrance whereby it may be penetrated and enlightened'[58].

And just because the preacher alone proclaims Christ's gospel, is there no mention of a good shepherd in Ezekiel 34. 'For the bad shepherds were contrasted, not with the good, but with the one and only good Shepherd, Who contains them all. Hence He feeds wherever they feed. The friends of the bridegroom do not speak with their own voices but instead rejoice in His voice. His voice dwelleth within them, and they are filled with His love. The shepherds give praise, but they praise the Lord. Hence they feed for Christ, in Christ, with Christ, and never without Him[59]. And thus the promise is fulfilled: "And I will make them and the places round about my hill a blessing, and I will cause the shower to come down in his season"[60]. Christ is the hill, and hence He is in our midst. He is a gently glowing hill, which is simple to climb as long as we are not too proud. And God will send the shower in his season—the shower of God's Word'[61].

Hence St. Augustine warned his congregation to look to it that God's Word was preached truly by their preachers. Only on the mountains of God's Word do His sheep find safe pasture. 'Whatever you hear upon it, mind that you take it to heart. Reject all that you hear from outside. Listen to the voice of the Shepherd lest you be lost in the mists. Gather on the mountains of the Holy Scriptures[62]. God's great anger with the false shepherds who feed themselves, is just, indeed. For if we feed ouselves, we care not for the sheep. But if we preach Christ's Word, Christ Himself feeds through us[63]. Paul said: "Am I therefore become your enemy because I tell you the truth?"[64] He spoke not of his own truth, but of Christ's[65]. Far be it

[57] Enarratio in Ps. 103, I, II,
[58] Enarratio in Ps. 118 XVIII, 4.
[59] Sermo 46, 39.
[60] Ezek. 34:26.
[61] Sermo 47, 24.
[62] Sermo 46, 24.
[63] ib. 2.
[64] Gal. 4:16.
[65] Sermo 46, 7.

from us to say "Live as ye would, and take no care. God will let no one stray so long as he only holds fast the Christian faith. He would not allow those to be lost whom He has redeemed, for whom He has shed His blood. And if you should desire to taint your hearts with idle spectacles, what harm can there be? And as for the feasts that are held in all the cities, you too may enjoy them, for God's mercy is great and all-forgiving. Gather up the roses before they wilt". Should we speak to you thus, we might find greater favour with you, but we should not be proclaiming God's Word or Christ's Word—we should simply be feeding ourselves'[66].

There are some preachers who fear to offend those to whom they preach and who not only fail to warn against temptation, but promise all manner of earthly reward not vouchsafed by God. These preachers have built their house upon sand, and their house will fall before the floods and the winds[67]. God's Word must be preached in its fullness, even in His anger and admonitions. No tittle must be omitted to please man's vanity. When, after a solemn sermon on the occasion of the anniversary of his consecration as bishop, St. Augustine called on the assembled congregation to become humble and to search their hearts, he added: 'I know full well that some of you will accuse me of having accused and condemned you. Far from it, I have tried to ease your burden of guilt. It is unkind and reprehensible, not to say wicked, evil, and despicable to believe that I have deceived you though God has not deceived me. God has threatened evil-doers with death, with hell, with eternal damnation. How can you expect me to promise what God has not promised? Shall the crier vouchsafe you safety? What if the landlord refuses to honour my promise? I am but an agent, a mere slave, and yet you wish me to tell you: Live as you would, for the Lord will preserve you. The crier's promise would be null and void. Oh, that the Lord Himself made you secure, and I, for my part, made you uneasy. What else is your security and mine but to listen to the Lord's commandment and to await the fulfilment of His promises faithfully?'[68]

The Donatists applied a different rule, altogether. Being mainly concerned with the preacher's own sanctity, they judged the effects of sermons and the administration of the sacraments entirely by the

[66] ib. 8.
[67] Matth. 7:24–27; Sermo 46, 11.
[68] Frangipani II, 9 (ed. Morin).

suitability of the ministers. Carnal men could not possibly gender spiritual men, the dead could never bestow life, the crippled could never teach walking, the blind could never bestow eyesight, the naked could never clothe, and the wicked could never sanctify[69]. According to the Donatists, the Catholic Church had become infested with a mundane spirit, so much so that even many of her bishops lived a godless and idle life. Such faithless hypocrites could not be expected to lead men to faith, but only to sin[70]. For had not Christ Himself said: "Every good tree bringeth forth good fruit, but a corrupt tree bringeth forth evil fruit"?[71]

St. Augustine had no wish to excuse these bishops. Faithless shepherds kill their flock by bad precept. For had not Paul directed Titus to show himself a pattern of good works in all things[72], and Timothy to be an example to the believers?[73] Even the strong sheep will generally look to his leader, albeit he live badly. He diverts his eyes from the commandments of the Lord, and says: if my leader liveth thus who am I to do otherwise? Thus the false leader killeth strong and weak sheep alike[74]. Still, St. Augustine saw no reason here for any schisms. However rightly we may condemn their misdemeanour, we have no grounds for destroying the unity of Christ's Church. Did not Christ Himself, when speaking out against those scribes and Pharisees who had the keys to the kingdom of heaven and yet neither entered it themselves nor allowed others to enter it, say: 'All therefore whatsoever they bid you observe, but do not ye after their works, for they say and do not"?[75] They are scribes but know nothing of the kingdom of God[76]. Yet it may be objected that an evil man can speak none but evil, since Christ Himself has said that an evil man out of the evil treasure of his heart bringeth forth evil things[77]. Or: "How can ye, being evil, speak good things?" Or again: "Whatsoever they bid you observe, but do not ye after their works, for they say and do not". If they say and do not, they are evil, and cannot any but evil things. What then must we do when

[69] Contra Parmenianum II, 23, 32.
[70] De baptismo IV, 1 ff.
[71] Contra litteras Petiliani II, 13.
[72] Titus 2:7.
[73] 1 Tim. 4:12.
[74] Sermo 46, 9.
[75] Matth. 23:3.
[76] Sermo 74, 2.
[77] Matth. 12:35.

we hear them speak? 'Whatever an evil man utters from himself is evil, whatever he speaks from his own heart is evil. How can such evil men then bring forth good things? Because they sit in Moses' seat. Had He not told us that they sit in Moses' seat,[78] He would never have commanded us to heed them. What they brought forth from the evil treasure of their hearts is always other than what they heard in Moses' seat. For what the crier proclaims on the judge's behalf is never attributed to the crier himself. What the crier says in his own house is quite other than what he says on behalf of the judge, for willy-nilly he is bound to pass on the judge's sentence even over his best friend, or the judge's acquittal of even his worst enemy. Were he to speak from his own heart, he would surely acquit his friend and condemn his enemy, but since he passes on what has been said from the judge's seat he condemns the friend and acquits the enemy. Let the scribes bring forth what is in their own hearts, and you will hear them say: "Let us eat and drink for tomorrow we shall die"[79], but let them speak from the seat of Moses and you hear them say: "Thou shalt not kill; thou shalt not commit adultery; thou shalt not steal; thou shalt not bear false witness; honour thy father and thy mother[80], love thy neighbour as thyself"[81]. All we have said is true also of the bad shepherd. He will always proclaim the Word of God, for better or for worse, if only to get at the milk in the bottle, so that his sheep will not be fed by him but by God'[82]. St. Augustine returned to this point on a number of occasions. Clearly, the Donatists' citation of Christ's own words had made a great impression on the simpler members of St. Augustine's congregation. St. Augustine therefore enjoined them not to become confused by Christ's saying that "every tree is known by his own fruits. For of thorns men do not gather figs, nor of a bramble bush gather they grapes"[83]. The question whether a scribe can bring forth good is best answered with: "Whatever they bid you observe". Do we therefore gather grapes from a bramble bush, after all? 'Nay, but take heed that the vine as it creeps over the earth does not—as so often happens—become choked by the brambles. A vine will often cling to the bramble hedge

[78] Matth. 23:2.
[79] Isa. 22:13.
[80] Exod. 20:12, 16.
[81] Lev. 19:18; Sermo 74, 3.
[82] Sermo 46, 22.
[83] Luke 6:44.

for better support, and wind its way among the thorns so that its grapes will hang between them. Those who can see the grapes will pluck them, not from the brambles, but from the hidden vine. Thus the scribes are like brambles but since they sit in Moses' seat, the vine clings to them, and they support the grapes, that is they speak good words, and give good precepts. Pluck the grapes, and the bramble will not prick you. Hence, whatever they bid you observe, but do not ye after their works lest the thorns wound you'[84].

And when Petilian quoted the same texts[85] to his own purpose, St. Augustine told him that Christ's words applied to man's works alone: 'When a man preaches the Word of God, or administers the sacraments of God, he does not, if he is a bad man, preach or minister out of his own treasure; but he will be counted among those of whom it is said, "Whatsoever they bid you observe, that observe and do; but do not ye after their works", for they bid you observe what is God's, but their works are their own'[86].

Apart from giving this interpretation of Christ's Words, St. Augustine was also wont to counter the attacks of the Donatists with two texts taken from the Epistles of Paul: "For if I do this thing willingly I have a reward, but if against my will, a dispensation of the gospel is committed unto me"[87], and: "Some indeed preach Christ even of envy and strife; and some also of good will. The one preach Christ of contention, not sincerely, supposing to add affliction to my bonds: But the other of love, knowing that I am set for the defence of the gospel. What then? Notwithstanding, every way, whether in pretence or in truth, Christ is preached, and I therein do rejoice, yea, and will rejoice"[88]. From the first text it is clear—so St. Augustine told Parmenian—that even if it is preached unwillingly, Christ's Word bestows blessings on all who listen, though not on those who preach it hypocritically. Such servants forfeit their reward, but do not rob those to whom they serve the Lord's food albeit badly[89]. 'Therefore, a minister, that is, a dispenser of the Word and the Sacraments of the Gospel, if he is a good man, becomes a fellow-partner in the working of the Gospel; but if he is a bad man, he does

[84] Sermo 46, 22. Cf. Sermo 74, 4; 101, 10; 137, 13.
[85] Matth. 7 : 17, 18 and 12 : 35.
[86] Matth. 23 : 3; Contra litteras Petiliani II, 13.
[87] Cor. 9 : 17.
[88] Phil. 1 : 15–18.
[89] Contra Parmenianum II, 24.

not therefore cease to be a dispenser of the Gospel[90]. Peter and the other disciples announce the good tidings, as being good themselves. Judas did it against his will, but yet, when he was sent, he announced it in common with the rest. But they who received the Gospel at the mouth of all those witnesses, could not be cleansed and justified by him that planted, or by him that watered, but by Him alone that gives the increase[91]. If Judas did not baptize, at any rate we must acknowledge that he preached the Gospel. But if you consider this a trifling function and of no importance, see what you must think of the apostle Paul himself, who said, "For Christ sent me not to baptize, but to preach the Gospel"[92]. Who does this unwillingly, has no reward for himself, but he dispenses yet the treasure of the Lord'[93].

As regards the second text, St. Augustine told Parmenian, that Paul said of those who do not proclaim the Gospel with a clean heart, not for Christ's sake but for the sake of their own reward: I will not rejoice over them, but over those whom their preaching has preserved. Did he prevent them from preaching the Gospel, albeit they failed to spread it with true purity of heart? Did not he rather rejoice over their sermons, inasmuch as they benefited those who heard what was good and true in them? For where Christ, Who is the truth, is not preached, falsehood and lies reign supreme. "If any man preach any other gospel unto you", Paul told the Galatians, "than that ye have received, let him be accursed"[94]. And to Timothy he wrote: "As I besought thee to abide still at Ephesus, when I went into Macedonia, that thou mightest charge some that they teach no other doctrine..."[95] As for those who act from contention and strife, greed, obstinacy and impurity, Paul not only let them be—the Holy Ghost scorned their hypocrisy but never their service—but rejoiced over their action[96]. 'They were seeking their own, not the things which are Jesus Christ's, but the gospel which they preached was pure[97]. Such a minister is reckoned with the devil; but the gift of Christ is not contaminated, which flows through him pure,

[90] 1 Cor. 9:17.
[91] 1 Cor. 3:6, 7.
[92] 1 Cor. 1:17.
[93] Contra litteras Petiliani III, 67.
[94] Gal. 1:9.
[95] 1 Tim. 1:3.
[96] Contra Parmenianum II, 24.
[97] Contra litteras Petiliani II, 11.

which passes through him liquid and comes to the fertile earth. Suppose that he is stony, that he cannot from water rear fruit; even through the stony channel the water passes to the garden beds; in the stony channel it causes nothing to grow, but nevertheless it brings much fruit to the gardens'[98]. And therefore, the true mother (the Catholic Church) may rest content since even the hypocrites in the Church feed her child with the milk of the divine Scriptures of the Catholic faith[99]. And the sheep are safe, if only they heed the voice of the good Shepherd, the voice of Christ, no matter if it is spoken through the voice of a good man or bad'[100].

By these arguments, St. Augustine had clearly set Christ's Church on a firm path for all time. Amidst the confusion of his day he knew how to steer a clear course, simply because he read the Scriptures with a pure heart and saw in them the only safe anchorage for God's people. The Word, and Christ's gospel alone contained enough food for all sermons, and enough physic for all man's ills, and from it the servant and dispenser of God's mysteries must bring forth things new and old, the new things being the preaching of the kingdom of heaven. A servant by himself gives forth no light, for he must draw on his master above, on God's Holy Words. If only he holds fast to them, he will not be feeding himself as he will whenever he speaks from his own heart or looks more to men than to the Word of God. Only where the Scriptures are preached does Christ Himself feed and does His Holy Spirit come into its own. Paul's curse shows that, where Christ's gospel is falsified or denied, there can be no true service. While Christ's congregation must see to it that the gospel is preached truly, they must not set up criteria outside the authority of the Scriptures. Thus the Donatists with their stress on the purity and sanctity of God's servants are wrong to make the effects of Christ's Gospel dependent on the holiness and good intentions of the ministers. Masterfully, St. Augustine refuted their viewpoint which had made so great an impression on the African people, with Scriptural weapons alone. While he fully appreciated the importance of purity and sanctity in God's servants, and shared the Donatists' horror of those who set a bad example to their flock, he did not share the Donatists' conclusions. Wherever the true Gospel

[98] Tractatus in evangelium Joannis V, 15.
[99] Sermo 10, 8.
[100] Sermo 46, 32.

of Christ is preached, Christ's Spirit does not depart from the service, though it may well leave the bad servant. The water runs over the field, albeit the stones do not profit by it. The grapes are plucked in the midst of brambles. The sheep are safe if only they listen to the voice of the good Shepherd. Thus St. Augustine showed the path for all centuries, and his arguments were to be quoted by the Church, time and again.

3. *The central message.*

It is a matter for argument, whether St. Augustine knew of a central message in the preaching of God's Word. His sermons are often strangely confused, resembling a gushing torrent rather than a narrow runnel. The reactions of the congregation frequently forced him to deviate from his main theme, and his exegesis proclaims all the failings of the decadent age in which he lived. The context is often ignored in favour of a single word, a number, or a small detail in the text. We must agree with Van der Meer—though we should have added the word 'often' for there are many brilliant exceptions—that St. Augustine's interpretations resemble the way in which a myopic person reads a letter, word by word[101]. Thus a single word could cause him to launch into a magisterial discussion of a topic which, though Scriptural, had no clear connection with the main text. Moreover, St. Augustine often interspersed his sermons with a great many doctrinal and practical discussions, from which it may be inferred that the thought of a central message was far from his mind. Thus, in his sermons on the Gospel according to St. John, he discussed the Trinity, the Word, God's many virtues, predestination, grace, freedom of the will, Christ and His Body, the Sacraments, asceticism and mysticism, the contemplative and active life, and many other subjects. All sorts of heresies and false doctrines were pilloried, and he attacked Donatists, Pelagians, Manicheans, Photinians, Arians, Sabellians, Patripassians, Marcionites, and Stoic and Neoplatonic philosophers alike. He seemed to make no distinction between his study and his pulpit, and broadcast his learned conclusions regularly and forcefully to the congregation, thus putting them into popular circulation. If there were

[101] F. van der Meer, op. cit. p. 388; see also Marrou, op. cit. p. 422 ff.; Pontet, op. cit., p. 195 ff.

things amiss with his own flock or with other congregations—which happened but too frequently in Carthage—he would use the slightest hint in the text to lecture the congregation on their misdemeanour at length. Niebergall[102] puts it as follows: 'Many objections can be raised against St. Augustine's method of preaching. His allegorical interpretations often read more into, than from, the text; the brilliant strokes of his own genius often outshine the light of the Scriptures; his delight in words often violates the Word, his glorious formulations darken the glory of the Scriptures; his sermons, generally made up on the spur of the moment often fail to do justice to the Scriptural text which they were supposed to interpret; his tendency to pay heed to the reaction of his audience often misleads him into paying more attention to them than to the Scriptures'. These are hard words, indeed, the truth of which no one well-versed in St. Augustine's sermons would care to deny.

And yet we make so bold as to speak of a central message in St. Augustine's sermons[103]. True, all the criticisms we have mentioned are valid, but we contend nevertheless that he increasingly, and particularly during his struggle against the Pelagians, set Christ and His Gospel of grace in the centre of his message. How could it be otherwise since, as we saw in Chapter III, St. Augustine looked upon all Scripture as the witness of Christ and of His Church, the fruit of His redemption. Hence he could state quite unequivocally that preaching Christ would alone lead to the goal, and that those who fail to preach Christ, broke into the fold like thieves in the night. 'When I seek to get into you, that is, into your heart, I preach Christ; were I preaching something else, I should be trying to climb up some other way[104]. Christ, therefore, is my gate to you; by Christ I get entrance, not to your houses, but to your hearts. It is by Christ I enter: it is Christ in me that you have been willingly hearing. And why is it you have thus willingly hearkened to Christ in me? Because you are the sheep of Christ, purchased with the blood of Christ. You acknowledge your own price, which is not paid by me, but is preached by my instrumentality. He, and only He, is the

[102] op. cit., p. 232.
[103] Niebergall himself mitigated his own harsh judgment by going on to characterize St. Augustine as the pastor who dispensed God's Word according to the light that he had gained after much struggle.
[104] Joh. 10:12.

buyer, who shed precious blood[105]. Christ Himself says, "As the Father knows me, even so know I the Father"[106]. He knows the Father by Himself, and we by Him. That He has knowledge by Himself, we know. That we also have knowledge by Him, we have likewise learned, for this also we have learned by Him. For He Himself has said: "No man hath seen God at any time; but the only-begotten Son, who is in the bosom of the Father, He hath declared Him"[107]. And so by Him do we also get this knowledge, to whom He has declared Him. In another place also He says: "No one knows the Son, but the Father; neither knows any one the Father, save the Son and to whomsoever the Son will reveal Him"[108]. As He then knows the Father by Himself, and we know the Father by Him: so into the sheepfold He enters by Himself, and we by Him'[109]. Thus St. Augustine, here as elsewhere, stressed the clear passages of Scripture in which Christ is shown to be He, by whom alone we can know the Father. He applied this to the preacher's task, by continuing: 'We were saying that by Christ we have a door of entrance to you. And why? Because we preach Christ. We preach Christ and therefore we enter by the door. But Christ preacheth Christ, for He preacheth Himself; and the shepherd entereth by Himself. When the light shows the other things, that are seen in the light, does it need some other means of being made visible itself? Whatever we understand, we understand with the intellect: and how save by the intellect, do we understand the intellect itself? In the same way as the intellect sees itself, so also doth Christ preach Himself. If He preaches Himself, and by preaching enters into thee, He enters into thee by Himself. And He is the door to the Father, for there is no way of approach to the Father but by Him. For there is one God and one Mediator between God and men, the man Christ Jesus[110]. Remember, then, how the Lord Jesus Christ is both the door and the shepherd: the door in presenting Himself to view; the shepherd in entering in by Himself. And indeed, because He is the shepherd, He has given to his members to be so likewise. For both, Peter and Paul, and the other apostles were, as all good bishops are, shepherds. But

[105] Tractatus in evangelium Joannis XLVII, 2.
[106] Joh. 10:15.
[107] Joh. 1:18.
[108] Matth. 11:27.
[109] Tractatus in evangelium Joannis XLVII, 3.
[110] 1 Tim. 2:5.

none of us calls Himself the door. This—the way of entrance for the sheep—He has retained as exclusively belonging to Himself. In short, Paul discharged the office of a good shepherd when he preached Christ, because he entered by the door'[111]. And once again, St. Augustine took the opportunity to warn against schisms, all of which were signs of adherence, not to Christ, but to men. 'But when the undisciplined sheep began to create schisms, and to set up other doors before them, not of entrance to their joint assembly, but for falling away into divisions, saying, some of them, "I am of Paul", others, "I am of Cephas", others, "I of Apollos", others, "I of Christ", terrified for those who said "I am of Paul"—as if calling out to the sheep, Wretched ones, whither are you going? I am not the door—the apostle said, "Was Paul crucified for you? or were you baptized in the name of Paul?"[112] Only those who said "I am of Christ" have found the door'[113].

Precisely because St. Augustine was so filled with this Scriptural truth, did he stress it so often in his sermons. The Scriptures, and hence his sermons have as their centre Christ, the Path, the Truth, the Life, the Shepherd, and the Door, and hence he looked upon most of the Psalms[114], as being completely Christocentric, and preached them accordingly. To do so, he often had recourse to allegorical jugglings with words, and these jugglings themselves are proof positive that he was propounding a central message. In his sermons on Christ and His Gospel we can see clear signs of his spiritual development. At first—and he never went back on this viewpoint, though he denied its dominant importance later on—Christ was to him, above all, the great Physician who by His humility softened our pride and freed us from the source of all evil. Thus he said in a sermon, given in about 396 A.D.: 'Pride is the head and cause of all offences. The beginning of all sin is pride. On account of this vice, on account of this great sin of pride, God came in humility. This cause, this great sin, this mighty disease of souls, brought down the Almighty Physician from heaven, humbled Him even to the form of a servant, exposed Him to despiteful treatment, hung Him on the tree; that by the saving strength of so great medicine this swelling

[111] Tractatus in evangelium Joannis XLVII, 3.
[112] 1 Cor. 1:12–13.
[113] Tractatus in evangelium Joannis XLVII, 3.
[114] Not all, as is often claimed.

might be cured. Let man now at length blush to be proud, for whose sake God has become humble'[115]. In another sermon of uncertain date, he even preached: 'Christ said: "Learn of me, for I am meek and lowly in heart"[116]. This is all the medicine we need'[117]. And in a sermon of 411 A.D., he still said: 'He came as the Almighty Physician to cure our conceit. From east to west, all mankind lay stricken with a mighty disease. Smitten as it was, with pride, it needed a great Physician to cure it by His example. Shame on thee, therefore, O man to continue in pride, for whose sake God has humbled Himself. And greatly, indeed, has He humbled Himself even when He was born for your sake. He even saw fit to die for you. The Jews said: if He be the Son, let Him descend from the cross and we will believe in Him. But He remained humble. Therefore did He refuse to come down. He had the power, but showed them His patience instead. By His example He desired to teach you humility and patience'[118].

Now and then, St. Augustine preached that Christ in order to turn men into gods, turned Himself, though God, into man[119]. 'God alone is truly God. But then who are those gods, or where are they, of whom God is the true God? It is evident that He has called men gods[120], that are deified of His grace, not born of His substance. For He doth justify, who is just through His own self, and not of another: and He doth deify who is God through Himself, not by the partaking of another. But He that justifieth doth Himself deify, in that by justifying He doth make sons of God. For He hath given them power to become sons of God. If we have been made sons of God, we have also been made gods; but this is the effect of grace adopting, not of nature generating'[121].

But as his understanding of man's sinfulness and of God's anger at

[115] Enarratio in Ps. 18 II, 15.
[116] Matth. 11:29.
[117] Sermo 142, 7.
[118] Ex collectione Quelferbytana XXII, 5; see also R. Arbesmann, *Christ the Medicus humilis in St Augustine,* in: Augustinus Magister, Paris 1954, Part II, pp. 623–629.
[119] Sermo 192, 1.
[120] Cf. Ps. 81.
[121] Enarratio in Ps. 49, 2. The very complex question of St. Augustine's views on deification, can only be discussed fully during our treatment of his doctrine of grace, when we shall examine, in particular, Hendrick's *De leer van de vergoddelyking in het oud-christelyk geloofsbewustzyn* (Genade en Kerk, Utrecht, 1953, p. 143 ff.) and J. A. A. A. Stoop's *Die deificatio hominis in die sermones en epistulae van Augustinus* (Leiden 1952).

our injustices increased, St. Augustine came to stress, even in his sermons, that Christ was the Mediator, who shed His blood for our sakes, who wiped out the handwriting that was against us, mediated between God and us, corrected our will into righteousness, bending his sentence into mercy[122]. 'If Thou, the Psalmist says, wilt be extreme to mark what is amiss, who, O Lord, may abide it? But there is propitiation with Thee[123]. And what is this propitiation, except sacrifice? And what is sacrifice, save that which has been offered for us? The pouring forth of innocent blood blotted out all the sins of the guilty; so great a price paid down redeemed all captives from the hand of the enemy who captured them. With Thee, then, there is propitiation. For if there were not mercy with Thee, if Thou choosest to be Judge only, and didst refuse to be merciful, Thou wouldest mark all our iniquities, and search after them. Who could abide this? Who could stand in Thy judgment? There is therefore one hope: For with Thee there is propitiation'[124]. When the Psalmist says in Ps. 65, "Our impieties Thou shalt propitiate", St. Augustine points out 'Let your love observe, it is not said except to some priest offering somewhat, whereby impiety may be expiated and propitiated. For impiety is then said to be propitiated, when God is made propitious to the impiety. What is it for God to be made propitious for the impiety? It is His becoming forgiving, and giving pardon. But in order that God's pardon may be obtained, propitiation is made through some sacrifice. There hath come forth therefore, sent from God the Lord, One our Priest; He took upon Him from us that which He might offer to the Lord; we are speaking of those same first-fruits of the flesh from the womb of the Virgin. This holocaust He offered to God. He stretched out His hands on the cross as the lifting up of the hands by the evening sacrifice. As ye know, the Lord about eventide hung on the cross: and our impieties were propitiated; otherwise they had swallowed us up. Our impieties thou wilt propitiate. Thou art the Priest, Thou the victim; Thou the offerer, Thou the offering'[125].

In a sermon on Rom. 8:1–4, he said: 'And in the flesh, He condemned sin by sin. By what sin? I know but too well, that He has

[122] Enarratio in Ps. 103 IV, 8.
[123] Ps. 130:2.
[124] Enarratio in Ps. 129, 3.
[125] Enarratio in Ps. 64, 6.

condemned sin, I know that the Lamb of God taketh away the sin of the world[126]. He has condemned all sin, all our sin. But through what sin? He Himself had no sin, Who had no sin, neither was guile found in His mouth[127]. And of Whom it was said: "For He hath made Him to be sin for us, who knew no sin, that we might be made the righteousness of God in Him"[128]. What does that mean? A great mystery surely. Christ our Lord, Jesus our Saviour and Redeemer, has become sin, so that we might become God's righteousness in Him. But how? Listen to the Law. In it the offerings are called sins that are offered up for our sins[129]. And what is Christ but an offering for sin? 'As Christ', St. Paul says, 'hath given Himself for us as an offering and a sacrifice to God for a sweet-smelling savour'[130]. By the offering, that He became for our sin He has condemned sin. This is the law of the Spirit of Life which has freed us from the law of sin and death'[131].

'Of Him therefore can be said in Psalm 45 "Grace is shed abroad on Thy lips". We read in the Gospel of John "The law was given by Moses; Grace and truth came by Jesus Christ"[132]. He came unto us with the word of grace, with the kiss of grace. What is there more sweet than that grace? To what purport is that grace? Blessed are they, whose iniquities are forgiven, and whose sins were covered[133]. He coming with 'grace', did not exact what was due, but paid that which He did not owe. For was not the forfeit of 'death' due from the sinner? Or was there anything but punishment 'due' to you, being a sinner? He has remitted thy debt, and He has paid that which He did not owe. Marvellous grace! Wherefore grace? Because it is given gratis, freely. Thou wert lost: He sought thee, and having found thee, restored thee. He did not impute to thee the past. He promised thee the future. Verily, grace, grace is shed abroad on Thy lips'[134].

This view of Christ is also used to evaluate His rich blessings, and,

[126] Joh. 1:29.
[127] 1 Pet. 2:22; Sermo 152, 9.
[128] 2 Cor. 5:20, 21; Sermo 152, 10.
[129] Cf. Levit. 4.
[130] Eph. 5:2.
[131] Rom. 8:2; Sermo 152, 11.
[132] Joh. 1:17.
[133] Ps. 32:1.
[134] Enarratio in Ps. 44, 7. See also pp. 227 ff., for a fuller discussion of Christ's work as our Redeemer.

above all, the forgiveness of our sins—a blessing that is stressed far more greatly in St. Augustine's theology and sermons than is generally believed[135]. Thus he frequently told his congregation that Christ shed His blood for the forgiveness of sin[136]. 'The sacrifice for sin has been made, the sin has been wiped out. The blood of the Redeemer has been shed, and the claim of the Creditor has been met. This is the blood that has been shed for the many, for the forgiveness of their sin[137]. By bearing punishment without guilt, He removed the guilt in the punishment. He removed guilt by the forgiveness of sin, the punishment by resurrecting us from the dead[138]. Therefore Christ said to His disciples after His resurrection, "It behoved Christ to suffer, and to rise again the third day, and that repentance and remission of sins should be preached in His name[139]". Whence and how far? Among all nations (He saith) beginning at Jerusalem. But what mercy do we all expect more abundant from the Lord, than that our sins be forgiven? Therefore it is said that the earth is full of the mercy of God, because God everywhere forgives sins, because He has sent the heavens (an image of the preachers) to water the earth'[140].

In addition to being indebted to Christ for this great act of forgiveness, we are greatly in His debt also for what Psalm 103:4–5 calls 'the healing of our diseases' in the hostel of the Church, for receiving us in the true dwelling, and for freeing us from our iniquities and greed. The healing, together with forgiveness from sin, apply to life on earth, the freedom to life eternal[141]. Or else, St. Augustine summed up Christ's blessings according to Rom. 8:30–31: predestination, calling, justification, and glorification, of which the first three have already been given us and the last still awaits fulfilment[142].

All these blessings were constantly stressed in the sermons, though the accent often fell on the blessings that still await us in the New Jerusalem. Precisely because the pilgrim in St. Augustine hankered so zealously after the fatherland, his faith after contemplation, and

135 See my thesis, pp. 89 f.
136 Tractatus in evangelium Joannis 92, 1; 98, 2.
137 Sermo 134, 5.
138 Sermo 240, 3.
139 Luke 24:46, 47.
140 Enarratio in Ps. 32 II, Serm. II, 7.
141 Sermo 131, 6, 7.
142 See particularly Sermo 158.

the fighter in him after the peace of perfection, did he speak of future salvation, so often and so readily[143].

Thus while the servant must preach Christ's Word and His Gospel, he cannot leave it at that. He must also preach the judgment, God's anger at sin, and His threat of hell-fire and damnation, whenever the voice of the Gospel and true godliness are scorned by men. St. Augustine took his permanent cue from Ezekiel 33 and 34. Even in 394, when he came to Thagaste as a presbyter to preach against the notorious Feast of Laetitia and its shameful excesses, his sermons were already influenced by those chapters[144]. And in another sermon, which he delivered on the anniversary of his ordination as bishop, probably in his old age[145], and in which he discussed his office as preacher, it was once again this call of God which he stressed[146].

Thus the preacher, as the dispenser of God's hidden mysteries, must preach redemption and damnation, life and death, peace and desolation. But St. Augustine never failed to show how greatly Christ and His Gospel outweighed the dark shadow of our perfidy and damnation. For grace precedes the judgment. God came to save the world through His mercy, to delay His final judgment[147]. For this reason, preaching the judgment has the sole aim of recalling us to God and of causing the sinner to confide in His mercy. God threatens punishment, so that He may find no one guilty on Judgment Day. The prophets foretold this judgment, so that we might bethink ourselves. Had he wished to judge us truly, He would have kept silent. No one who wishes to do injury to another, will advise him to be on his guard. Yet whatever the Scriptures tell us about God's judgment, reflects God's advice to us to be on our guard[148]. 'Now is the time to listen, for the time of judgment has not yet come. He Who speaks is also silent. He speaks in His commandments and is silent in His judgment. Thus He speaks in His Laws, in His many mysteries, in many pages of so many Books. He has not kept us ignorant of the final judgment. No one who wishes to condemn us would warn us beforehand, no one who wishes to strike us would reveal his intention. It is thus that God proclaims his goodness.

[143] See Enarratio in Ps. 148, 8; Sermo 103; 104; 169, 17, 18; 179; 255 et al.
[144] See Epistula 29, 8.
[145] This is borne out by more than one comment in the sermon.
[146] Frangipani II.
[147] Sermo 5, 1.
[148] Sermo 22, 3.

Let no one despise His long-suffering[149]. Let us therefore listen as sheep while He speaks and (still) keeps silent, while He (still) warns us and suspends His judgment, while it is still given to us to listen, and indeed even to read'[150].

4. *God's work by and in the preaching of His Word.*

God's work is with and in the preaching of His Word. St. Augustine based this belief on Paul's saying: "I have planted, Apollos watered, but God gave the increase"[151]. We could cite more than seventy texts in which St. Augustine quotes, explains, and is swayed by, this passage.

'God alone gives increase, and hence His preachers, who like farmers can but tend their flock from the outside, are entirely in His hands. If there were no one who worked from within, no seed would take root in the earth, no blade of grass would cover the land, no twig would grow into a branch, and no branch would bear leaves or fruit. For this reason Paul said rightly that if God had not given increase from within, the sound (of the sermon) would be empty'[152]. 'God's husbandry ye are, God's building ye are. God is the husbandman. We are the labourers of that husbandman. God Himself both filleth and giveth the increase, but a human husbandman tilleth a vineyard only so far as to plough, prune, apply other means which belong to the diligence of husbandmen: to rain upon his vineyard he is not able. But if perchance he is able to water, of whose power is it? Himself indeed guideth the water into a channel, but God filleth the spring. Lastly in his vineyard he cannot give increase to his tender shoots, he cannot shape the fruit, he cannot qualify the seeds, he cannot rule the seasons of production. But God, who can do all things, is our husbandman; we are secure'[153].

St. Augustine ascribed this work of God to the Trinity. Marie Comeau's claim that he attributed it especially to Christ as the inner teacher[154], is contradicted by the very work she has chosen to examine. For in Tractate 77 which treats of "the Comforter which is the Holy Ghost, whom the Father will send in my name, he shall

[149] Rom. 2:4, 5.
[150] Sermo 47, 4, 5.
[151] 1 Cor. 3:6, 7
[152] Sermo 152, 1.
[153] Enarratio in Ps. 66, 1.
[154] Marie Comeau, op. cit., p. 315 ff.

teach you all things to your remembrance, whatsoever I have said unto you"[155], St. Augustine asked: 'Is it, then, that the Son speaks, and the Holy Spirit teaches, so that we merely get hold of the words that are uttered by the Son, and then understand them by the teaching of the Spirit? as if the Son could speak without the Holy Spirit, or the Holy Spirit teach without the Son: or is it not rather that the Son also teacheth and the Spirit speaketh, and, when it is God that speaketh and teacheth anything, that the Trinity itself is speaking and teaching? And just because it is a Trinity, the persons required to be introduced individually, so that we might hear it in its distinct personality, and understand its inseparable nature. Listen to the Father speaking in the passage where thou readest, "The Lord said unto me, Thou art my Son". Listen to Him also teaching in that where thou readest, "Every man that hath heard and hath learned of the Father, cometh unto me". The Son, on the other hand, thou hast just heard speaking; for He says of Himself, "Whatsoever I have said unto you": and if thou wouldest also know Him as a Teacher, bethink thyself of the Master, when He says, "One is your Master, even Christ". Furthermore, of the Holy Spirit, whom thou hast just been told of as a Teacher in the words, "He shall teach you all things", listen to Him also speaking, where thou readest in the Acts of the Apostles, that the Holy Spirit said to the blessed Peter, "Go with them, for I have sent them". The whole Trinity, therefore, both speaketh and teacheth; but were it not also brought before us in its individual personality, it would certainly altogether surpass the power of human weakness to comprehend it. For as it is altogether inseparable in itself, it could never be known as the Trinity, were it always spoken of inseparably'[156].

As for the Donatists, who exaggerated the importance of God's. servants, calling them mediators, fathers, the head and the origin, and the root and branch of the faithful, St. Augustine told them clearly that the work of Christ alone was the origin, root, and head of all Christians[157].

'Paul was not the head and origin of those whom he had planted, or Apollos the root of those whom he had watered, but God who gave the increase, and Christ who says, "I am the vine, ye are the

[155] Joh. 14:26.
[156] Tractatus in evangelium Joannis 77, 2.
[157] Contra litteras Petiliani I, 6.

branches"[158]. It is Christ always that justifieth the ungodly, by changing his ungodliness into Christianity; it is from Christ always that faith is received, Christ is always the origin of the regenerate and the head of the Church[159]. He is the origin, the root, and the head of him who is being born[160], in order that he that glorieth should glory in the Lord'[161].

And the Pelagians, who belittled the work of the Holy Ghost, were referred to the operations of the Holy Spirit, in applying the work of Christ to individual sinners. In one of his earliest writings against them, St. Augustine told them: 'No small gift, therefore, must you suppose to have been conferred upon you, by the circumstances that Christ is in you, for His Spirit dwelleth in you. And all will be perfected by the grace of Christ, in other words, by His Spirit, that dwelleth in you'[162]. 'He bringeth to light what was hidden, and maketh agreeable what was unpleasant'[163]. 'His grace works within us our illumination and justification'[164]. Thus St. Augustine felt impelled to emphasise to Pelagius the work of the Spirit and the hidden mercy which, in God, gives us increase[165].

However, these appropriations did not detract from his belief that we must always worship the undivided work of the Holy Trinity.

It is much more difficult to determine what St. Augustine considered this work of God to be. On the one hand, he stated clearly those who are called according to God's purpose, come to believe through, and with the preaching of the Word of God. This doctrine was developed particularly in his writings against the Pelagians. Thus he showed in his *De praedestinatione sanctorum* how, at the beginning of his episcopate, he had not yet very carefully worked out importance of this call. At that time he still believed that, having preached the Gospel, we were free to obey or reject the calling[166]. He then went on to show how the Holy Scriptures and particularly John 6[167] had taught him otherwise: 'Every man that has

[158] ib.
[159] ib. 8.
[160] ib. II, 11.
[161] ib. III, 42.
[162] De peccatorum meritis et remissione I, 7.
[163] ib. II, 26, 27; De spiritu et littera 5.
[164] De peccatorum meritis et remissione I, 7, 10.
[165] Epistula 177, 7; 194, 18.
[166] De praedestinatione sanctorum 7.
[167] Particularly verses 22, 26, 27, 43–45.

heard of the Father, and has learned, comes into Christ; every one who does not come, has not heard of the Father. Far removed from the perceptions of the flesh is this teaching in which the Father is heard and teaches to come to the Son. Engaged herein is also the Son Himself, because He is His Word by which He thus teaches; and He does not do this through the ear of the flesh, but of the heart. Herein engaged, also, at the same time, is the Spirit of the Father and of the Son; and He too teaches and does not teach separately, since we have learned that the workings of the Trinity are inseparable. But this is especially attributed to the Father, for the reason that of Him is begotten the Only Begotten and from Him proceeds the Holy Spirit. Very far removed, I say, from the perceptions of the flesh is this instruction wherein God is heard and teaches. We see that many come to the Son because we see that many believe in Christ, but when and how they have heard this from the Father, and have learned, we see not. It is true that that grace is exceedingly secret, but who doubts that it is grace? This grace, therefore, which is hiddenly bestowed in human hearts, is rejected by no hard heart, because it is given for the sake of first taking away the hardness of the heart. When, therefore, the Father is heard within and teaches, so that a man cometh to the Son, He taketh away the heart of stone and giveth a heart of flesh[168]. Because He thus maketh them children and vessels of mercy which He hath prepared for glory[169]. When the Gospel is preached, some believe, some believe not; but they who believe at the voice of the preacher from without, hear of the Father from within, and learn; while they who do not believe, hear outwardly, but inwardly do not hear nor learn. By Him who said, "No one cometh to me except it were given him of my Father", not the hearers of the Gospel were distinguished from those who did not hear, but the believers from those who did not believe[170]. God indeed calls many of his children not with that calling with which they were called who would not come to the marriage. With that calling were called also the Jews, to whom Christ crucified is an offence, and the Gentiles, to whom Christ crucified is foolishness[171]. But with that vocation He calls them predestinated whom the

[168] Ezek. 11:19.
[169] De praedestinatione sanctorum 13.
[170] ib. 15.
[171] 1 Cor. 1:24.

apostle distinguished when he said that he preached Christ, the wisdom of God, and the power of God, to them that were called, Jews as well as Greeks. For thus he says, "But unto them which are called" in order to show that there were some who were not called; knowing that there is a certain definite calling of those who are called according to God's purpose[172]. It was this that he had in view when he said, "The gifts and calling of God are without repentance"[173]. Not with that calling of which it is said, "many are called", but with that whereby the chosen are called in order that they believe[174]. For whom He predestinated, them He also called, with that calling, to wit, which is according to His purpose. He did not call others, therefore, but those whom He predestinated, them He also called; nor others, but those whom He so called, them He also justified[175]. There are many passages in the Holy Scripture in which God is declared to prepare and to convert men's wills, even for the kingdom of heaven and for eternal life'[176].

In the *De gratia Christi* he declares: 'This grace of God by which strength we not only believe what ought to be loved, but that we love what we have believed, if it is to be called a doctrine, let it at any rate be so called in such wise that God may be believed to infuse it, along with an ineffable sweetness, more deeply and more internally, not only by their agency who plant and water from without, but likewise by Himself too who ministers in secret His own increase in such way that He not only exhibits truth, but likewise imparts charity. For it is thus that God teaches those who have been called according to His purpose, giving them simultaneously both to know what they ought to do, and to do what they actually know'[177]. He turns the unwilling into the willing, for unlike the teacher who threatens and cajoles his hearers, God works from within. For when the teacher waters and plants with his words, we can say: The hearers may believe him or not. But when God gives them increase, they will believe unquestioningly and make progress. This is the difference between law and promise, between letter and

[172] Rom. 9:12.
[173] Rom. 11:29; De praedestinatione sanctorum 32.
[174] ib. 33.
[175] ib. 34.
[176] Ps. 119:36, 37; 37:13; Ezek. 11:19; 26:27 et al. De praedestinatione sanctorum 42.
[177] De gratia Christi 14.

spirit[178]. The Pelagians claimed that God helped by His commandments, blessings, sanctifications, corrections, admonitions, which, according to the Scriptures, could also be bestowed by men. But God gives only increase, i.e. obedience to His commands through love[179] which comes from God alone[180].

Thus St. Augustine had learned from the Scriptures and from experience that the sermon had a double effect. At first, he had believed that this effect depended on an individual reaction, since every man could apparently accept or reject what he had heard. Then he recanted, and distinguished two kinds of callings: the 'inner' and the 'outer', two terms borrowed from Neoplatonism. It was also a remnant of his Neoplatonic beginnings, that he was anxious to explain how far the Word of God the Father was removed from the ears of the flesh, which Neoplatonic philosophers held in low repute. The great difficulty of this distinction is that it gives rise to the impression that preaching God's Word "which is quick and powerful and sharper than any two-edged sword" was an 'outer' act, powerless by itself. This approach is good Neoplatonism but poor Christianity according to which "God's Word goeth forth out of His mouth: it shall not return void". Those who speak of outer and inner calls always run the very real danger of suggesting that the outer call of the Word is received alike by the pious and by the impious, by the faithful and the godless, while, in fact, the inner call is evoked in man's innermost soul. Now this is anything but Scriptural. "The Gospel is the power of God unto salvation"[181]. "It is not the word of men, but the word of God which effectually worketh also in you that believe"[182]. "It is a two-edged sword[183], which bestows countless blessings, e.g. regeneration[184], faith[185], and illumination[186], and saves by the foolishness of the preaching of the cross"[187]. St. Augus-

[178] Opus imperfectum II, 157.
[179] Eph. 4:16.
[180] Opus imperfectum III, 114.
[181] Rom. 1:16; 1 Cor. 1:18; 2:4. See H. Bavinck, *Gereformeerde Dogmatiek* IV[2], p. 503 ff., in which the author tries, unsuccessfully, to grapple with the same problem.
[182] 1 Thess. 2:13.
[183] Hebr. 4:12.
[184] 1 Pet. 1:23.
[185] Rom. 10:17.
[186] 2 Cor. 4:4–6.
[187] 1 Cor. 1:18.

tine would have been the last to deny the truth of these remarks. His frail terminology was meant to characterise two things only. The first of these was that man's heart must be affected before he can even hear God's Words. His heart of stone must be turned into a heart of flesh, rebellion must give way to glad acceptance of the kingdom of heaven and eternal life. The eyes and the ears of the heart must be opened up so that the truth may be received and love be allowed to enter. But on the other hand, St. Augustine refused to admit mysticism, and wished to hold fast to the bond with the preached Word, by which the Father moved and taught in mysterious ways. And it is precisely the inner call which enables us to hear and learn the message of the Gospel in our hearts. For what else is the difference between law and promise, letter and Spirit? Through the promise and the Spirit, our will turns towards Christ and His kingdom, and we embrace His message with wonderful tenderness and loving faith. It is through the subjective work of the spirit in our innermost heart, that the heart becomes concentrated on the preaching of the truth. Hence does it respond to the call, is it called by God's Word and Holy Spirit. St. Augustine preserved his distinction the better to describe what was subsequently called, the work of the Trinity through and with the Word. True, this does not solve the problem, but it does emphasise by two words the hidden and mysterious connection between two effects of God.

On the other hand, St. Augustine, particularly in his sermons on the Gospel according to St. John, referred frequently to this work of God so as to make it appear as if the Word of God as proclamation had the sole function of admonishing, alluding, and of hinting symbolically, while all real teaching belongs purely to Christ, the inner Teacher. According to many scholars, and Roman Catholic scholars in particular, St. Augustine had simply applied Neoplatonic epistemology, developed in *De Magistro*, to the preaching of God's Word. We have discussed this point in Chapter I[188], and also at the beginning of this Chapter[189]. There is no doubt that this view contains more than a grain of truth. But as against the belief that St. Augustine never outgrew this stage of his development, we have upheld the thesis that in his second stage, while never denying his former convictions, he nevertheless became largely converted to a

[188] See p. 26 ff.
[189] See p. 120

belief in the majestic power of God's living Word, so much so that the Neoplatonic approach largely gave way to Biblical concepts of God's Word[190]. Sometimes the Neoplatonic influence is negligible, and the Biblical reality of God's speaking becomes all-pervasive. But even in those texts where language, choice of words, and terminology are reminiscent of the Neoplatonic school there can often be no question of complete identification. An excellent example is the quotation from Tractate 19, which Marie Comeau has cited as a clear case of the dominance of Neoplatonic epistemological concepts over Biblical data[191], viz.: 'Hear ye the Master, while dawning upon us, and as our Sun gliding in upon our hearts; not such as the eyes of flesh desire to look upon, but on whom the eyes of the heart fervently long to be opened'[192]. In fact, this quotation cannot be read out of its context, in which St.Augustine discussed Christ's saying: "Verily, verily, I say unto you, the hour is coming, and now is when the dead shall hear the voice of the Son of God, and they that hear shall live". St. Augustine interpreted this text, as follows: 'Our Lord Jesus Christ, our heavenly Master, the Word of the Father and the Truth, distinguishes two resurrections, the one of the last day and the other in this life. How then, do we understand these two resurrections? Do we, perhaps, understand that they who rise now will not rise then; that the resurrections of some is now, of some others then? It is not so. For we have risen in this resurrection, if we have rightly believed; and we ourselves, who have already risen, are looking for another resurrection in the end. Moreover, both now are we risen to eternal life, if we perseveringly continue in the same faith; and then, too, we shall rise to eternal life, when we shall be made equal with the angels. But let Himself distinguish and open up what we have made bold to speak: how there happens to be a resurrection before a resurrection. He will open it clearly'. Then follow the words quoted by Marie Comeau, which, in turn, are followed by: 'To Him, then, let us give ear: "Verily, verily, I say unto you, The hour cometh and now is, when the dead"—you see that a resurrection is asserted—"shall hear the voice of the Son of God; and they that hear shall live"'[193].

[190] See p. 122 ff.
[191] See also the rest of the argument, op. cit. p. 310 ff.
[192] p. 312; Tract. 19, 10. The reference to Tract. 18 is a printer's error.
[193] Joh. 5 :25.

'Why has He added "they that hear shall live"? Because by hearing we come back to life! We must understand them to be living, since they could not hear unless they lived. No, saith He, not because they live they hear; but by hearing they come to life again: "Shall hear, and they that hear shall live"[194]. What then is "shall hear" but "shall obey"? They that obey, shall live: let them be sure and certain of it, they shall live. Christ the Word of God is preached to us; the Son of God, by whom all things were made, who, for the dispensation's sake, surely took flesh, was born of a virgin, was an infant in the flesh, a young man in the flesh, suffering in the flesh, dying in the flesh, rising again in the flesh, ascending in the flesh, promising a resurrection to the flesh, promising a resurrection to the mind—to the mind before the flesh, to the flesh after the mind. Who heareth and obeyeth, shall live; whoso heareth and obeyeth not, that is, heareth and despiseth, heareth and believeth not, shall not live[195]. Who hear and live, whence live, except by hearing? For "the friend of the bridegroom standeth and heareth Him and rejoiceth greatly because of the bridegroom's voice", not because of his own voice; that is to say, they hear and live by partaking, not by coming into being; and all that hear live, because all that obey live'[196].

Thus the text actually speaks of Jesus Christ as the heavenly master, who distinguishes, opens up, and lets in the daylight. He is called our sun gliding in upon our hearts, on whom the eyes of the heart fervently long to be opened. These expressions by themselves may strike one as being purely Neoplatonic, but their context has nothing in common with that position. Our heavenly Master endows us with spiritual understanding through the Bible, for this, St. Augustine always stresses, is what Christ Himself has taught. The hearing and hence the new life take place under the preaching of the great acts of salvation: His birth, crucifixion, and resurrection. Christ revealed nothing beyond the Word of God, but explained and revealed the Gospel, the Word of God, the Holy Scripture. And the friends of the bridegroom brought the same Gospel, not out of their own hearts but by partaking in, and spreading, its great message, by speaking of the birth, crucifixion, and resurrection of the Word that had become Flesh. And it is by hearing that Word that

[194] Tractatus in evangelium Joannis 19, 9.
[195] ib. 10.
[196] ib. 14.

the dead are brought back to life and obey the call of this glorious Gospel.

We must therefore be very careful not to conclude without further ado from the mere presence of Neoplatonic sounds, that St. Augustine was materially influenced by them, let alone that his doctrine was identical with the Neoplatonic. After careful analysis of various texts[197], we feel that three facts deserve emphasising:

1. In his epistemology, constructed under the influence of Neoplatonic ideas and in his discussion of the preaching, St. Augustine liked to speak of *admonere*, to admonish. The task of the master is restricted to admonition—even the sensible world is merely a means of arousing us—and the preacher can do no more than admonish his congregation—he cannot resurrect the dead, convert the godless, or give faith and love to the faithless. Under the influence of Neoplatonism, St. Augustine usually left it at that in the passages we have quoted. And yet even these passages indicate clearly that he would have been the last to claim that this approach covered the preaching of God's Word fully. What the preacher himself is unable to do, God's Word does in the sermon, since it causes the dead to rise up, bestows rebirth out of the everlasting seed, and fires love and faith by proclaiming the glory and loving kindness of Christ Who is *the* Truth, *the* Righteousness, and *the* Redemption. Even when St. Augustine spoke of the preacher alone, he never denied the effectiveness of God's Word in his sermons.

2. St. Augustine's epistemology and his doctrine of preaching both involve the concept of illumination. In *his* epistemology, illumination is never caused by sensory perception. Ideas are never obtained by Aristotelian abstractions. Illumination is immediate, so that no intermediary is needed between God, who illumines, and man, the illumined. The details of this process are open to argument. The Neoplatonic view is clear: the soul, which is itself divine, beholds ideas in the *nous*. But St. Augustine considered that God, or Christ as the *logos*, was the seat of ideas. It would have been more logical to assume with Plotinus that illumination led to the immediate perception of ideas in God or Christ as the Logos, but this path was

[197] Cf. Tractatus in evangelium Joannis 20, 3; 26, 4–9; 40, 9; 96, 4; 97, 1; In epistolam Joannis Tractatus 3, 13; 4, 1; Sermo 102, 2; 179, 7; Enarratio in Ps. 126, 2 et al. These texts are usually quoted as proof of a Neoplatonic influence.

barred by Biblical considerations, since the Holy Scriptures say nothing of the contemplation of God on earth. St. Augustine gave no clear answer as to the correct view, and the question has, in fact, remained controversial to this day.

Now for the preaching itself. Christ, the Holy Spirit, and God the Father, enlighten, make known, teach, call and inspire us, not immediately through the inner Word of the mystics, but always through the agency of the Word of God as it is revealed in the sermon. The sermon tells of the *magnalia Dei*, God's intervention into history, of which God's Word is the only true witness. Neoplatonism, on the other hand, is concerned with ideas, as *a priori* truths, alone.

3. St. Augustine and the Neoplatonists alike called for introspection, but with what a difference! Philosophic introspection is tantamount to turning one's back upon the visible world and looking instead into the depths of one's soul, where truth lives in the intellect, the sovereign and most important part of the psyche. But when the call to introspection re-echoes in the sermon, it calls for communion with the heart and hence with the roots of life. In the heart, we experience the effect of the Word and in it are born our faith and love in and for Christ.

In short, the real difference, which is often implicit rather than explicit, is that the sermon proclaims the Word of God, through which all concepts apparently agreeing with the Neoplatonic view are altered in meaning and christianised. What is involved here is an act of God which transcends all the thoughts of the ancient philosophers.

5. *The work of the preacher.*

St. Augustine was forced to take up the cudgels not only against the Donatists, who overestimated the role of the dispensers of the Word and the Sacrament, but also against those who went to the other extreme. In the preface to his *De doctrina Christiana*, he mentions people who claimed that they could understand the Scriptures by direct divine inspiration and without human help. St. Augustine attempted to clip their wings, observing with sharp irony that they must have learned their alphabet, at least, from human teachers, while Antony the hermit learned Scripture by ear alone. Reliable people had told him that there was a slave who had learned his alphabet directly from God, and so he did not dismiss the untutored understanding of the Scriptures out of hand. He even considered it a great gift of God if, in fact, it occurred. Still he thought it the exception, rather than the rule: 'Suppose we advise all our brethren not to teach their children any language, because on the outpouring of the Holy Spirit the apostles immediately began to speak the language of every race; and warn every one who has not had a like experience that he need not consider himself a Christian, or may at least doubt whether he has yet received the Holy Spirit? No, no; rather let us put away false pride and learn whatever can be learnt from man; and let him who teaches another communicate what he has himself received without arrogance and without jealousy. And do not let us tempt Him in whom we have believed, lest being ensnared by such wiles of the enemy and by our own perversity, we may even refuse to go to the churches to hear the Gospel itself, or to read a book, or to listen to another reading or preaching, in the hope that we shall be carried up to the third heaven. Let us beware of such dangerous temptations of pride and let us rather consider the fact that the apostle Paul himself, although stricken down and admonished by the voice of God from heaven, was yet sent to a man to receive the sacraments and be admitted to the church; and that Cornelius the centurion, although an angel announced to him that his prayers were heard and his alms held in remembrance, was yet handed over to Peter for instruction. And without doubt it was possible to have done everything through the instrumentality of angels, but the condition of our race would have been much more degraded if God had not chosen to make use of men as the ministers of his Word to their fellow-men. For how could that be true which is written, "The temple of God is holy, which temple ye are"[198], if God gave forth no oracles from his human temple, but communicated everything by voices from heaven? Moreover, love itself, which binds men together in the bond of unity, would have no means of pouring soul into soul and mingling them one with another, if men never learnt anything from their fellowmen. Everyone after all who boasts that he through divine illumination understands the obscurities of Scripture, why does he himself undertake to interpret for others? Why does he not rather send them direct to God, that they too may learn by the inward teaching of the Spirit without the help of men?'[199]

[198] 1 Cor. 3 : 17.
[199] De doctrina Christiana, Praefatio. See also Quaestiones Evangelica II, 40.

A somewhat different, yet essentially similar, attitude is found in those who consider it unnecessary to instruct the future teachers of the Church, claiming that only the Holy Spirit can instruct such men truly. 'You may as well say that we need not pray, since our Lord says, "Your Father knows what things ye have need of before ye ask Him"[200]. Or that the apostle Paul should not have given directions to Timothy and Titus as to how or what they should teach others. These three apostolic epistles ought to be constantly before the eyes of everyone who has obtained the position of a teacher in the church. In the first epistle to Timothy do we not read: "These things command and teach"[201]? What these things are, has been told previously. Do we not read there: "Rebuke not an elder, but entreat him as a father"[202]? Is it not said in the second epistle: "Hold fast the form of sound words, which thou hast heard of me"[203]? And is he not there told: "Study to show thyself approved unto God, a workman that needeth not to be ashamed, rightly dividing the word of truth"[204]? And in the same place: "Preach the word; be instant in season, out of season; reprove, rebuke, exhort, with all long-suffering and doctrine"[205]. And so in the epistle to Titus, does he not say that a bishop ought to "hold fast the faithful word as he has been taught, that he may be able by sound doctrine both to exhort and to convince the gainsayers"[206]? There, too, he says, "But speak thou the things which become sound doctrine: that the aged men be sober" and so on[207]. What then are we to think? Does the apostle in any way contradict himself, when, though he says that men are made teachers by the operation of the Holy Spirit, he yet himself give them directions how and what they should teach? Or are we to understand, that though the duty of men to teach even the teachers does not cease when the Holy Spirit is given, yet that neither is he who planneth anything, nor he who watereth, but God who gives the increase?[208] Wherefore though holy men are our helpers, or even holy angels assist us, no one learns aright the things that pertain to

[200] Matth. 6:8.
[201] 1 Tim. 4:11.
[202] 1 Tim. 5:1.
[203] 2 Tim. 1:13.
[204] 2 Tim. 2:15.
[205] 2 Tim. 4:2.
[206] Tit. 1:9.
[207] Tit. 2:1–2.
[208] 1 Cor. 3:7.

life with God, until God makes him ready to learn from Himself[209]. For as the medicines which men apply to the bodies of their fellow-men are of no avail except God gives them virtue (who can heal without their aid, though they cannot without His), and yet they are applied; so the aids of teaching, applied through the instrumentality of men, are of advantage to the soul only when God works to make them of advantage, who could give the Gospel to man even without the help or agency of men'[210].

God, who could easily dispense with preachers, has chosen otherwise. In his struggle against the Donatists, who called their preachers 'the fathers of the faithful', St. Augustine had emphasised that God alone could bestow increase. But he refused to go to the other extreme, and insisted always that God employs His preachers as instruments to proclaim His Kingdom. Thus, St. Augustine, when speaking of their role, always uses the preposition *per*, and never the preposition *ab*, by which he would have indicated that they, the instruments, had become independent dispensers of salvation. When Parmenian cited John 20:22–23 to prove that preachers may forgive sins, St. Augustine told him that he would only admit these words of Christ as evidence against the Catholic position, if the Scriptures forced us to hold that sin was forgiven *ab*, i.e. by, them, rather than *per* them, i.e. by their agency. But clearly, forgiveness of sin is wrought not by them but by the Holy Ghost through them. 'For it is not ye that speak, but the Spirit of your Father which speaketh in you'[211]. Now the Spirit enters the preacher or the servant of the Church in such a way that, if he is not a hypocrite, the Holy Ghost uses him as His agent, to the preacher's eternal credit and to the reward and eternal salvation of those who receive the Sacrament and the Gospel from him. But if he be a hypocrite, he will receive no reward, though the Holy Spirit will not depart from his ministering[212], if only he continues to preach Christ[213].

'If, therefore, what is in itself pure is preached in purity, then the preacher himself also, in that he is a partner with the word, has his share in begetting the believer: but if he himself be not regenerate, and yet what he preaches be pure, then the believer is born not from

[209] 2 Tim. 3:14.
[210] De doctrina Christiana IV, 33.
[211] Matth. 10:20.
[212] A reference to Phil. 1:15–18 and to 1 Cor. 9:17.
[213] Contra Parmenianum II, 24.

the barrenness of the minister, but from the fruitfulness of the Word[214]. The minister of Christ is something in one point of view and nothing in another. For ministering and dispensing the Word and Sacrament he is something, but for purifying and justifying he is nothing'[215]. Thus could Paul consider himself a father to the Corinthian, and refuse this title to those who came after him[216]. For in Christ Jesus he had begotten them through the Gospel[217]. Moreover, faith once it had been awakened, must be watered, fed, and supported. Hence we (the preachers) busy ourselves with speaking, admonishing, teaching and urging. Thus we plant and water, but we cannot give increase[218]. We break the true bread of the Holy Scriptures before you[219]. And therefore the ministering of the Word and Sacrament is needed, for Christ's flock could not live without it[220]. Without this ministering men can neither become nor remain Christians'[221].

Beyond that, St. Augustine was wont to warn the dispensers of God's mysteries, not to pride themselves on their work. Rather must they always remember that "God hath chosen the foolish things of the world to confound the wise, and the weak things of this world to confound the things which are mighty. And base things of the world and things which are despised hath God chosen, yea, and things which are not, to bring to nought things that are"[222]. St. Augustine applied this text to the preachers, saying: 'Christ, who is God, came to benefit all, but He chose to benefit the emperor by means of a fisherman, not the fisherman by means of the emperor[223]. He chose neither senators, orators, or emperors, but simple fishermen, so that those who glorify, do so in the Lord[224]. Because in the wisdom of God, the world by its wisdom knew not God, it pleased God by the foolishness of preaching to save them that believe[225]. If they who

[214] Contra litteras Petiliani II, 11.
[215] ib. III, 66.
[216] 1 Cor. 4:15; 1:14.
[217] Contra litteras Petiliani III, 67.
[218] Sermo 43, 8.
[219] Sermo 95, 1.
[220] Epistula 228, 2.
[221] ib. 4.
[222] 1 Cor. 1:26–28.
[223] Enarratio in Ps. 149, 13.
[224] Sermo 43, 6.
[225] 1 Cor. 1:21.

believe were to be saved by the foolishness of the preaching, God hath chosen certain mortal things, He hath chosen men mortal and doomed unto death; using the human tongue, He hath spoken in a human voice; using the stewardship of mortals, He hath used mortal instruments and He hath made a heaven (an allusion to the Scriptures) in thy sight, that thou mightest in what is mortal recognise the immortal Word, and that thou also by sharing in the same Word mightest become immortal. Moses, Jeremiah and so many prophets have died; and their words though they be dead abide even to our posterity, because they were not theirs, but of God. The apostle Paul is released from this life, but by what instrument did He bestow upon us what we read? By what was mortal, by mouth, by tongue, teeth, hands[226]. So He who destroys the wisdom of the prudent, overthrows it by that foolishness of preaching whereby believers are healed[227]. There is a false wisdom, wherefore Christ the Crucified, Who is the strength and the wisdom of God, has become foolishness. And hence it pleased God to save by the foolishness of the preaching those who believe, for God's foolishness is wiser than men'[228].

And precisely because God saves by preaching, and uses the servants of His words as the instruments of His Kingdom, has He given them a clear mandate, and precise instructions to which they must adhere faithfully. Their task is to dispense the Word of God, the full Word of God, and nothing but the Work of God, thereafter to account to Him for their stewardship. St. Augustine discussed this point in detail in his sermon on the anniversary of his episcopate, which we have cited before, and in his well-known sermons on the Shepherds. He began the first by saying how conscious he was of the weight of his burden, and how, with growing age, he wondered more and more what account he could give the Lord of his flock. For while they, the people, had to account for only themselves, the preacher bore the double burden of being responsible not only for his own but also for his congregation's life. Hence his is the greater glory, but also the greater punishment, if he fail[229].

He then showed that this burden was enjoined upon the preacher in Ezekiel 33:2–10. 'It is God's will that the preacher proclaim it, for

[226] Enarratio in Ps. 103 I,8; the Neoplatonic influence of this sentence, is opposed by the text as a whole.
[227] De natura et gratia, 47.
[228] Epistula 120, 6.
[229] Frangipani II, 1.

else he should have to give a poor account of his guardianship. Hence we proclaim—and you know that have always done so and have never kept silent[230]: "God sayeth, I wish not for the death of the godless, but his return to the paths of righteousness". For what did the godless say? "Our transgressions and our sins be upon us, and we pine away in them, how should we then live?"[231] He abandoned hope, but the Healer has told him: "Thou shalt live, if only thou put aside thy vanity and trust in My Word alone"[232]. Yet there are some who rely solely on God's inexhaustible mercy, saying what if we do evil, commit injustices, live in sin, and show no repentance, God will not abandon the many, to rescue the few'. Thus St. Augustine realised that danger threatened from two sides. While he referred those representing the first threat to the quoted text from Ezekiel, he told the others: 'Or despisest thou the riches of his goodness and forbearance and longsuffering; not knowing that the goodness of God leadeth thee to repentance?'[233]. The true servant of the Word must rouse the fainthearted, console the meek, strengthen the weak, refute the foe, repel the besiegers, teach the unlearned, shake the indolent, constrain the litigious, humble the proud, pacify the angry, help the poor, free the slaves, reward the good, punish the wicked, and watch over all[234].

How they can do this, was shown by St. Augustine poignantly in the sermon on the shepherds in which he went more deeply into the meaning of Ezekiel 34:3: 'Neither do ye strengthen the weak sheep, nor heal the sick, nor bind up the wounded, nor return the stray to the flock, nor seek out the lost, but ye kill the strong'. In this text, St. Augustine saw his life's mandate as a preacher and shepherd, a mandate which, by the help of God's Word, he tried to carry out to the best of his ability.

The sheep, he argued, is weak when it fails to remember future temptations. The negligent shepherd will not say: My son, if thou wishest to serve the Lord, walk in righteousness and steel your heart against temptation[235]. Whoever says this strengthens the weak and

[230] Note the relevance of this point to the central message in St. Augustine's sermons.
[231] Ezek. 33 : 10.
[232] Frangipani II, 2.
[233] Rom. 2 :4; Frangipani II, 3.
[234] Sermo 340, 1 (delivered immediately after Sermo 339=Frangipani II).
[235] Eccles. 2 : 1.

turns them into the steadfast who seek not their own profit. Else he builds not on the rock, but on sand. The rock, however, is Christ[236]. We strengthen the weak when we tell them to expect temptation, in their day, but that the Lord will save them, if their heart is surrendered to Him. For it was in order to strengthen their hearts that He suffered, and died, was spat upon, was crowned with thorns, suffered insult, and was nailed to the cross[237]. Perhaps they, too, will begin to pale and tremble, and would gladly have done with their suffering, but we can tell them: "God is faithful, who will not suffer you to be tempted above that ye are able"[238]. To promise this and to preach Kingdom Come is to strengthen the weak. For it is binding up their wounds, if we tell the fearful and oppressed that they may count on God's Mercy. Bind up their wounds with solace, make whole what is broken and say: 'He in whom you believe will not abandon you to your temptation. God is faithful, who will not suffer you to be tempted above that ye are able'. These words are not mine, but the apostle's who also said: 'Since ye seek a proof of Christ speaking in me[239], examine yourselves and, if you are in faith, you will hear (in me) the voice of Christ, of the shepherd of Israel'[240]. There are many who are sick and lame. This is their consolation: God is faithful who will not suffer them to be tempted above that they are able, but who offers escape together with temptation, so that you can withstand it[241]. Nothing could show more clearly how much St. Augustine placed God's Word into the centre of his ministry. He did not dispense the wise counsels of learned men, but drew on the medicine-chest of God.

'And you failed to call back the stray sheep and to warn them against the threats of the heretics. And you failed to call them back, or to search out those that were lost. Therefore we associate for better or for worse under the hand of the robbers, and in the teeth of voracious wolves, and we ask that you pray for us in this our danger. The sheep, however, have no shame when they are found astray. Why do you seek us out, they ask? Just because you have strayed, I shall call you back. Because you are lost, I will find you. But we wish

[236] 1 Cor. 10:4.
[237] Sermo 46, 10.
[238] 1 Cor. 10:13.
[239] 2 Cor. 13:3.
[240] Sermo 46, 12.
[241] ib. 13.

to stray and court perdition, they tell me. All the more do I not want it, for I have heard the apostle say: Preach the word in season and out[242]. You wish to stray and to perish, I do not wish it. He who has sent me wishes it neither. Should I fear you more than Him? For we must all appear before the judgment seat of Christ[243]. I shall call back the strays, I shall seek out the lost. I shall do it in and out of season. No matter if the brambles will bruise me, I shall creep through all the narrow places and all the hedges. For inasmuch as the Lord, whom I fear, will give me strength I shall penetrate all. If you do not wish me to harass you, do not stray or lose your way[244]. If I were to keep silent, I would not be a true shepherd[245]. God's watchmen must heed Ezekiel'[246].

Without this mandate and command of God, St. Augustine would gladly have cast this heavy burden from his shoulders. 'But if I did not share my wealth with you, the Gospel would frighten me. For I might say: What good does it do me to cause people annoyance? Or to tell the wicked: Do not act thus, live thus, and behave thus? What does it benefit me to be so great a burden to men? I know how I must live inasmuch as I have received the commandment and the law. Let me keep what I have received. What good does it do me to have to account for others? But the Gospel frightens me! No one needs to entice me into living that wonderful kind of free and peaceful life. Nothing is better, nothing sweeter, than to contemplate God's divine treasure in peace. Such a life is sweet indeed. But preaching, accusing, punishing, edifying, and wearing oneself out for each and everyone is a heavy burden, a hard task, a great labour. Who would not escape from it? But the Gospel frightens me. "And another came, saying: Lord, behold here is thy pound, which I have kept laid up in a napkin. Thou art an austere man, thou takest up what thou layedst not down, and reapest that thou didst not sow"[247]. Take thine own. None of it is missing. And if it be all there, be thou no burden to me. But the master said: Out of thine own mouth will I judge thee, thou wicked servant. Thou knewest that I was an austere man, wherefore

[242] 2 Tim. 4:2.
[243] 2 Cor. 5:10.
[244] Sermo 46, 14.
[245] Sermo 46, 15.
[246] ib. 19.
[247] Luke 19:20 ff.

then gavest thou not my money into the bank, that I might have required mine own with usury? If I was anxious about giving it to you, what right had you not to lend it?[248] In all my words, I hold a mirror before you. They are not mine own, for it is at the Lord's behest that I speak out rather than keep silent, for I go in fear of Him. Whoever would not prefer to keep silent and not to have to account for you? But we (the preachers) have taken up the burden, which we cannot nor will not cast off from our shoulders'[249].

But side by side with the burden and the heavy responsibility, St. Augustine also knew the joy and the treasures which lie hidden in faithful service. Thus he said in one of his sermons, that 'by the reading of the lesson, we, the preachers, are faced with a mirror in which we can behold ourselves. That is what we have done. I do what I have heard therein. The prophet says that if you have failed to warn the righteous and to tell the godless that they will surely die their deaths; if you have failed to ask of them to cease from wickedness, the wicked will assuredly die in sin, but their blood will be on your hands. If however you warn them and they heed you not, they will die in sin but no blame will attach to you. If I keep silent, my own soul is in danger, but if I speak out and do as I am bid, you ignore me at your own risk. What then do I desire? What do I ask? Why do I speak? Why am I here? Why do I live? With no other purpose than that we may live together with Christ. That is my desire, my honour, my glory, my joy, and my rich treasure. But even if you do not heed me, I shall not keep silent hoping to save my own soul. I do not ask to be saved without you'[250].

Faithful to the Lord's mandate, St. Augustine zealously guarded the keys to the kingdom. His own life was a witness to what he wrote in *De doctrina Christiana:* 'A Christian orator, while he says what is just, and holy, and good (and he ought never to say anything else), does all he can to be heard with intelligence, with pleasure, and with obedience; and he need not doubt that if he succeed in this object, and so far as he succeeds, he will succeed more by piety in prayer than by gifts of oratory; and so he ought to pray for himself, and for those he is about to address, before he attempts to speak. And when the hour is come that he must speak, he ought,

[248] Frangipani II, 4.
[249] Sermo 82, 15.
[250] Sermo 17, 2.

before he opens his mouth, to lift up his thirsty soul to God, to drink in what he is about to distribute. For, as in regard to every matter of faith and love, there are many things that may be said, and many ways of saying them, who knows what it is expedient at a given moment for us to say, or to be heard saying, except God who knows the hearts of all? And who can make us say what we ought, and in the way we ought, except Him in whose hand both we and our speeches are?'[251]

Of the pleasure his own heart found in God's Scripture, he himself said that it so filled him that he could not but try to move the ears and the spirits of others[252]. And if God then lent them increase, his stewardship became a source of deep joy. This subject, as he observed in a sermon, was discussed in Paul's Epistle to the Hebrews[253]. 'When do we do it with joy? Whenever we see men advancing in God's Word. When does the husbandman till his field with joy? Whenever his trees bear fruit, whenever his field produces a rich harvest. Then he has not laboured in vain, bent his back in rain, blistered his hands and suffered heat and cold for no reason'[254].

But he regretted that so many failed to turn to God, or deferred their open conversion from day to day. St. Augustine would often be moved by this thought, right in the middle of a sermon, when he would struggle with all his might to transmit the full impost of the threat and the liberation, of the judgment and the salvation. He found it difficult to be forced, time after time, to have to scold his congregation because of their sinful lives, but he did it nevertheless, since 'God strengthens those who speak out without fear of contradiction'[255]. A preacher is, after all, no court musician who has to please his audience with sweet song. Far better say bitter things now, which will later taste sweetly to the heart[256].

He was equally severe on those who put off their conversion from day to day. By saying *cras*, *cras*, (tomorrow, tomorrow) they had become like so many ravens. 'But I say unto you, whenever you set up your croakings, you are lost. For the raven, whose voice you imitate, left the ark never to return'[257]. All delay was foolish, for no

[251] De doctrina Christiana IV, 32.
[252] Sermo 37, 1.
[253] Hebr. 13:17.
[254] Sermo 82, 15.
[255] Sermo 9, 3.
[256] ib. 5.
[257] Gen. 8:7; Sermo 224, 4.

one had promised them a morrow. Hence the time was short. 'These words are not mine own and yet they are mine own also. Inasmuch as I love you, they are as mine, though they are Holy Scripture. Be it known that I quote the word of the Scriptures. Oh, evil procrastinators, evil hankerers after the morrow, listen to the Words of the Lord, to the preaching of His Holy Scriptures. Make no tarrying to turn to the Lord, and put not off from day to day for suddenly shall the wrath of the Lord come forth, and in thy security thou shalt be destroyed and perish in the day of vengeance'[258]. And St. Augustine pointed out that, do what he will, he could not keep silent about their dalliance. For when the doctor comes to tell a son that his father will surely die that night, if he be allowed to fall asleep, the son must most certainly keep him awake, first by gentle means, and if necessary by shaking him, or even by pinching him hard. 'He says, let me be, I want to sleep. But you know that the doctor said, No, do not let him sleep, even if he wants to. And the father says: Let me be, I want to die. But I do not wish it, says the son to the father. To whom? To one who wishes to die. And yet the son wishes to postpone his father's death, to linger on a little while with his old father who is bound to die. The Lord calls to you: sleep not, lest you sleep in eternity. Awaken so that you may live with me, so that you may have a Father who will never die. And you are deaf to his call!'[259]

Truly, this is a sphere quite other than the cold and serene detachment of Neoplatonic philosophy! For here the two keys to the kingdom are being wielded in obedience to God's mandate. Hence we need not be surprised to learn that St. Augustine's contemporaries spoke of him freely as the man with the burning heart.

6. *The effects of the preaching.*

On this subject, too, St. Augustine held forth in many of his sermons. He realised that the preacher by himself could not bestow faith with its rich blessings on any one. Van der Meer was right to say that St. Augustine knew full well that a preacher cannot knead men's hearts like so much wax[260]. But in his evaluation of the effects of his ser-

[258] Eccles. 5:7.
[259] Frangipani II, 7, 8.
[260] op. cit., p. 397; see also pp. 120 and 122.

mon, this knowledge played no more than a subsidiary role, for St. Augustine also knew that once God's Word is preached, it will never return empty-handed. If the Word does not elevate, it will cast down. If it is not a call of life unto life, it becomes a call of death unto death. If it does not acquit, it condemns. God Himself speaks whenever His Word is preached, and hence St. Augustine admonished his congregation to search their soul's reception of God's Word. God's Word (*sermo*) shines on all alike from heaven (an allusion to the Holy Scriptures). The Word of God comes down like a rain that falls on good and evil alike. But while the evil turn God's rain into bramble roots, the good turn it into fruit. The Lord always rains on field and brambles alike, but on the field for its grain, and on the brambles for their firewood. God's Word *(verbum)* rains on all alike. 'Let us all mind our roots, let us see what we have made of His good rain. If we take up the rain in order to bring forth brambles, is it the fault of God's rain?'[261] Christians must listen to God's Word *(verbum)* every day of their lives, as a necessary means of their instruction. Just as the lesson must be repeated daily, lest the evil in the world and the brambles in men's heart grow up to choke the seed that has been sown, so also the Word *(sermo)* of God, must always be repeated lest in our forgetfulness we say that we have not heard it[262].

Whenever a minister speaks out, he must remember that he is the minister of the Lord's Word, which is quick and strong and as a two-edged sword. He must also know, as St. Augustine was wont to stress, that the Word has proved its worth throughout the world in storming the bastions of the enemy, and in winning nation after nation for Christ's Gospel. Hence his servants can take courage and strength in wielding their weapons on behalf of Christ the King. If they do so, the result of their battle is a foregone conclusion. 'The ministers of the Word, bear the Word of God, as a sword twice sharpened, in their hands. So they received the Word of God in power, to speak where they would, to whom they would, neither to fear power, nor to despise poverty. For they have in their hands a sword; where they will, they brandish it, handle it, smite with it and all this is in the power of the preachers. Now, you see the saints armed: observe the slaughter, observe their glorious battles. For if there be a commander, there must be soldiers; if soldiers, an enemy;

[261] Sermo 4, 31.
[262] Sermo 5, 1.

if a warfare, a victory. What have these done who had in their hands swords sharpened on both sides? They do, says the Psalmist, vengeance on the nations[263]. Daily is it done. We do it ourselves by speaking. Observe how the nations of Babylon are slain. She is repaid twofold. The saints wage war, they draw their swords twice sharpened; thence come defeats, slaughters, severances: how is she repaid double? When she had power to persecute the Christians, she slew the flesh indeed, but she crushed not God: now she is repaid double, for the Pagans are extinguished and the idols are broken. How are the Pagans slain? How, save when they become Christians? Whence was Saul the persecutor slain, and Paul the preacher raised up? Wherewith? With the sword twice sharpened. As was done to him, so has been done through him. For when made a preacher, he also had put into his hand the sword twice sharpened[264]. Christ filled his apostles with His Spirit; He commanded them to spread the Gospel and to go throughout the whole world. The world roared, the lion lifted himself up against the Lamb, but the Lamb was found stronger than the lion. The lion was conquered in his rage, the Lamb conquered in his suffering[265]. The hearts of men were turned to fear Christ. They are bound in the fetters of God's Word, bonds of iron so long as they fear: let them love and they shall be golden[266]. The powerful of the world, kings and nobles, if they fear not God, what shall they fear? But the Word is preached to them and they are smitten with the sword twice sharpened. It is said to them, that there is One who setteth some on his right hand, others on his left, that He may say to those who are on the left, Go ye in the everlasting fire, that is prepared for the devil and his angels[267]. So God saves by the foolishness of preaching and draws many to salvation[268]. Crowds of common people, possessing no great strength of intellect, run to the Physician in the exercise of faith, with the result of being healed by Christ and Him crucified. And it comes in wondrous ways to pass, through the depths of the riches of the wisdom and knowledge of God and his unsearchable judgments, that on the other hand some who do discern between the material and

[263] Ps. 149:7.
[264] Enarratio in Ps. 149, 11, 12.
[265] An allusion to the persecution of the martyrs.
[266] Enarratio in Ps. 149, 13, 14.
[267] ib. 14, 15.
[268] Epistula 169, 3.

the spiritual in their own nature, while pluming themselves on this attainment, and despising that foolishness of preaching by which those who believe are saved, wander far from the only path which leads to eternal life'[269].

Thus the preaching of the Word, leads to the eternal life of all those for whom Christ died[270]. 'The seed of which we are born again is the Word of God, that is, the Gospel. Whence the apostle says, "For in Christ Jesus I have begotten you through the Gospel"'[271]. Through the Gospel, in the preaching of which dwells the Holy Ghost, God's sons are quickened[272].

Hence the dispensers of the Word and the Sacrament are indeed dispensers of eternal salvation[273]. Through the preaching of His Word, God calls the elect according to His purpose[274].

But ministering the Lord's Word not only awakens us to new life, its blessings accompany God's children wherever they may go. God Himself, St. Augustine said, always desires to feed his people on the hills of Israel, that is on the hills of the Holy Scripture. Gather upon these hills, he told his congregation, where is found balm for your heart, where there is no evil, and where the pastures are lush and green. Go thither, ye good sheep, to feed on the mountains of Israel, in all Israel's valleys and in all her dwelling places. From her mountains the river of the Gospel has sprung, and their line is gone out through all the earth[275]. All Israel's dwellings have become happy and rich pastures for the sheep. Here they will find their fold in which they may rest and say: How good it is here! How clear is the truth! Here we are not led astray. Here we may rest as in our folds. And here we may sleep, that is dwell in sweet joy[276].

Hence St. Augustine would often call the Word of God, as it is read and preached, the daily bread of the faithful. Particularly in his sermon on the Lord's Prayer, he considered the daily bread, next to the supper, as God's Word. The bread which fills our stomach, and which renews our flesh from day to day is bestowed by God

[269] ib. 4.
[270] ib.
[271] 1 Cor. 4:15; Contra litteras Petiliani II, 11; III, 68
[272] Contra Parmenianum II, 23.
[273] Epistula 265, 2.
[274] See p. 148 ff.
[275] Ps. 19:5.
[276] Sermo 46, 24.

on those who praise Him and blaspheme against Him alike. For He maketh His sun to rise on the evil and on the good and sendeth rain on the just and on the unjust[277]. No matter whether you praise Him or abuse Him, He will feed you. But is there not also the bread which the children desire and of which the Lord says in the Gospel: It is not meet to take the children's bread and to cast it to the dogs?[278] Most certainly. But what kind of bread is it? And why is it called daily? This bread, too, is essential. We cannot live without it. The daily bread of the children is the Word *(sermo)* of God, which is given them daily. That is our daily bread which feeds our soul and not our stomach. Our daily food on this earth is the Word *(sermo)* of God which is dispensed by the churches[279]. The Lord's Supper, the explanation of God's Word, the lesson, the hymns which are sung and heard—all these are our daily bread. They are all needed on our pilgrimage[280]. And the Word *(verbum)* of God which is daily revealed to you, and in a sense broken before you, is next to the eucharist, our daily bread which feeds our soul just as natural bread feeds our stomach[281]. When we interpret Holy Scripture, we break the bread for you. What I distribute, is not my own. What you eat, I also eat. Whereof you live I also live. Together we have our granary in heaven. Thence cometh the Word *(verbum)* of God[282].

'When the divine Word makes use of, by the necessity of declaring himself, the sound of the voice (of the preacher), whereby to convey himself to the ears of the hearers; in the same sound of the voice, as it were in husks, knowledge, like the wine, is enclosed; and so this grape comes into the ears, as in the pressing machines of the wine-pressers. For there the separation is made, that the sound may reach as far as the ear; but knowledge be received in the memory of those that hear, as it were in a sort of vat; whence it passes into discipline of the conversation and habit of mind, as from the vat in the cellar: where if it do not through negligence grow sour, it will acquire soundness by age[283]. And when the heart is in the book (the Holy Scripture), it shall not be moved by the wickedness in the

[277] Matth. 5:45.
[278] Matth. 15:26.
[279] Sermo 56, 10.
[280] Sermo 57, 7.
[281] Sermo 58, 5.
[282] Sermo 95, 1.
[283] Enarratio in Ps. 8, 2.

world beneath, as it is said, but our conversation is in heaven. Doest thou wish to imagine the heaven? Think of the book of God. Hear the Psalm, and in his law will he exercise himself day and night[284]. His heart is then in heaven: if his heart is in heaven, all the wickedness which taketh place for a season upon the earth, all the successes of the wicked, all the sufferings of the righteous, to him who exercises himself day and night in the law of God, are as nought; patiently he endures all and blessed shall he be, instructed by the Lord'[285].

For that reason the congregation must make a nest in their hearts for the sermon[286]. They must not be lazy and slothful, but gather and store the grain of the Lord's field, the Word of God, of God's Church, in their heart[287]. Then they may sleep by the brooks[288]. In inner solitude, there rise up the brooks of divine memories, memories, which dwell in all who hold fast to the Scriptures. If only men entrust what they have read and heard to their memories in purity and sanctity, and rest in their inner sanctuary, their good conscience, the memory of the Word of God will spring forth from the spirit, and run on surely, so that all the faithful may rest together safely, and say: Verily, I am comforted, here lies my hope, this has God promised to me. I am at peace[289].

But to those who reject the Word that is preached, God's Word is the savour of death unto death[290], so that the preacher becomes the instrument of their perdition[291]. The Word of God penetrates inexhorably to the very roots of our being and lays bare our hypocrisy, our evil longings and our wickedness[292]. The Word *(sermo)* of God hates our inner ague[293], and there is a very real danger that some may become incensed at the remedy, and refuse it[294]. St. Augustine frequently compared the effect of the preaching of the Word to the parable of the sower. The seed of the Word of God, which the heavenly husbandman sows in the field of our heart is often trodden

[284] Ps. 1:2.
[285] Enarratio in Ps. 93, 6.
[286] Ps. 84:4; Sermo 37, 1.
[287] Sermo 38, 6.
[288] Ezek. 34:25.
[289] Sermo 47, 23.
[290] 2 Cor. 2:16.
[291] Enarratio in Ps. 7, 15.
[292] Sermo 4, 31.
[293] *i. e.* our sins.
[294] Sermo 9, 10, 11.

upon by the feet of the unworthy, or else stifled under the rock-like foolishness of an obdurate heart, the brambles of desire, or by sinful cares[295]. And man's obduracy, which does not escape God's judgment[296], caused St. Augustine to feel a divine perturbation, whence he would constantly appeal to the conscience of the congregation to turn to God in truth. He knew full well that the conversion of men was wrought by the grace of God and not by His servants. Still, he never allowed this understanding to drive him into quietism and passive resignation. 'For we ought to hasten much more readily to see the works of God than our own works'[297]. And St. Augustine's love sought the preservation of all[298 and 299].

[295] Sermo 216, 3; 73, 3.

[296] Epistula 194, 10.

[297] Epistula 144, 1.

[298] Sermo 17, 2; 82, 15.

[299] Dr. Lorentz, in discussing this chapter (Theol. Litt. Zeitung 1957, p. 855) has questioned our claim that St. Augustine veered from a more highly Neoplatonic to a more Biblical evaluation of the Word as proclamation. According to him, St. Augustine's linguistic *(sprachphilosophische)* remarks (which were not exclusively derived from Neoplatonism) dominate the Biblical sense of the Word. Hence even the divine presence in the word of the preacher cannot be interpreted in the realist sense of the Reformers, since that presence is merely an indwelling in a sensual shell, which must be transcended. For further reference, Lorentz indicates two of his articles in the *Zeitschrift für Kirchengeschichte* (1955–56, pp. 29–60, 213–251) in which we find the statement: The methodical view of the transition from sensuality to being was a preoccupation of the young Augustine as he elaborated his disciplines, and of the older Augustine as he interpreted and preached Scripture as a bishop (p. 242). While we fully appreciate the considerable weight of this remark (see, for instance, pp. 26 ff., 150 ff., and 213), we must insist that the many quotations we have cited in this chapter show clearly that St. Augustine also had a much more Biblical conception of the Word as proclamation, which went far beyond the purely philosophic approach. The Word had become the *Sermo Dei*, sharper than a twoedged sword, by which God's people were struck in order to rise up, separated in order to be gathered in, wounded in order to be healed, and stricken in order to be quickened unto life. This approach to the Word cannot be fitted into any scheme of ancient linguistic philosophy, since it represents God's call, effects our re-birth, and awakens, feeds and supports our faith. Lorentz himself admits that, in the introductory passage of *De doctrina christiana* (quoted by us on p. 155 f), St. Augustine refused to take his doctrine (that no one can really learn anything from anyone else; cf. *De magistro)* to its logical conclusion, under the influence of Christianity (op. cit. p. 237 f.) Now this was the very influence which, in the doctrine of the proclamation of God's Word, broke through the philological arguments of the day. All those who have read St. Augustine's sermons on the anniversary of his episcopate and on the shepherds and their mandate, can clearly hear more than the injunction to pass from sensuality to being (see also Chapters VI and VII). Only by considering both chapters together, can we explain St. Augustine's real evaluation of the Word.

CHAPTER V

THE WORD OF GOD AND THE CHURCH

Under this heading, which immediately conjures up all sorts of associations, we shall discuss four different questions which have lost none of their importance in the age-old controversy between Catholics and Protestants.

The first question may be put as follows: What was St. Augustine's criterion of canonicity, i.e. by what means did he decide which of the Books are canonical? Did he consider the Church's magisterium so infallible, that what Books she called canonical, he accepted without question? Or did he rather look for the answer in the Scriptures themselves? Or again, was the whole question never considered by him at all? The problem has been studied mainly by Nebrada and Costello, Nebrada concluding that St. Augustine's chief criterion of the canonicity of the Holy Scriptures lay in the *authority* and the *tradition* and the *lessons* of the apostolic churches[1], and Costello that St. Augustine's criterion was church usage, apostolic tradition, and church authority[2]. Hence he differs from Nebrada in emphasis rather than substance. However, the shift in emphasis is anything but purely formal or accidental. Protestant scholars in their general discussion of this subject—and I know of no special Protestant discussion—usually agree with these findings[3].

The second question concerns the acceptance of the authority of the Holy Scriptures. Does God's Word derive its authority over Christians from that of the Church, either as Christ's Body which is suffused with the Holy Ghost, or else as the infallible teacher who assents to the Holy Scriptures, or does it rather rest, over and above the reliable testimony of the Church, on the *autopistia* of the Scrip-

[1] op. cit. Pars prima, Caput III, 45 and 57. The italics are Nebreda's.
[2] op. cit. University of Ottawa Review, 1932, p. 130 ff.; id. Diss., p. 77 ff.,
[3] Johannes Leipoldt, *Geschichte des neutestamentlichen Kanons*, Leipzig 1907. (see indexes in both volumes).

tures themselves, so that the Scriptures are as clear a proof of divinity and truth as white and black objects are of their colour, and sweet and bitter pills of their taste? Since the Reformation, all discussions of this point have mainly centered on St. Augustine's own dictum: 'For my part I should not believe the Gospel except as moved by the authority of the Church'[4]. Catholic scholars take this quotation as proof positive that St. Augustine chose the second answer, and many Protestants share their view fully[5]. Others again take the opposite view, pointing out—as they did particularly during the Reformation—that St. Augustine frequently used the imperfect where classical Latin writers would assuredly have chosen the pluperfect tense[6]. Thus, they point out that St. Augustine was merely speaking about his past, and that what he wrote was in fact: 'I should not have believed the Gospel except the authority of the Church *had* moved me'. Thus Calvin, in his *Institutio*[7] could point to a later passage in which St. Augustine stated clearly that, as he wrote his refutation of Manichaeus' so-called fundamental letter, he had already gone back on that point of view. Other Protestants claimed that Catholics were wrong to quote the passage in question, since St. Augustine did not use it in connection with an *auctoritas imperii*, attaching to the Church as an institution, nor with the Gospel as inspired Holy Writ. Instead he merely referred to the fact that the Church, as a preacher of the Gospel and as a respected institution was one of the means which the Holy Ghost uses in order to lead the reborn unto conscious faith in Christ[8].

The third question is whether St. Augustine held that the Church must base its faith on what is written in Scripture, or must Scripture be interpreted according to the active faith of the Church? Fritz Hoffmann has answered this point very pertinently when he wrote in his remarkable work on St. Augustine's Doctrine of the Church: '(He considered) the Church essential for interpreting the content of individual Books; this fact alone shows clearly that St. Augustine

[4] Contra epistolam Manichaei, quam vocant Fundamenti 6.

[5] Cf. J. Kunze, Glaubensregel, *Heilige Schrift und Taufbekenntnis*, Leipzig 1899; p. 304 ff.; id. *Evangelisches und Katholisches Schriftprinzip*, Leipzig 1899, p. 9 ff. Ad. von Harnack, *Lehrbuch der Dogmengeschichte* III[4], p. 79 ff.

[6] Cf. Daniel Chamier, *Panstratia Catholica*, Geneva 1626, Part I, p. 198 ff.

[7] I VII, 3. For the view of Protestant theologians, see the comprehensive survey of B. B. Warfield, *Augustine's Doctrine of Knowledge and Authority*. In: Studies in Tertullian and Augustine, New York, 1930, p. 199 ff.

[8] Cf. A. Kuyper, *Encyclopaedie der heilige godgeleerdheid*, Amsterdam 1894, II, p. 503.

did not find the *regula fidei* in the written Word, but in the active faith of the Church, i.e. in what came to be called the *traditio activa*. For it is not as if the faith of the Church had to adapt itself to what is written in the Scriptures but rather that the Scriptures must be interpreted according to the *traditio activa*. It is one of the main principles of Augustinian exegesis that the Scriptures cannot oppose the faith of the Church, and must hence and always be interpreted in accordance with it'[9]. All Catholic scholars have endorsed this opinion as reflecting the true position of St. Augustine[10]. Protestant scholars, on the other hand, have often challenged this view have in the old controversy-literature[11], and what few later writers have discussed the subject, have veered from one attitude[12] to the other[13]. On this subject, too, there is clearly no agreed opinion.

The final question is whether St. Augustine considered that the Church, as the direct creation of Christ, and as the Body of this Head with its own law and dynamic, was ontologically antecedent to the Scriptures, so that the Scriptures may be said to spring from her and to be verified in her fullness, or whether, instead, the Church is born out of God's Word, and is, in all her doings, bound to its authority. In other words, does the Church take pride of place over the Word, do they coexist, or does the Word come first, or did St. Augustine, perhaps, ignore the whole question? In the early controversies, Catholic authors placed the Church foremost, while the Reformers gave pride of place to the Word. Many Neo-Catholic theologians deny that there is a formal and material priority of the Holy Scriptures, as the Word of God, over the Church as the mystical Body of Christ. The Church, according to them, is the independent creation of Christ and His Spirit, the extension of the incarnation, and the continuous corporealization of the divine Christ of which the Scriptures are the witness. This view of the Church is, according to them based fully on the writings of St. Augustine[14]. Protestants have not

[9] op. cit., p. 298.
[10] See, for instance, Pesch, op. cit., p. 116; Portalié, op. cit., col. 2341.
[11] Cf. Chamier, op. cit. I, p. 5 ff.
[12] Kunze, *Glaubensregel, Heilige Schrift und Taufbekenntnis*, p. 304 ff.
[13] F. Kattenbusch, *Das apostolische Symbol*, Leipzig, 1900, p. 418 ff.
[14] See J. Vetter, *Der hl. Augustinus und das Geheimnis des Leibes Christi*, Mainz 1929, p. 55 ff.; O. Bauhofer, *Corpus Christi und Wort Gottes. Catholica* 1933, pp. 125–140: M. D. Koster, *Ekklesiologie im Werden*, Paderborn 1940; Emile Mersch, *Le corps mystique du Christ*, Paris 1951, II, p. 35–138; W. D. Jonker, *Mistieke liggaam en kerk in die nuwe Rooms-Katholieke Teologie*, Kampen 1955.

taken any stand on this matter, for though Jonker's thesis dealt with the question as such, it could not, within its terms, enter into the validity of this interpretation of St. Augustine's views.

These four questions, each of which deals with aspects of the relationship between God's Word and His Church, will now be examined in the light of St. Augustine's own writing.

1. *The question of the canonicity.*

St. Augustine was very fond of the word 'canonical', for, according to Costello, he used it on more than two hundred occasions[15]. St. Augustine always used the term in its exclusive sense, to refer to the Scriptures alone. God's Word is distinguished from all other writings by its canonicity. The canonical books have divine authority. Costello claims that he also used the word to mean Catholic and ecclesiastic, but none of his references would seem to bear out this contention[16]. True, 'canonical' may be tantamount to 'received into the official list of divine writings', but far more often it simply means 'of divine authority and hence self-evident'[17].

Moreover, St. Augustine distinguished clearly between canonical and apocryphal books. 'The apocryphal books', he said, 'are so called, not because of any mysterious regard paid to them, but because they are mysterious in their origin, and in the absence of clear evidence, have only some obscure presumption to rest upon'[18]. The meaning of this quotation is unequivocal. They lack clear evidence, possibly because they lack inner conviction, but more probably because their origin is not vouchsafed by any reliable witness. Elsewhere, St. Augustine showed that the Manicheans were wont to quote all sorts of apocryphal writings that were no more than a collection of fables published by some unknown authors under the name of the apostles. Manichaeus even produced a text which, he claimed, was written by Christ Himself. St. Augustine's reply was most instructive: 'These books would no doubt have been sanctioned by the Church at the time of their publication, if holy and learned men then in life, and competent to determine the matter,

[15] op. cit., p. 71.
[16] ib.; the references are to: Contra Faustum XXIII, 9; XXXIII, 6; De natura boni 24.
[17] Cf. Contra Faustum XI, 5; Epistula 82, 3, 7, 22, 24.
[18] Contra Faustum, XI, 2.

had thought the contents to be true[19]. As regards any writing professing to come immediately from Christ Himself, if it were really His, how is it not read and acknowledged and regarded as of supreme authority in the Church, which, beginning with Christ Himself, and continued by His apostles, who were succeeded by the bishops, has been maintained and extended to our own day, and in which is found the fulfilment of many former predictions, while those concerning the last days are sure to be accomplished in the future? In regard to the appearance of such a writing, it would require to be considered from what quarter it issued. Supposing it to have issued from Christ Himself, those in immediate connection with Him might very well have received it, and have transmitted it to others. In this case the authority of the writing would be fully established by the traditions of various communities and of their presidents. Who, then, is so infatuated as in our day to believe that the epistle of Christ issued by Manichaeus is genuine?'[20] We cannot help being struck by St. Augustine's sober commonsense. For him there was no doubt that all truly canonical writings must have a genuine stamp that would have been recognized by Christ's Church. Hence he dismissed, *a priori*, the possibility that any writing lacking a succession of reliable witnesses and appearing out of nowhere, should be canonical. Any of Christ's writings would have been broadcast by His disciples, there and then. St. Augustine considered it utter foolishness to assume that the intimate circle of Christ's Apostles could have been unaware of any of His works, and that they would have left their discovery to a Persian interloper who came more than two hundred years later. A book bearing the name of an Apostle—unlike false Apostolic letters, of which there must always have been many if we consider the precautions Paul had to take[21]—would surely have been investigated and established as having come from the Apostle's pen. Hence, St. Augustine stressed the credibility of the tradition rather than that of the content, though elsewhere he pointed out that the contents of a certain apocryphal manuscript[22]

[19] ib. XXII, 79.
[20] ib. XXVIII, 4.
[21] 2 Thess. 3:17.
[22] I.e. the *Apocalypsis Pauli*, of which St. Augustine said that it is crammed with all sorts of fables about St. Paul's pronouncements on the third heaven, which, according to St. Paul himself, it is not lawful for a man to utter; see Tractatus in evangelium Joannis, XCVIII, 8.

were in utter conflict with what is reported in the canonical Books. In the City of God, St. Augustine had this to say about apocryphal writings: 'Let us omit the fables of those scriptures which are called apocryphal, because their obscure origin was unknown to the fathers from whom the authority of the true Scriptures has been transmitted to us by a most certain and well-ascertained succession. For though there is some truth in these apocryphal writings, yet they contain so many false statements, that they have no canonical authority. We cannot deny that Enoch, the seventh from Adam, left some divine writings, for this is asserted by the Apostle Jude in his canonical epistle. But it is not without reason that these writings have no place in that canon of Scripture which was preserved in the temple of the Hebrew people by the diligence of successive priests; for their antiquity brought them under suspicion, and it was impossible to ascertain whether these were his genuine writings, and they were not brought forward as genuine by the persons who were found to have carefully preserved the canonical books by a successive transmission. So that the writings which are produced under his name, and which contain these fables about the giants, saying that their fathers were not men, are properly judged by prudent men to be not genuine; just as many writings are produced by heretics under the names both of other prophets, and, more recently, under the names of the apostles, all of which after careful examination have been set apart from canonical authority under the title of Apocrypha'[23]. Once again, he used the same argument: their origin is mysterious, because they lack a well-ascertained succession of witnesses, and because they are properly judged by prudent men not to be genuine.

While this approach contains many valuable hints about St. Augustine's true attitude to the problem we are investigating, his full view only emerges from an examination of his many utterances on the determination of the canonicity of the Books of the Bible. We had best treat these utterances, by dealing with his view firstly of the Hebrew canon of the Old Testament, secondly of the Septuagint and finally of the New Testament.

The references to the Hebrew canon are few and far between. From the last quotation we gave, it must be clear how firmly convinced St. Augustine was of the fact that successive generations of

[23] De civitate Dei XV, 23, 4.

priests had watched over the canon of the Books kept in the Temple. In Book XVIII of the City of God he writes 'that nation, that people, that city, that republic, these Israelites, to whom the oracles of God were entrusted, by no means confounded with similar licence the false prophets with the true prophets; but, agreeing together, and differing in nothing, acknowledged and upheld the authentic authors of their sacred books'[24]. And some chapters earlier, he had said: 'Many things are mentioned in the canonical Scriptures which are not explained there, but are said to be found in other books which the prophets wrote, the very names of these prophets being sometimes given, and yet they are not found in the canon which the people of God received. Now I confess the reason of this is hidden from me; only I think that even those men, to whom certainly the Holy Spirit revealed those things which ought to be held of religious authority, might write some things as men by historical diligence, and others as prophets by divine inspiration; and these things were so distinct, that it was judged that the former should be ascribed to themselves, but the latter to God speaking through them: and so the one pertained to the abundance of knowledge, the other to the authority of religion. In that authority the canon is guarded. So that, if any writings outside of it are now brought forward under the name of ancient prophets, they cannot serve even as an aid to knowledge, because it is uncertain whether they are genuine; and on this account they are not trusted, especially those of them, in which some things are found that are even contrary to the truth of the canonical books, so that it is quite apparent they do not belong to them'[25]. Hence whatever is accepted into the canon, is a true prophecy inspired by God, and has the authority of religion. And the true people of God, to whom the Words of God are entrusted, have the gift of distinguishing between true and the false prophets and between what was written by divine inspiration and what by human diligence. In this distinction they apparently applied the complete inner harmony of all the divine writings as a yardstick[26].

We now come to the Septuagint. St. Augustine's view of it, as Pontet has rightly remarked, was based on tradition rather than on

[24] ib. XVIII, 41, 3.
[25] ib. 38.
[26] For further details, see Nebreda's full discussion in Chap. III, *De canone Veteris Testamenti*.

any objective investigation of his own[27]. In this respect, there was a great difference between him and St. Jerome. Thus Cavallera could show that while St. Jerome was first and foremost a scholar who devoted his life to the passionate defence of Hebrew truth and the scrupulous rendering into Greek of the inspired Hebrew texts, St. Augustine was above all a churchman, a leader of his flock, and hence mainly concerned with preserving their peace of mind[28]. The truth of this comment is felt by all who read the correspondence between these two Fathers of the Church. In his very first letter, St. Augustine asked St. Jerome to make it quite clear in his translations of the sacred canonical books into Latin, where his version differs from that of the LXX, whose authority is worthy of the highest esteem. For his part, he could not sufficiently express his wonder that anything should still be found in the Hebrew manuscripts which escaped so many translators perfectly acquainted with the language. He went on to say that he was aware of his inability to pronounce a decided opinion on the harmony of mind of the LXX, except that a high authority must surely be conceded to them. And then he formulates this syllogism: the Hebrew texts are either obscure, in which case St. Jerome was as likely to be mistaken as others, or else they were plain, in which case the LXX could not possibly have been mistaken[29].

In a subsequent letter, he stated once again that a direct translation from the Hebrew (rather than from the Greek) might easily lead to differences between the Latin and the Greek churches. Thus a bishop of Oea, having introduced St. Jerome's version into his church, had caused such a tumult among the congregation, that he was compelled to correct that version, as he desired not to lose his flock[30]. Meanwhile, he would very much like to be told how it was that the Hebrew text differed so frequently from the Greek Septuagint, which, after all, had no mean authority, seeing that it had obtained so wide a circulation, and was the one which the apostles used[31].

In 404 A.D. St. Jerome at last replied to St. Augustine's questions[32]. He showed easily that St. Augustine's syllogism was never applied,

[27] op. cit., p. 220, Note 101.

[28] F. Cavallera, *Les 'Quaestiones hebraicae in Genesim' de Saint Jérôme et les 'Quaestiones in Genesim' de Saint Augustin.* In: Studi Agostiniani, Rome 1931, p. 359.

[29] Epistula 28, 2.

[30] Epistula 71, 4, 5.

[31] ib. 6.

[32] St. Augustine's two letters were written in 394 and 404 A.D. respectively.

not even by St. Augustine in his interpretations of the Psalms. Moreover his (St. Jerome's) translation from the Hebrew had no other object than to reveal the true meaning of the original text 'since the Jews had omitted or tampered with many things'[33]. St. Augustine replied that while he was convinced of the benefits of St. Jerome's translation inasmuch as the latter wished to bring to light what had been omitted or perverted by the Jews, he would gladly have known which Jews were meant. Moreover, he had merely objected to the introduction of St. Jerome's translation into the Church, lest the new version cause confusion among the flocks of Christ, whose ears and hearts had become accustomed to listen to that version to which the seal of approbation was given by the apostles themselves[34].

We cannot help being struck by a number of points in these letters. Firstly, St. Augustine never once mentioned that the Seventy were divinely inspired in their translation, although he had frequently suggested this inspiration elsewhere. He was also strangely circumspect in pronoucing on the 'fact' of their miraculous unanimity. Moreover he claimed that the apostles had approved the Septuagint, and ignored the fact that their quotations from the Old Testament often differed from the LXX. Nor did he acknowledge that St. Jerome, when speaking of omissions from, or perversions of, the original Hebrew text by the Jews, was undoubtedly referring, *inter alia*, to the Septuagint[35]. And finally we must note his confession that he cannot explain the difference between the Hebrew text and that of the Seventy.

Unfortunately, St. Augustine—unskilled as he was in this field—did not always leave it at that. Thus in his *De doctrina Christiana* II, written in 397 A.D., he claimed that 'the seventy translators enjoyed so much of the presence and power of the Holy Spirit in their work of translation, that among that number of men there was but one voice'. In support of this contention, he stated that many not unworthy of confidence assert that they were separated during the work of translation, each man in a cell by himself, and yet their translations differed in no respect[36].

In his *De Consensu Evangelistarum*, published in 400 A.D., he ex-

[33] Epistula 75, 20.
[34] Epistula 82, 34, 35.
[35] See Pontet, op. cit., p. 223, Note 107; Cavallera, op. cit. p. 361.
[36] De doctrina christiana II, 22.

plained the occasional differences between the Hebrew text and the Septuagint by saying that the Seventy had most probably composed their translation under the influence of the very Spirit by whose inspiration the things which they translated had been originally spoken. This is confirmed by their marvellous consent[37]. He even made this unanimity the subject of his sermons: 'But the Septuagint translators, whose authority is such that they may deservedly be said to have interpreted by the inspiration of the Spirit of God owing to their wonderful agreement, conclude, not by mistake, but taking occasion from the resemblance in sound between the Hebrew words expressing these two senses, that the use of this word is an indication of the sense of the Hebrew word'[38]. In yet another sermon, he said: 'The gods of the Gentiles are devils. It is said[39] that this is not the reading in Hebrew; but the gods of the Gentiles are idols. If this be true, much the more must the Seventy be believed to have interpreted by the divine Spirit, the same Spirit as He by whom these things were said in the Hebrew. For by the working of the same Spirit this also should be said which was said, The gods of the Gentiles are devils, that we might understand what had been expressed in the Hebrew, The gods of the Gentiles are idols, meaning rather the devils which dwell in the idols'[40]. And as late as 426, he continued to defend the same point of view, and to believe in the pseudo-miracle of their strange consent. If anything, his conviction had grown stronger, for he wrote: 'It is reported, indeed, that there was an agreement in their words so wonderful, stupendous, and plainly divine, that when they had sat at this work, each one apart (for so it pleased Ptolemy to test their fidelity), they differed from each other in no word which has the same meaning and force, or in the order of the words; but, as if the translators had been one, so what all had translated was one, because in very deed the one Spirit had been in them all. And they received so wonderful a gift of God, in order that the authority of these Scriptures might be commended not as human but divine, as indeed it was, for the benefit of the nations who should at some time believe, as we now see them doing'[41].

[37] De Consenu Evangelistarum II, 128.
[38] Enarratio in Ps. 87, 10. The Septuagint renders 'giant' as 'physician'. The Hebrew for both is 'raphah'.
[39] St. Augustine, who knew no Hebrew, could not check this fact himself.
[40] Enarratio in Ps. 135, 3.
[41] De civitate Dei XVIII, 42.

He knew fully well that there were other translations, and even stated that the Jews looked upon St. Jerome's translation as faithful while they considered the Septuagint to be full of omissions. But he dismissed them with: 'The churches of Christ judge that no one should be preferred to the authority of so many men, chosen for this very great work by Eleazar, who was then high priest; for even if there had not appeared in them one spirit, without doubt divine, and the seventy learned men had, after the manner of men, compared together the words of their translation, that what pleased them all might stand, no single translator ought to be preferred to them; but since so great a sign of divinity has appeared in them, *certainly*, if any other translator of their Scriptures from the Hebrew into any other tongue is faithful, in that case he agrees with these seventy translators, and if he is not found to agree with them, then we ought to believe that the prophetic gift is with them. For the same Spirit who was in the prophets when they spoke these things was also in the seventy men when they translated them, so that assuredly they could also say something else, just as if the prophet himself had said both, because it would be the same Spirit who said both; and could say the same thing differently so that although the words are not the same, yet the same meaning should shine forth to those of good understanding; and could omit or add something, so that even by this it might be shown that there was in that work not human bondage, which the translator owed to the words, but rather divine power, which filled and ruled the mind of the translator. If then, as it behoves us, we behold nothing else in these Scriptures than what the Spirit of God has spoken through men, if anything is in the Hebrew copies and is not in the version of the Seventy, the Spirit of God did not choose to say it through them, but only through the prophets. But whatever is in the Septuagint and not in the Hebrew copies, the same Spirit chose rather to say through the latter, thus showing that both were prophets. Further, whatever is found in both editions, that one and the same Spirit willed to say through both, but so that the former preceded in prophesying and the latter followed in prophetically interpreting them; because, as the one Spirit of peace was in the former when they spoke true and concordant words, so the self-same Spirit has appeared in the latter, when, without mutual conference, they yet interpreted all things as if with one mouth'[42].

[42] ib. 43.

Note the adverb 'certainly'! What had been a probable assumption, a possibility worth pondering, had become an article of faith. Even though St. Augustine never said so explicitly, he clearly held that the Seventy were inspired infallibly by the Holy Spirit. And yet there is no evidence whatsoever that St. Augustine, like St. Jerome, made any attempt to check the reliability or the origin of this translation. For had he done so he would have had to concur with St. Jerome, that the alleged circumstances of the translation were pure fable and nothing else. This is all the more unfortunate in that this pseudo-miracle was always cited as evidence for the inspired nature of the Septuagint. Only complete ignorance of the actual truth could have persuaded St. Augustine to hold that all differences between the Septuagint and the Hebrew text were due to prophetic visions. Thus he conjured up the most far-fetched allegories to explain what a mere glance at the original text would have explained without any trouble[43], and stuck to his completely baseless[44] and confabulated account of a divinely inspired translation through thick and thin. All these allegorical fantasies might never have sprung from his pen, had he but adhered to his own precept: 'When in both books (the Hebrew Bible and the Septuagint) any diversity is found, since both cannot be true to fact, we do well to believe in preference that language out of which the translation was made into another by translators'[45].

His belief that the Septuagint was divinely inspired, led him to hold that anything in it not found in the Hebrew original was of divine origin, and hence canonical. Thus St. Augustine held that the LXX had superseded the Hebrew canon, though it must be admitted that, in many of his utterances he showed a certain reserve when discoursing upon this subject. In so early a work as the *De doctrina christiana*, he mentions an interpreter who had read all the sacred writings, those at least that are called *canonical*[46]. Moreover, he wrote to St. Jerome: I confess that I have learned to yield respect and honour only to those books of Scripture which already are called canonical[47]. It must be most assuredly believed that no lies

[43] See Cavallera, op. cit. for some simple examples.

[44] Arthur Allgeier, *Der Einfluss des Manichäismus auf die exegetische Fragestellung bei Augustin.* Festschrift Mausbach, p. 12.

[45] De civitate Dei XV, 13, 3.

[46] De doctrina christiana II, 12.

[47] Epistula 82, 3.

are found in the authors of holy writings, *especially of the canonical Scriptures*[48]. These passages were written in 396 and 405 A.D. respectively, but even towards the end of his life (427 A.D.) he still wrote: 'This reckoning of the dates (from this time, when the Temple was rebuilt, down to the time of Aristobulus) is found, not in the Holy Scriptures which are called canonical, but in others, among which are also the books of the Maccabees. These are held as canonical, not by the Jews, but by the Church, on account of the extreme and wonderful sufferings of certain martyrs'[49]. And some chapters earlier: 'The story of Judith... Which they say the Jews received not into their canon'[50]. No doubt, this was the reason why he could write about these 'deutero-canonical' books in a way which he would never apply to the canonical writings. Thus he said of the Books of the Maccabees, that the Jews did not receive it like the Law, the Prophets and the Psalms of which the Lord Himself has said through His prophet that they must all be fulfilled. However these Books were received by the Church, *not with disadvantage*, provided only that they were read and heard *soberly*, and with an eye to the Maccabees as true martyrs of God[51]. And in his *De octo Dulcitii quaestionibus*, St. Augustine, after having shown from Ecclesiasticus that Samuel prophesied after his death, went on to say that if we were to reject this evidence simply because Ecclesiasticus is not part of the Hebrew canon, what can we say about Moses who died a mortal death according to Deuteronomy, and of whom the Gospel nevertheless says that he appeared with Elias, who had not died?[52] Thus St. Augustine's reaction to any doubt of the canonicity of those books, which are not part of the Hebrew canon, is quite other than his attitude to those who reject the books of the Hebrew canon. For the latter act in a godless manner and have no claim to be called Christians[53].

But side by side with these somewhat hesitant utterances, St. Augustine also used expressions by which he unequivocally accepted all these books as being canonical. We cannot cite his list of canonical

[48] ib. 22.
[49] De civitate Dei XVIII, 36.
[50] ib. 26.
[51] Contra Gaudentium I, 38.
[52] De octo Dulcitii quaestionibus VI, 5.
[53] See Costello's thesis, p. 87 ff., where Costello has tried to get over this difficulty most unsatisfactorily.

books in *De doctrina Christiana* as evidence, since that evidence itself had first to be judged by the criteria given in Christian Doctrine II, 12[54]. In his *Speculum*, however, he ended his discussion of Ezekiel by saying that, while he had been quoting exclusively from Books which the Jews themselves held to be canonical, those books which are established to have been written before the coming of the Saviour, but which were not embraced by the Jews, cannot be ignored since the Church has, indeed, received them[55]. In the *City of God* he observed that Solomon was a prophet as his works, namely the Proverbs, the Canticles, and Ecclesiastes prove, all of which are canonical. But Ecclesiasticus and the Book of Wisdom are only called his, for some similitude between his style and theirs. Yet the Churches of the West hold them of great authority, and have done so long[56]. In his *De praedestinatione sanctorum* he mentioned that a quotation from the Book of Wisdom was rejected by the Pelagians as being taken from a non-canonical book. Hence the Book could not have been generally accepted, even in his day. Once again, St. Augustine's reaction was characteristic. Having observed that the subject is clear, even without the additional evidence of the Book, he went on to say: '*And since these things are so*, the judgment of the Book of Wisdom ought not to be repudiated, since for so long a course of years that book has deserved to be read in the Church of Christ, from the position of the readers of the Church of Christ, and to be heard by all Christians, from bishops downwards, even to the lowest lay believers, penitents and catechumens, with the veneration paid to divine authority'[57]. He then pointed out that various interpreters of the Holy Writings, who lived shortly after the Apostles, and who embraced the Book of Wisdom, were convinced of paying veneration to divine authority[58]. And in the very next chapter he observed once again that this Book was considered by illustrious commentators to have been divine testimony[59]. Hence it would appear that St. Augustine's criterion of canonicity was time-hallowed Church usage.

It is particularly interesting to learn what St. Augustine had to

[54] De doctrina christiana II, 13 and 12.
[55] Migna P.L. 34, col. 946, 7.
[56] De civitate Dei XVII, 20, 1.
[57] De praedestinatione sanctorum 27.
[58] ib. 28.
[59] ib. 29; my italics.

say about the canonicity of the New Testament. His point of view emerges most clearly in his arguments against Faustus, who challenged the authenticity and integrity of many books of the New Testament, claiming, for instance, that the Gospel according to St. Matthew and various Epistles of St. Paul were a mixture of truth and lies. As regards the Gospel according to St. Matthew, St. Augustine pointed out that it was handed down from the days of Matthew in the Church, without any break in the connection between that time and the present, and was hence inherently credible. The Manicheans, on the other hand, placed their faith in the book of a Persian, written long after Christ, in which it is written that Christ was not born of Mary. Hence while believing the writings of Manichaeus, they denied the true origins of the Gospel according to St. Matthew. And St. Augustine told them plainly: 'As I believe your book to be the production of Manichaeus, since it has been kept and handed down among the disciples of Manichaeus, from the time when he lived to the present time, by a regular succession of your presidents, so I ask you to believe the book which I quote to have been written by Matthew, since it has been handed down from the days of Matthew in the Church, without any break in the connection between that time and the present. The question then is', he goes on to say, 'whether we are to believe the statements of an Apostle who was in the company of Christ, while He was on earth, or of a man away in Persia, born long after Christ. But perhaps you (Faustus) will quote some other book bearing the name of an Apostle known to have been chosen by Christ; and you will find there that Christ was not born of Mary. Since, then, one of the books must be false, the question in this case is, whether we are to yield our belief to a book acknowledged and approved as handed down from the beginning in the Church founded by Christ Himself, and maintained through the apostles and their successors in an unbroken connection all over the world to the present day; or to a book which this Church condemns as unknown, and which, moreover, is brought forward by men who prove their veracity by praising Christ the falsehood'[60]. 'Or, if the question is of Matthew being the real author, who would not believe what he finds in the Church which has a distinct history in unbroken connection from the days of Matthew to the present time, rather than a Persian interloper, who comes more than two

[60] Contra Faustum XXVIII, 2.

hundred years after?' The Church, for one, does not embrace her tradition lightheartedly, and would not have accepted the evidence of an unknown man without much scrutiny. 'Even in the case of the Apostle Paul, who was called from Heaven after the Lord's ascension, the Church would not have believed him, had there not been Apostles in life with whom he might communicate and compare his gospel with theirs, so as to be recognised as belonging to the same society. When it was ascertained that Paul preached what the Apostles preached and that he lived in fellowship and harmony with them, and when God's testimony was added by Paul's working miracles like those done by the Apostles, his authority became so great, that his words are now received in the Church, as if, to use his own appropriate words, Christ was speaking in him[61]. And therefore Manichaeus ought not to think that the Church of Christ should believe what he says in opposition to the Scriptures, which are supported by such strong and continuous evidence, and in which the Church finds an emphatic injuction, that whoever preaches to her differently from what she has received, must be anathema'[62].

No less instructive was St. Augustine's reply to the question how we may know with certainty that the Epistles of the New Testament were, in fact, written by the apostles themselves. That certainty, he claimed, is obtained in the same way, in which the Manicheans know that Manichaeus' books were written by his own hand. 'Suppose someone should raise a question on this point and should contend, that the books which they attribute to Manichaeus are not of his authorship: their only reply would be, to ridicule the absurdity of thus gratuitously calling in question a matter confirmed by successive testimonies of such wide extent. As, then, it is certain that these books are the production of Manichaeus, and as it is ridiculous in one born so many years after to start objections of his own and so raise a discussion on the point; with equal certainty may we pronounce it absurd, or rather pitiable, in Manichaeus or his followers to bring such objections against writings originally well authenticated, and carefully handed down from the times of the apostles to our own day through a constant succession of custodians[63]. All the certainty of the authorship of any book disappears, if we doubt the

[61] Gal. 2:1–10; 2 Cor. 13:3.
[62] Contra Faustum XXVIII, 4.
[63] ib. XXXII, 21.

apostolic origin of those books which are attributed to the apostles by the Church which the apostles themselves founded, and which occupies so conspicuous a place in all lands, and if at the same time we acknowledge as the undoubted production of the apostles what is brought forward by heretics in opposition to the Church, whose authors, from whom they derive their name, lived long after the apostles'[64].

St. Augustine then used the analogy of profane literature: 'Do we not see', he says, 'in profane literature that there are well-known authors under whose names many things have been published after their time which have been rejected, either from inconsistency with their ascertained writings or from their not having been known in the lifetime of the authors, so as to be handed down with the confirmatory statement of the authors themselves, or of their friends?'[65] Thus St. Augustine held clearly that the authenticity of some doubtful books must be established by internal as well as by external criteria. Either their language, style, or contents can be compared with those of the authentic books, and judged on that score, or else they must be judged on traditional grounds. As an example, he quoted a book ostensibly published by Hippocrates, which was subsequently rejected as false by the physicians, on the grounds that a comparison with the authenticated writings of Hippocrates showed them to be forgeries, certain similarities notwithstanding. Moreover, the book in question was not known at the time when his other works were published.

There remains the question how we can be so certain of the authenticity of what are believed to have been Hippocrates' genuine works. St. Augustine is quite clear on this point: 'For a succession of testimonies to the books from the time of Hippocrates to the present day makes it unreasonable either now or hereafter to have any doubt on the subject. How do we know the authorship of the works of Plato, Aristotle, Cicero, Varro, and other similar writers, but by the unbroken chain of evidence? So also with the numerous commentaries on the ecclesiastical books, which have no canonical authority, and yet show a desire for usefulness and a spirit of inquiry. How is the authorship ascertained in each case, except by the author's having brought his work to public notice as much as

[64] ib. XXXIII, 6.
[65] ib.

possible in his own lifetime, and, by the transmission of the information from one to another in continuous order, the belief becoming more certain as it becomes more general, up to our own day; so that when we are questioned as to the authorship of any book, we have no difficulty in answering? But why speak of old books? Take the books now before us: should anyone, after some years, deny that this book was written by me, or that Faustus' was written by him, where is evidence for the fact to be found but in the information possessed by some at the present time, and transmitted by them through successive generations even to distant times?' Therefore he concluded: 'From all this it follows that no one who has not yielded to the malicious and deceitful suggestions of lying devils, can be so blinded by passion as to deny the ability of the Church of the Apostles—a community of brethren as numerous as they were faithful—to transmit their writings unaltered to posterity, as the original seats of the Apostles have been occupied by a continuous succession of bishops to the present day, especially when we are accustomed to see this happen in the case of ordinary writings both in the Church and out of it'[66].

From these quotations we can see clearly that St. Augustine was firmly convinced that in Christ's Church, the apostles are the authentic witnesses of Christ. Whatever can be traced back to them is authoritative, and hence canonical. Nothing was accepted by the old Christian Church unless it agreed with the evidence of the apostles. Even Paul had to receive apostolic approbation before his testimony was accepted as being inspired by Christ. Paul's case convinced St. Augustine of the great care and circumspection with which the early Church treated such matters. Hence every Book that was written or accepted by the apostles, has divine authority.

But who can guarantee that the early Church did, in fact, approve certain Books? The answer is much the same as in judging a work of literature: every community transmits its tradition by means of an unbroken succession of accredited men. Similarly with Christ's Church. St. Augustine never associated this tradition with the infallibility of the magisterium of the Church, rather did he consider that the uninterrupted succession of apostolic bishops was in itself proof that the Christian community had been continuous since the Apostles. The transmission of the traditions of the Books of

[66] ib.

the New Testament is due to the same kind of love and respect which every philosophical school shows towards its master. Hence all pseudo-epigraphic Books are rejected on internal and external grounds. Every book which is open to dispute is held up against what is indisputable, and every book lacking a tradition is rejected out of hand, since the community of true Christians had not observed it from olden times.

We can now summarise St. Augustine's attitude to canonicity, as follows:

1. Those who claim, like Diekamp[67], that, according to Catholic doctrine, the infallible magisterium of the Church is the infallible guarantee of the divine inspiration and canonicity of the Holy Scriptures, cannot cite St. Augustine in their support. Nor was Nebreda right to suggest that St. Augustine considered Church authority the primary factor in transmitting the *criteria canonicitatis*. Moreover we cannot even agree with Costello when he reversed the order, if by Church authority he meant *ecclesia docens*.

2. True, St. Augustine fully accepted what Grosheide has called the formal tradition, for[68], he recognised this service of the Church on the basis of Romans 3:2 where St. Paul remarks that the oracles of God were committed to the Church. But St. Augustine considered this tradition to be purely formal, to the extent that he compared the handing on of Church tradition to the handing on of great works in profane literature. Still, he held that what could be said of profane literature was true *a fortiori* of the Church, since the apostolic Church as the faithful, numerous, and unanimous community of brothers, had the best possible chance of handing on Holy Scripture to successive generations, the more so since the established succession of bishops was a guarantee of its unbroken transmission from the time of the apostles. And Warfield remarked justly that a gradual difference does not prove a difference of type, so that what matters is 'the validity of the testimony of the Church, not of the dogmatic authority of the Church'. Warfield also wrote that 'Augustine's appeal to the Church as authenticating the Scriptures is to the Church as a witness, not as an authorizer[69].

3. Despite its purely formal nature, this tradition, according to

[67] F. Diekamp, *Katholische Dogmatik*, Munster. 1930, I[6], p. 42 ff.
[68] F. W. Grosheide, *Algemene Canoniek*, Amsterdam 1935, p. 143 ff.
[69] op. cit., p. 196, 199.

which the Church is no more than the servant of the Word of God, and as such cannot canonise any writings, nevertheless has a material content, received originally by its first witnesses. As regards the Old Testament according to the Hebrew canon, the God-fearing people of Israel knew how to tell true books from false. God's people could clearly distinguish between what was written by divine inspiration and was therefore endowed with religious authority and what was written by human diligence. Moreover Scripture itself was used as a yardstick, inasmuch as all sacred writings have an inner and mutual harmony[70]. Also, St. Augustine was wont to point out that the canonicity of the Law, the Prophets, and the Psalms were vouchsafed by Christ Himself. As for the New Testament, its authority is guaranteed by the apostolic authority. Only what is accepted by apostolic choice is handed on by the Church.

This consistent approach is partially impaired by the unjustified acceptance of the Septuagint as a translation of the Old Testament inspired by the Holy Spirit. From its alleged origins, St. Augustine assumed that those parts of the Septuagint which were not found in the Hebrew canon were the work of the Spirit Himself. However, he never claimed that these parts were therefore to be considered canonical, and whenever he quoted them, with some hesitation, he took as the criterion of their canonicity their Church usage since the time of the apostles. In this criterion, St. Augustine obviously deviated from his own precepts for judging the canonicity of the Old and New Testaments, and thus laid the foundations for the later views of the Catholic Church. Still we have justly called this approach a partial deviation, since, on quite a few occasions, he cited apostolic approval of the Septuagint as the final criterion of its canonicity.

4. Although we have summed up St. Augustine's main position, we cannot but point out that he was not entirely unaware of the fact that 'this formal tradition based on a succession of reliable witnesses' was not by any means as unanimous and harmonious as his theory postulated. This was particularly true of those parts of the Septuagint not contained in the Hebrew canon, on which the witnesses were far from being agreed. On one occasion, St. Augustine himself made a remark to the effect that the Eastern and Western

[70] Note the past tense. Canonical questions cannot be decided by means of the *Testimonium Spiritus Sancti.*

Churches sometimes handed on different traditions about the books of the New Testament. This fact faced him with a difficulty which even later theologians were unable to solve.[71] In his sole discussion of this problem—in 397—he suggested the following rule: 'In regard to the canonical Scriptures, we must follow the judgment of the greater number of Catholic Churches, and among these, of course, a high place must be given to such as have been thought worthy to be the seat of an apostle and to receive epistles. Accordingly, among the canonical Scriptures we shall judge according to the following standard: To prefer those that are received by all the Catholic Churches to those which some do not receive. Among those again, which are not received by all, we shall prefer such as have the sanction of the greater number and those of greater authority, to such as are held by the smaller number and those of less authority. If, however, we shall find that some books are held by the greater number of Churches, and others by the Churches of greater authority (though this is not a very likely thing to happen) I think, that in such a case the authority on the two sides is to be looked upon as equal'[72]. Now, though we must not attach too much importance to this rule which was put forward on only one occasion, the mere fact that it was put forward at all is significant. On the one hand it shows once again that St. Augustine recognised no infallible magisterium of the Church which could solve such problems[73], and on the other hand it indicates that St. Augustine's belief in the harmonious unity of the Holy Scriptures, in the gift of discrimination vested in God's chosen people, in apostolic authority, and in the uninterrupted succession of the formal tradition, did not help him to overcome the concrete difficulties. But which of us, familiar with subsequent polemics on the subject of the acceptance and conclusion of the canon and the complicated problems they involved, would hold that against him? For my part, I have become increasingly convinced that St. Augustine has set us on the right road in the four ways I have shown, and that the inadequacy of this method in the concrete situation of his time was due mainly to the fact that the

[71] See Herman Ridderbos, *Heilsgeschiedenis en Heilige Schrift*, Kampen 1955.

[72] De doctrina christiana II, 12.

[73] The list of Canonical books adopted by the Councils of Hippo and Carthage was no more than a recommendation to overseas bishops, and applied, in any case, to a restricted field and liturgical usage alone. (See Leipoldt, op. cit., p. 230.)

Church herself had left the correct path, and had broken the chain of traditions for a variety of reasons[74].

2. *Motive or ground?*

We have seen that since the days of the Reformation, all discussions of St. Augustine's approach to the Word have been dominated by his famous dictum: 'For my part, I should not believe the gospel except as moved by the authority of the Church'. To understand this statement, we must remember its date (about 397) and its context. St. Augustine began with the declaration that he, for his part, could not inveigh against the Manicheans, as he himself had been entangled in their errors for nine years. 'Let those treat you angrily', he declared, 'who had never been led astray in the same way that they see that you are. For my part, I'who, after much and long-continued bewilderment, attained at last to the discovery of the simple truth; who, unhappy that I was, barely succeeded by the help of the Lord, in refuting the vain notions of my mind, gathered from theories and false doctrines of various kind; who so late sought the cure of my mental obscuration, in compliance with the call and the tender persuasion of the all-merciful Physician; who long mourned, till the immutable and inviolable Substance vouchsafed to convince me inwardly of Himself, in resounding of the sacred books—I can on no account treat you angrily'[75]. Thus he ascribes his conversion, in full agreement with his account in the Confessions[76], to the working of Christ, the Physician, who called and tenderly invited; to the immutable and inviolable Substance[77], who evoked in him the inner conviction through the working of the Holy Scriptures. The Church is not mentioned in this context. A firm, inner, and true conviction is a matter between God, the merciful Physician Christ, the Word of God and man's inner life[78].

Next he said—and this is completely overlooked in moxt explanations of his well-known words—: 'Let neither of us assert that

[74] See Herman Ridderbos, op. cit. p. 86 ff.; W. C. van Unnik, *Het kort geleden ontdekte 'Evangelie der Waarheid' en het Nieuwe Testament*, Mededelingen der Koninklijke Nederlandse Akademie, New Series, Part 17. No. 3, 1954.
[75] Contra epistulam Manichaei, quam vocant Fundamenti 3, 4.
[76] Both Books date from the same period.
[77] This reference to God helps to date the passage.
[78] Contra epist. Man. 4.

he has found truth; let us seek it as if it were unknown to us both'. Truth can only be found in the absence of any rash assumption that it has already been found and ascertained. Therefore St. Augustine asked the Manicheans to bring forward in all matters relating to salvation only the clear arguments of reason. This was an entirely legitimate demand since it was the pretension of the Manicheans that they could prove all their teachings by reason, whereas the Catholics made faith the basis of true understanding.

Hence St. Augustine acted as the spokesman of the Catholics. As such, he pointed out that he distinguished between two groups in the Catholic Church. On one side are a few spiritual men who attain in this life the purest wisdom without any uncertainty. On the other side are a multitude of men, who derive their entire security not from acuteness of intellect, but from simplicity of faith. Siding with the latter, he showed how many things keep him in the bosom of the Catholic Church, as a Catholic Christian who acts and speaks for those who do not know the truth but merely believe[79]. 'The consent of peoples and nations keeps me in the Church; so does her authority, inaugurated by miracles, nourished in hope, enlarged by love, established by age. The succession of priests keeps me, beginning from the very seat of the Apostle Peter down to the present episcopate. And so, lastly, does the name itself of Catholic, which, not without reason, amid so many heresies, the Church has still retained. Such in number and importance are the precious ties belonging to the Christian name which keep a believer in the Catholic Church, as it is right they should, though from the slowness of our understanding, or the small attainment of our life, the truth may not yet fully disclose itself'. And to the Manicheans he said: 'You again have none of those things to attract or retain me, and your only claim is to teach the truth. Now if the truth is so clearly proved as to leave no doubt, it must be set before all the things which keep me in the Catholic Church; but if there is only a promise without any fulfilment, no one shall move me from the

[79] T. van Bavel, *Revue d'histoire ecclésiastique* 1956, p. 946, and W. F. Dankbaar, *Nedl. Theol. Tijdschrift* 1956, p. 54 have remarked that St. Augustine, though one of the spiritual men, counted himself at one with simple Christians. Bavel quotes two texts which clearly illustrate this point. But the first quotation (in Epist. Joannis Tract. 98, 6) dates from 418 or a little later, while the second dates from 416. During the interval the contrast on which we have remarked had disappeared; not so, however, when he wrote his anti-Manichean books.

faith to which Christian ties, so many and so strong, bind me'[80].

This preamble is of fundamental importance for the understanding of what follows. In it, St. Augustine, far from speaking about himself, put himself in the shoes of one who does not yet understand the truth, but acts on faith and authority alone. Moreover, the oppositions on which the argument is based, are clear evidence of the philosophical world in which he still moved. We refer to the distinction between the small group of spiritual men and the multitude, and particularly of the criterion whereby this distinction is made. Equally important is the distinction between blind faith based on Scriptural authority alone, and understanding of truth and wisdom, a distinction which did not yet involve the appreciation of the Biblical meaning of faith and which least reflects St. Augustine's radical change of outlook during that very year, i.e. the year in which he wrote *De diversis quaestionibus ad Simplicianum*[81]. It redounds greatly to St. Augustine's credit that he honestly confessed his preference for the clear demonstration of truth to Church adherence based on faith alone.

At the start of his argument against the Manicheans, he therefore held them strictly to their promise of giving knowledge of truth without demanding faith. For that purpose he examined their Book of Fundaments, and quoted its first sentence: 'Manicheaus, an apostle of Jesus Christ, by the appointment of God the Father'. He at once turned on his opponents, saying: 'I do not believe Manichaeus to be an apostle of Christ. Who then is this Manicheaus? You will reply, An apostle of Christ. I do not believe it. Now you are at a loss what to say or do; for you promised to give knowledge of the truth, and here you are forcing me to believe what I have no knowledge of. Perhaps you will read the Gospel to me and will attempt to find there a testimony to Manichaeus. But should you meet with a person not yet believing the Gospel, how would you reply to him were he to say, I do not believe?' And it is, as the spokesman of those who remain within the Catholic Church by reliance on authority alone, that St. Augustine went on to say: 'For my part, I should not believe the Gospel except as moved by the authority of the Catholic Church. So when those on whose authority I have consented to

[80] ib. 5.

[81] A. D. R. Polman: *De praedestinatieleer van Augustinus, Thomas van Aquino en Calvijn* 1936, p. 49 ff.

believe in the Gospel tell me not to believe in Manichaeus, how can I but consent? Take your choice. If you say, Believe the Catholics: their advice to me is to put no faith in you; so that believing them I am precluded from believing you;—If you say, Do not believe the Catholics: you cannot fairly use the Gospel in bringing me to faith in Manichaeus; for it was on the testimony of the Catholics that I believed the Gospel;—Again if you say, You were right in believing the Catholics when they praised the Gospel, but wrong in believing their condemnation of Manichaeus: do you think me such a fool as to believe or not to believe as I like or dislike, without any reason? It is therefore the fairest and the safest plan for me, having in one instance put faith in the Catholics, not to go over to you, till, instead of bidding me believe, you make me understand something in the clearest and most satisfactory manner. To convince me, then, you must find proof elsewhere than in the Gospel. If you keep to the Gospel, I will keep to those who led me to believe the Gospel, and in obedience to them I can never believe you. Then, should you succeed in finding in the Gospel an incontrovertible testimony to the apostleship of Manichaeus, you will weaken my regard for the authority of the Catholics; and the effect of that will be that I shall no longer be able to believe the Gospel either, for it was through the Catholics that I got my faith in it; and so, whatever you bring from the Gospel will no longer have any weight with me. Thus, supposing no clear proof of the apostleship of Manichaeus to be found in the Gospel, I will believe the Catholics rather than you. Again, supposing you to find some passage clearly in favour of Manichaeus, I will believe neither them nor you: not them, for they deceived me about you: nor you, for you quote to me that Scripture which I believed on the authority of those deceivers'[82]. Thus St. Augustine remained quite consistent, since to one who believes in the Gospel on the authority of the Catholic Church alone, dependence on the Church is so complete that faith cannot remain faith outside that authority. Should Church authority fail, the whole framework comes tumbling down, for authority is vested in the Church alone, and there is no personal tie with the Scriptures, and no firm inner conviction kindled by God in man's heart through response to the Scriptures. Hence the Reformers' claim that St. Augustine's imperfect tense should, in fact, have been rendered by the pluperfect—

[82] ib. 6.

even though perhaps technically correct in view of St. Augustine's idiom—must definitely be rejected as an explanation of St. Augustine's real meaning. The same is true of Dr. A. Kuyper's interpretation in his Encyclopedia (see p. 174), which was probably based on De Moor's well-known commentary[83], and, in any case, not on the text itself. The entire tenor of St. Augustine's argument leaves no doubt that he could not possibly have spoken of himself. Nörregaard rightly pointed out that the Confessions, which were written at the same time, contain no such views, either in the Prologue (I, 1–5), where he dealt with the question of how man finds God and in which the Church is only mentioned in passing, or in the account of his own conversion. In Rome and Milan he finished up by questioning almost everything, and even threatened to fall prey to scepticism. For a moment he even thought of giving up his search for a personal conviction altogether and of simply submitting to the authority of the Church. However, he bethought himself in time. Not the Church, but Neoplatonism, not the Gospel, but philosophy led St. Augustine to intellectual certainty. Afterwards the achieved complete surrender of his heart and will by consulting the Bible (notably Paul, whom he now read with utterly different eyes) and by his experience in a garden of Milan where he heard the voice of a singing child as the voice of God, and the words of the song as a message from Heaven. For this reason, it is absolutely impossible that he should have proclaimed his belief in the Gospel on Church authority alone[84].

But by simply stating that the text in question does not offer a

[83] De Moor. Commentarius perpetuus 1761, p. 160.

[84] Nörregaard. *Drei Augustin Worte*, Studien der Luther Akademie, No. 8, Gütersloh 1939, p. 6 ff., 14 ff. It was not until some years after writing the Dutch original that I came across this publication and realised that, as early as 1934, Nörregaard had arrived at the same conclusions, and by the same argument. This is how Nörregaard put it:

1. It (St. Augustine's statement) is neither a dogmatic nor a religio-psychological proposition, but a single statement within a polemic argument.

2. 'Ego' is not Augustine, but the authority-bound Catholic, who is coupled with a Manichean in a fictitious dialogue. The statement is therefore not universal, but particular.

3. Even as it stands, it expresses 'rational' rather than 'blind' faith in authority. Even the simplest of Christians can cite good reasons why he believes in Church authority.

4. And finally, St. Augustine, in that very context, stresses that there is, in fact, a far deeper interpretation of Christianity, which he leaves out of the

satisfactory solution of the problem, we have done little towards answering it. It is even doubtful whether, as Bavel observed[85], this problem which was, in fact, thrown up by later theological discussions, can ever be solved finally by reference to St. Augustine's writings, in which the problem was never posed in these terms. Hence it would be unfair to saddle him with our dilemma, and to deduce a particular answer from a number of scattered statements.

Bearing this fact fully in mind, we venture to make the following observations:

1. From the beginning of the fifth century, St. Augustine held, at all events, that there was an intimate relationship between the Word of God, the Church, and the faithful. By the Word of God, he meant, first and foremost, the Holy Scriptures, which are communicated to the faithful by Church lessons and sermons and to some by personal reading. To him the Church was not an objective and impersonal entity, not, above all, the sacramental apparatus, nor the Church hierarchy, nor the empirical Church, but the bride of Christ, in whose close garden (Song of Songs 4:12–13) the saints, the true believers in Christ, and the children of promise, live in God's City, and form a royal priesthood[86]. The faithful were subsequently divided into spiritual and carnal men, the former changing from an intellectual élite, into the saints, who in faith, hope and charity live out the sum of the law, and the latter becoming the dull, inert and lazy Christians (though not the chaff), who must still be fed with milk[87].

2. St. Augustine held that God's Word was self-evident, since it

discussion, simply because that interpretation is reached by only a few. For Christianity can be represented as a *sincerissima sapientia,* so that it may be known beyond all doubt, even though this knowledge may only be piecemeal, as ordinary mortals never attain perfection. Not even many of the spiritual men attain this state. Hence, St. Augustine's statement was never meant to have the scope, often attributed to it, and it in no way contradicts his description in the Confessions of his conversion to Christianity, nor his religio-philosophic approach in the Prologue. 'It was no more than an aside' (p. 181 ff.).

It may be permissible to quote what Löhrer *(Der Glaubensbegriff des hl. Augustins in seinen ersten Schriften bis zu den Confessiones,* 1953, p. II) had to say in similar circumstances: 'Since we have arrived at our view independently of N., the agreement between our interpretations, may be considered a confirmation of its validity'. See also Warfield's contribution (mentioned above) which arrives as the same result, though in a different way (p. 203).

[85] op. cit., p. 946.

[86] F. Hoffmann *Der Kirchenbegriff des hl. Augustinus* 1933, p. 265 ff.

[87] Cf. Löhrer op. cit. p. 216 ff.

was divinely inspired[88]. Hence he told Faustus, that 'there is a distinct boundary line separating all productions subsequent to apostolic times from the authoritative canonical books of the Old and the New Testaments. The authority of these books has come down to us from the apostles through the succession of bishops and the extension of the Church, and from a position of lofty supremacy claims the submission of every faithful and pious mind. Scripture has a sacredness peculiar to itself and in consequence of this distinctive peculiarity of these sacred writings we are bound to receive as true whatever the canon shows to have been said by even one prophet or evangelist'[89]. In support of this argument, he cited the inner harmony of all the writings included in the Bible[90], but especially the evidence provided by Scripture itself in that it constantly fulfils its predictions and promises. 'The established authority of Scripture', he wrote, 'must outweigh every other; for it derives new confirmation from the progress of events which happen, as Scripture proves, in fulfilment of the predictions made so long before their occurrence'[91]. This was one of St. Augustine's favourite arguments, which he used and amplified countless times. He was firmly convinced that the Scriptures provide their own evidence, for even the blind can see that the things foretold in them are being fulfilled[92]. 'Let us suppose', he told Faustus, 'a conversation with a heathen: If we say to him, Believe in Christ, for He is God, and, on his asking for evidence, produce the authority of the prophets, if he says that he does not believe the prophets, we can prove the truth of the prophets from the actual fulfilment of their prophecies. He could scarcely be ignorant of the persecutions suffered by the early Christians from the kings of this world; or if he was ignorant, he could be informed from history and the records of imperial laws. But this is what we find foretold long ago by the prophet, saying, "Why do the heathen rage, and the people imagine a vain thing? The kings of the earth set themselves, and the princes take counsel together against the Lord and against his Christ". The rest of the Psalm shows that this is not said of David. For what follows might convince the most stubborn

[88] Cf. H. Lorenz *Die Wissenschaftslehre Augustinus*, Zeitschr. f. Kirchengeschichte 1955–56, p. 218.
[89] Contra Faustum XI, 5.
[90] ib. XI, 6.
[91] Contra Faustum, XIII, 5.
[92] Art. 5 of the Confessio Belgica.

unbeliever: The Lord said unto me, Thou art my Son. Ask of me and I will give Thee the heathen for thine inheritance, and the ends of the earth for Thy possession[93]. This never happened to the Jews, but is now plainly fulfilled in the subjection of all nations in the name of Christ. This and many similar prophecies would surely impress the mind of the inquirer. He would see these very kings of the earth now happily subdued by Christ, and all nations serving Him; and he would hear the words of the Psalm in which this was so long before predicted: "All the kings of the earth shall bow down to Him, all nations shall serve Him"[94]. Hearing these prophecies and seeing their actual fulfilment, I need not say that he would be affected; for we know by experience how the hearts of believers are confirmed by seeing ancient predictions now receiving their accomplishment'[95]. He then gave some further examples and ended with the conclusion: 'After considering these instances of the fulfilment of prophecy about kings and people acting as persecutors, and then becoming believers, about the destruction of idols, about the blindness of the Jews, about their testimony to the writings which they have preserved, about the folly of heretics, about the dignity of the Church of true and genuine Christians, the inquirer would most reasonably receive the testimony of these prophets of the divinity of Christ. No doubt, if we were to begin by urging him to believe prophecies yet unfulfilled, he might justly answer, What have I to do with these prophets of whose truth I have no evidence? But in view of the manifest accomplishment of so many remarkable predictions, no candid person would despise either the things which were thought worthy of being predicted in those early times with so much solemnity, or those who made the predictions. To none can we trust more safely, as regards either events long past or those still future, than to men, whose words are supported by the evidence of so many notable predictions having been fulfilled[96]. And so is our belief determined by the declarations of Scripture, resting as they do on foundations of the strongest and surest evidence'[97].

3. Side by side with this self-evidence of Scripture, there is the evidence of the Church. Particularly in his apologetic writings,

[93] Ps. 2:7, 8.
[94] Ps. 72:10.
[95] Contra Faustum, XIII, 7.
[96] ib. XIII, 14.
[97] ib. XXVI, 3.

St. Augustine strongly emphasised the antiquity, sacredness and catholicity of the Church, which furnishes conclusive evidence of the truth of Scripture[98]. 'Do you think', he asked in his *De utilitate credendi*, 'that little has been done for the benefit of men, that not some few learned men maintain by argument, but also an unlearned crowd of males and females in so many and different nations both believe and set forth, that we are to worship as God nothing of earth, nothing of fire, nothing lastly which comes into contact with the senses of the body, but that we are to seek to approach Him by the understanding only? That chastity is carried even unto the contempt of marriage and family; that patience even unto the setting light by crosses and flames; that liberality even unto the distribution of estates unto the poor; that, lastly, the contempt of this whole world even unto the desire of death? This has been brought to pass by the divine Providence, through the prophecies of the Prophets, through the manhood and teaching of Christ, through the journeys of the Apostles, through the insults, crosses, blood of the Martyrs, through the praiseworthy life of the Saints, and, in all these, according as times were seasonable, through miracles worthy of so great matters and virtues. When therefore we see so great help of God, so great progress and fruit, shall we doubt to hide ourselves in the bosom of that Church, which even unto the confession of the human race from the apostolic chair through successions of bishops has held the summit of authority. To be unwilling to grant to her the first place, is either surely the height of impiety, or is headlong arrogance'[99]. And in his very interesting work *De fide rerum quae non videntur*, he writes: 'Even if there went before no testimonies concerning Christ and his Church, whom ought it not to move unto belief, that the divine brightness has on a sudden shone on the human race, when we see the one true God invoked by all? And that this has been brought to pass by One Man, by man mocked, seized, bound, scourged, smitten with the palms of the hand, reviled, crucified, slain; His disciples, for whom He chose common men, and unlearned, and fishermen, and publicans, that by their means His teaching might be set forth, proclaiming His resurrection, His ascension, which they asserted that they had seen, and being filled with the Holy Ghost, sounded forth this gospel in all tongues. And of them

[98] Löhrer, p. 147 ff.
[99] ib. 35.

who heard them, part believing, part, believing not, fiercely withstood them who preached. Thus while they were faithful even unto death for the truth, strove not by returning evil, but by enduring, overcame not by killing, but by dying: thus was the world changed unto this religion, thus unto this gospel were the hearts of mortals turned, of men and women, of small and great, of learned and unlearned, of wise and foolish, of mighty and weak, of noble and ignoble, of high and low, and throughout all nations the Church shed abroad so increased, that even against the Catholic faith itself there arise not any perverse sect, any kind of error, which is found to oppose itself to Christian truth, as that it affect not and go not about to glory in the name of Christ. How would the Crucified have availed so greatly, had He not been God that took upon Him Man, even if He had through the Prophet foretold no such things to come? But when now this so great mystery of godliness has had its prophets and heralds going before, by whose divine voices it was before proclaimed; and when it has come in such manner as it was afore proclaimed, who is there so mad as to assert that the Apostles lied concerning Christ? Who therefore, unless blinded by amazing madness, or hard and steeled by amazing obstinacy, would be unwilling to put faith in the sacred Scriptures, which have foretold the faith of the whole world?'[100] Both quotations show clearly how closely St. Augustine thought Church and Scripture were intertwined. Scripture testifies to the truth of the Church and the Church in her turn testifies to the truth of Scripture. The two testimonies are never discordant, nor are they balanced against each other. Questions as to whether the Church is superior, equal or inferior to Scripture were never even raised by St. Augustine. Both work in harmony. The Words of God are entrusted to the Church, so that from her hands we may safely receive the divine books and submit to their authority. As Dankbaar said, she puts the truth of the Scriptures beyond all doubt, makes plain their obscure passages and fills in their gaps[101]. At the same time, the Church receives from the Scriptures the clear testimony of her authority, so that she becomes the fulfilment of God's promises and Christ's work as Saviour. Objective criteria such as the fulfilment of the prophecies, conversion of the nations by Christ, the blood of the martyrs, and the lives

[100] ib. 10.
[101] Dankbaar op. cit., p. 51.

of the saints, vouchsafe the truth of both Scripture and the Church.

4. Of the two groups of believers, the carnal men will assent to the statement: For my part, I should not believe the Gospel except as moved by the authority of the Church. Not so the spiritual men, who both personally and also in permanent communion with one another, have a living bond with the Word of God, established by the Holy Ghost dwelling within them. They are re-born by the powerful effects of the spoken Word, they rest in the promises of this Word, preserve it in good faith, judge the spoken Word by it and make its service bear fruit by prayer and supplication. Thus they say: 'O Lord, is not this Thy Scripture true, since Thou art true, and being Truth hast set it forth? And Thou repliest unto me, for Thou art my God, and with strong voice tellest unto Thy servant in his inner ear, O man, that which My Scripture says, I say.[102] Verily within me, within the chamber of my thought, Truth, without the organs of voice and tongue, without the sound of syllables, would say, He (Moses in the Scripture) speaks the truth and I, forthwith assured of it, confidently would say, Thou speakest the truth'[103]. And at the same time the authority of the Church, above all as the communion of the saints who are the constant evidence of the power and truthfulness of the Word of God, is a firm support and strong motive for keeping faith with God's Word. But those of firm faith will say with St. Augustine: 'We ought to have no fears, even if as yet the Lord has made none of His promises good. Lo! let us henceforth think thus; He has promised us every thing; He has not yet given us possession of any thing; He is a responsable Promiser, a faithful Paymaster'[104].

3. *The Word of God and the* regula fidei.

The problem of God's Word and the rule of faith is best approached with a remark by Kattenbusch in the very readable chapter of his book dealing with St. Augustine and the Symbol. In it, Kattenbusch shows that St. Augustine used the term *regula fidei* in three different

[102] Confess. XIII, 44.

[103] ib. XI, 5. This is one of the passages referred to by J. Pannier (*Le témoignage du Saint Esprit,* Paris 1893) when he tries to prove that St. Augustine cited the testimony of the Spirit in confirmation of the authority of Scripture.

[104] Enarr. in Ps. 39, 2. See also Chapt. VI, and especially p. 214 ff.

senses: 1) to refer to Holy Scripture 2) to refer to the apostolic symbol and 3) to refer to the basic ideas of Holy Writ[105].

As regards 1), we have been unable to find any direct references in St. Augustine's writings to the effect that he fully equated Scripture with the rule of faith, in the way that, for instance, such Fathers of the Church as Clement Alexandrinus, Athanasius, Origen, Chrysostom, and Hilary of Poitiers did[106]. True, there are some passages in which he called Scripture the 'rule of truth'[107], and others where the whole context would lead one to suppose that he must have considered the Sacred Writings the rule of faith, as well, for instance in the passage mentioned by Kattenbusch, of St. Augustine's *De nuptiis et concupiscentia*. In it, St. Augustine countered the Pelagians' denial of original sin by quoting Romans 5:12, asserting that the acceptance of the doctrine of original sin was contained in the oldest and unvarying rule of the Catholic faith[108]. This reference cannot have been to anything but the Holy Scriptures. In another of his anti-Pelagian books, he remarked: 'You see with what confidence this great man (Cyprian) expresses himself after the ancient and undoubted rule of faith'[109]. If we read the quotations in that book[110] together with Cyprian's epistle to Fidus[111] from which they were taken, we see that the ancient and undoubted rule of faith could only have referred to Scripture, since Cyprian bases his entire argument on God's Word. Thus when Fidus asked whether the children of the New Covenant were to be baptized on the eighth day on which those of the Old Covenant were circumcised, or immediately after birth, St. Cyprian's reply was taken entirely from Scripture[112]; viz. from Luke 9:56, Tit. 1:15 and Acts 10:28.

This reference to Scripture as the rule of truth or the rule of faith, was, in fact, quite natural for St. Augustine, since he took the view that the things plainly laid down in the Scriptures contained everything relevant to faith and morals[113]. He even went so far as to

[105] op. cit., p. 417.
[106] See Kunze op. cit. for a full discussion.
[107] Most particularly in Sermo 30, 2.
[108] De nuptiis et concupiscentia I, 1.
[109] De peccatorum meritis et remissione III, 11.
[110] ib. 10.
[111] Cyprian's epistle 64.
[112] ib. 3.
[113] De doctrina christiana II, 14.

subscribe to Paul's curse on all those who, concerning Christ or His Church or any matter whatsoever which is connected with faith and life preach any gospel outside the lawful and evangelical Scriptures[114]. And we do him wrong, if we take it that Scripture, because of its obscurity, was to him the *source*, and the symbol the *rule* of faith for, according to St. Augustine, Scripture was the rule of faith and truth precisely because of the plain passages. Kunze held this to be true of St. Augustine's predecessors, but not of St. Augustine himself[115], though the references he quotes do not bear him out[116], inasmuch as they were all based on the plain revelation of Scriptures, to which St. Augustine constantly appealed. All those who apply the distinctions: source vs. rule, or remote vs. nearest rule use a later vocabulary of which St. Augustine himself was ignorant.

We must, however, agree that St. Augustine usually applied the term 'rule of faith' to the apostolic symbol[117]. He was never concerned with the origin of that symbol[118], but simply declared that it was derived from the Holy Scriptures. Thus he told a group of catechumens in a sermon on the symbol, to receive the rule of faith which is called the symbol. 'The words expressed in the symbol, are found throughout the divine Scriptures whence they are collected so that the memories of the indolent be not too heavily taxed, and so that every man be able to state and to keep what he believes'[119]. In another sermon to the catechumens, he said that whatever is heard in the symbol, is contained in the divine words of the Holy Scriptures, but since, brought together thus and given that form, it may not be written in words, God's promise is expressed by His prophet as: "Behold, the days come, saith the Lord, that I will make a new covenant in their inward parts and write it in their hearts"[120]. And St. Augustine went on to say that this writing was the symbol which

[114] Contra litteras Petiliani III, 7.
[115] op. cit., p. 292.
[116] viz. De symbolo ad catechumenos 2, 3; De fide et symbolo 19, 20.
[117] Tractatus in Joannis evangelium 98, 7; De fide et operibus II, Sermo 186, 2; 213, 1; 362, 7; Epistula 193, 11. Cf. C. P. Caspari, *Quellen zur Geschichte des Taufsymbols und der Glaubensregel*, Christiania 1869, II, p. 264, 265. Note 1., and particularly Kattenbusch, op. cit. II, p. 403–421.
[118] Caspari is wrong to see indirect proof in St. Augustine's writings, that he accepted the legend which arose in his time of the apostolic origin of the symbol (op. cit. II, p. 99).
[119] De symbolo ad catechumenos 1.
[120] Jeremiah 31:31.

the Scriptures and Church sermons had impressed upon the catechumens[121]. In another sermon discussing the symbol, St. Augustine quoted the apostle's saying: "If thou shalt confess with thy mouth the Lord Jesus, and shalt believe in thine heart that God hath raised him from the dead, thou shalt be saved. For with the heart man believeth unto righteousness, and with the mouth confession is made unto salvation"[122]. The symbol thus inculcates true faith and hence leads to salvation. 'Even what you will shortly receive to store up in your memory and to confess with your mouth, is not new or unknown to you. For you are accustomed to hear these things, since they are found in many ways in the Holy Scriptures and in our sermons. But they must be handed to you in condensed form and, in fixed order, so that your faith be well-founded, your confession be prepared and your memory be not burdened'[123]. For that very reason he could say in another sermon that everything which we hold from the rule of faith is held from truth (which, in that context, was Scripture)[124]. And on advising on the interpretation of an obscure Scriptural passage, he counselled: 'Let the reader consult the rule of faith which he has gathered from the plainer passages and from the authority of the Church'[125].

This stressing of the plain passages is of the utmost importance to our investigation, for they show that St. Augustine considered the apostolic symbol, i.e. the rule of faith, as a *verbum abbreviatum*, a short summary of what is clear in the Scriptures. Hence, those who confess the symbol, confess God's Words briefly. In all St. Augustine general comments on the symbol[126], he always emphasised that it was taken, part and parcel, from the Scriptures, and nowhere is there even a hint that the *regula fidei* is based, not on God's written Word, but on the active faith of the Church, as Hoffmann has asserted[127].

[121] Sermo 212, 2.
[122] Rom. 10:9, 10.
[123] Sermo 214, 1.
[124] Sermo 362, 7.
[125] De doctrina Christiani III, 2. Remigius Storf has given a 'truly' Roman Catholic translation of the original: *Consulat regulam fidei quam de Scripturarum planioribus locis et Ecclesiae auctoritate percepit*, when he rendered it as: Let him consult the plainer passages of the Scriptures or the rule of faith received from Church *doctrinal* authority. *Die Christliche Lehre* in *Bibl. der Kirchenväter*, p. 128 (my italics).
[126] E.G. De fide et symbolo; De agone Christiana, Enchiridion.
[127] op. cit., p. 187.

This is not the place to discuss whether Kattenbusch is right to claim that St. Ambrose, St. Vincent, and with them the Western Church in general, held the Holy Scriptures and the apostolic symbol to exist *side by side*, each having its proper authority and each being independent. We can, however, agree with him when he says that St. Augustine did not share that opinion; and that he looked upon the symbol as being derived entirely from the investigation of Scripture[128]. Hence we find it strange that Harnack should say that 'the old, though at the time unconscious, opposition between symbol and Scripture was acerbated by St. Augustine, who did much to obscure the relationship between Scripture and the symbol, even though he made so great a contribution to familiarising the Church with the Scriptures'[129].

Precisely because St. Augustine held the apostolic symbol to be no more than a summary of the plainer Scriptural texts, could he enjoin his congregation not to interpret the obscure texts in a way that would contradict the symbol. This was never said of the plain texts themselves, and hence his rule for interpreting the obscure parts of Scripture is no more than a modification of his general rule of explaining the obscure places by the plain[130].

It is in this light that we must also view the text which Hoffmann has cited as the main evidence for his approach[131], viz. a quotation from a chapter of the incomplete *De Genesi ad litteram*. In it, St. Augustine asserted that, since we recognise the mysteries of nature as the work of Almighty God, we may enquire about them but must make no positive assertions about them, quite particularly when they are mentioned in the Books transmitted to us by divine authority, for misrepresentations of these run the risk of being sacrilegious. Questioning[132] must never go beyond the bounds of the Catholic faith. And since many are accustomed to interpret the Scriptures according to opinions which are irreconcilable with the

[128] op. cit., p. 404 ff.

[129] *Lehrbuch der Dogmengeschichte* III, p. 96; Romeis has rightly criticised this view (op. cit., p. 2 ff.)

[130] Cf. De doctrina christiani III 2, 37, 38; Enrichiridon 67, 68; De Genesi ad litteram V, 23, De civitate Dei XX, 5, 4; Confessiones XII, 33, 34.

[131] op. cit., p. 298.

[132] Here Hoffmann quotes. After the words *Quaerendi dubitatio* he adds in parenthesis: 'of Scriptural interpretations'. This generalisation is, however, not applicable in the context in which the words were written, since St. Augustine was dealing with only the obscure places treating of nature's mysteries.

Catholic faith, the Catholic view must be made clear before the Scriptures are expounded[133]. This is followed by a summary of the twelve articles[134]. And, indeed, the facts seem to support Hoffmann's views, though nothing in the whole passage asserts that *the Church* is indispensable for the explanation of the separate books, nor that St. Augustine saw the *regula fidei* in the active faith of the Church rather than in the Word of God. Nor did St. Augustine ever assert that the *faith of the Church* must not be based on the Scriptures, or that there cannot be any contradiction between them and Church dogma. The fact that he nevertheless held all true exegesis to be bound up with Catholic dogma, might well be explained by considering that he looked upon Catholic dogma as being based exclusively on the Scriptures and hence as being a sacred guide, the *norma normata* derived from the plain texts of Scripture[135]. As we have seen this assumption is, in fact, borne out by St. Augustine's subsequent writing[136].

As regards the third usage of *regula fidei*, mentioned by Kattenbusch, the texts indicated by him fail to show that St. Augustine ever used the term in that way. In three of these texts, St. Augustine spoke of the ecclesiastic rule of faith[137], and in the fourth quotation the rule of faith referred plainly to the Holy Scriptures[138]. In the fifth quotation, he spoke of the 'rule of the well-established truth' which in that context could only have meant the Scriptures once again[139].

The third question we have asked we can therefore answer as

[133] De Genesi ad litteram. Liber imperfectum 1.

[134] ib. 2–4.

[135] In the book under discussion (dated 393 A.D.!), the question is left unanswered. True it contains a paraphrase of the twelve articles, which makes it clear that St. Augustine was still a tyro in explaining the Scriptures (see his own comments in *Retract.* I: 18). We need only mention his views of sin (original sin was not yet known to him) and of the Church.

[136] We can ignore Hoffmann's further quotations in support of his views. There is no doubt that, in *Sermo* 7, 3, the rule of faith and the rule of truth referred exclusively to Scripture. In *De doctrina christiana* III, 2, we are told unequivocally that the rule of faith is derived from the plain texts of Scripture. Hoffmann's third quotation, from *Contra Faustum* XXXII, 19, has nothing to do with the subject, but deals with the acceptance or rejection of Scripture through subjective feelings. The rule of faith is not discussed.

[137] De peccatorum meritis et remissione I, 28; Contra Julianum I, 17, 22.

[138] De peccatorum meritis et remissione III, 11, see p. 204.

[139] Contra Julianum I, 16, cf. the previous paragraph.

follows: St. Augustine held clearly that the faith of the Church must be based entirely on Scripture, and more particularly on the plain passages. The *regula fidei* rests not on the active faith of the Church, but on plain Scriptural texts, and all Scriptural interpretations are bound to this *regula fidei* as their *normata*.

4. *Is the Church subject to, or equivalent with, the Word of God?*

Only when discussing St. Augustine's ecclesiology, can we answer this question fully. Here we shall therefore content ourselves with only two observations:

1. St. Augustine taught clearly that Christ's Church was born out of the preaching of God's Word. This is how he put it in a sermon on Psalm 45: 'All the souls that have been born through the preaching and evangelizing of the apostles are as daughters of kings and the churches as daughters of apostles are daughters of kings. For Christ is the King of kings, the apostles themselves kings, of whom it was said, You shall sit upon twelve thrones, judging the twelve tribes of Israel. They preached thc Word of truth and begat churches not for themselves, but for Christ. The apostle Paul says, For in Christ Jesus, through the Gospel, have I begotten you[140]. The apostles have begotten you. They were sent, they were the preachers, they are the fathers. But it was impossible for them to be with us in the body for ever. Is the Church then left desolate by their departure? God forbid. There have been appointed bishops. The Church itself calls them fathers; the Church itself brought them forth, and placed them on the thrones of the fathers. God has established His temple everywhere, has laid everywhere the foundations of the prophets and apostles'[141].

2. No one can doubt that St. Augustine always stressed the unity of Christ and His Body. Hoffmann says rightly that St. Augustine placed the idea of the unity of all the faithful with Christ and the Holy Spirit, expressed most fittingly by the symbol of 'the whole Christ, Head and Body', in the centre of his entire theology[142]. But the consequences which Neo-Catholic theologians have drawn from this Augustinian approach are not, as far as we have been able to

[140] 1 Cor. 4:15; Enarratio in Ps. 44, 23.
[141] ib. 32; see also Chapter IV of this book.
[142] op. cit., p. 148.

verify, corroborated by St. Augustine's own dicta. This is shown by the fact, that they themselves are unable to cite any unequivocal passages from St. Augustine in their support. Thus, to take only one example, while Mersch discussed St. Augustine's belief in the prolongation of the Incarnation at length, he failed to prove it by any of his many quotations from St. Augustine[143].

[143] Mersch was apparently very keen on this term. See, for instance, pp. 76, 78 ff., 135 ff.

CHAPTER VI

THE WORD OF GOD AND THE SPIRITUAL LIFE OF THE INDIVIDUAL

When, in his old age, St. Augustine wrote his thirty-two meditations on Psalm 119, and when he came to the well-known text: "Thy Word is a lamp unto my feet, and a light unto my path"[1], he went on to ask: 'What then means Thy Word? Is it He who was in the beginning God with God, that is, the Word by whom all things were made? It is not thus. For that Word is a light, but is not a lantern. For a lantern is a creature, not a creator; and it is lightened by participation of an unchangeable light. What is then this Word, which is thus called a light and a lantern at the same time? It is the Word which was sent unto the prophets, or which was preached through the apostles; not Christ the Word, but the Word of Christ, of which it is written, Faith comes by hearing and hearing by the Word of God[2]. For the apostle Peter also, comparing the prophetical word to a lantern, says: We have also a more sure word of prophecy; whereunto you do well that you take heed, as unto a lantern, that shines in a dark place[3]. What therefore he here says, Thy Word is a lantern unto my feet and a light unto my paths, is the Word which is contained in all the Holy Scriptures[4]. The Psalmist says, Quicken me, O Lord, according to Thy Word: that is, according to Thy promises. For the Word of the promises of God is a lantern to the feet, and a light to the paths'[5].

In this short, but important passage, St. Augustine has covered nearly all the subjects we have been discussing: the Word Christ, the Word of Christ, the Holy Scriptures containing the Word, the

[1] Ps. 119:105.
[2] Rom. 10:17.
[3] 2 Pet. 1:19.
[4] Enarratio in Ps. 118 XXIII, 1.
[5] ib. 3.

Word as proclamation, and finally the Word of promise which is what the Psalmist had in mind quite particularly when he said that the Word of the Lord is 'a lantern to the feet and a light to the path', which helps to quicken us. By it, he refers to the meaning of God's Word in our own spiritual life. While we have mentioned this subject before, we should now like to dwell on the special way in which St. Augustine thought that the Word of the promises of God, or as he was wont to call it the 'chirography of God's promise' affects our soul.

Thus, in a sermon on Psalm 110, he said that God has set aside a time of promising and a time of fulfilment. The time of promise extends from the Prophets to St. John the Baptist; the time of fulfilment from him and thenceforth unto the end of the world[6]. Hence he looked upon his own and future generations as living in the age of fulfilment, under the New Testament. Once again, we can point to an inner struggle between the Neoplatonic view, with its emphasis on 'not yet' and 'in hope', and the distinction between *verbum* and *res*, and the realistic Biblical view, according to which the new age was the time of fulfilment because Christ had come. While the former view predominated, as predominate it did at first, St. Augustine failed to appreciate the full historical significance of Christ. His faith still had a strong intellectual tinge, and was merely the preparatory stage for contemplation; hope was no more than longing, and love was the exponent of both. During the second stage, the pilgrim continued to hanker after the promised land, but could look back on the great victory, the total redemption by Christ, and Christ's grace which sprang from it[7]. The Sacred Scriptures were now fully understood as the seal of God's promise. Thus could St. Augustine introduce his sermon on Psalm 110 with the following words: 'God is faithful, who made Himself our Debtor; not by accepting any thing from us, but by promising us great blessings. Promise was not enough. He even chose that He should be bound by writing, creating for us a kind of bond for His promises. So that when He began to fulfil His promises, we might contemplate in Scripture the order of their accomplishment'[8].

And in preaching on the text in Ps. 145:17 "The Lord is righteous

[6] Enarratio in Ps. 109, 1.

[7] See Gustaf Ljunggren, *Zur Geschichte der christlichen Heilsgewissheit*, Göttingen 1920, p. 1–156, in which St. Augustine's inner struggle is described most movingly.

[8] Enarratio in Ps. 109, 1.

(faithful) in all his works (words)", he said: 'Faithful is the Lord in His words, for what has He promised that He has not given? Hereto there are certain things which He has promised, and has not given; but let Him be believed from the things which He has given. We might well believe Him, if He only spake: He willed not that we should believe Him speaking, but that we should have His Scriptures in our hands: as though thou shouldest say to a man when thou promisedst him something, 'Thou believest me not, behold, I write it for thee'. For because one generation goeth and another cometh and so these generations hasten by as men retire and succeed one another, it was needful that the Scriptures of God should remain as a kind of bond of God's, which all who pass by might read, and might keep to the paths of its promise'[9]. St. Augustine was to return to this point over and over again. What God has promised He has sealed with His Word, thus making Himself our Debtor. We may therefore ask Him to fulfil the promises He has made to our fathers, the promise He has sealed with His Word, so that all of us may read it[10]. He has seen fit to become our Debtor, and to pledge His seal in the death of Christ. Would He who sacrificed His Son for the godless, deny the promise of His death to the pious and faithful?[11] He Himself has appointed Himself our Debtor. His Book is His seal[12].

And God's children must live by the seal of His promise—they must read it again and again, heeding reverently and faithfully what God has already fulfilled, and what He is about to fulfil. All of them live in the days of fulfilment and can everywhere see the truthfulness and faithfulness of God. Even if God had not fulfilled any of His promises, we could fully rely on His repaying His debt[13]. Even if He had paid us nothing so far, He Who created heaven and earth would yet be a virtuous debtor. He is, after all, rich enough to pay us in full, and cannot deceive us since He is the Truth. Hence we need no tangible proof of His solvency. Thus did our fathers believe in Him; thus did Abraham believe in Him. Indeed, Abraham should be our example since he had received nothing from God and yet believed His promise, while we, who have received so much, do not yet believe. Abraham believed at once; he demanded no payment

[9] Enarratio in Ps. 144, 17.
[10] Sermones Moriniani XIII, 4, 5.
[11] ib. XVI, 7.
[12] ib. VIII, 5.
[13] Enarratio in Ps. 39, 2.

in advance. When God said to him: 'Get thee out of thy country, and from thy kindred unto a land that I will show thee, and I will make of thee a great nation', he obeyed without question. Yet God did not give the land to Abraham himself, but kept it for his seed[14]. Hence, St. Augustine admonished the congregation: 'If you should have any friend stern and wise, how would you say? He has spoken these things, there must needs come to pass that which he has spoken: the man is stern, no levity he used, not easily from his resolution is he moved aside, that which he has promised is steadfast. But nevertheless a human being he is that sometimes will to do that which he has promised, and is not able. Of God there is not anything that you may fear; that truthful He is, is certain; that all-mighty He is, is certain: to deceive thee He is not able, He has means whence He may perform[15]. God is faithful, He cannot deny Himself[16]. We have then a faithful God also: but let us well distinguish faithful God from faithful man. Man is faithful when he trusts in God promising; God is faithful because He performs what He promised to men. Let us hold Him a Debtor most faithful, since we hold Him a Promiser most merciful'[17].

For that very reason we should have to believe in Him, even if He had fulfilled none of His promises. As it is, we live in the time of fulfilment. In awed astonishment and in great reverence for all the great deeds God had wrought in the past, St. Augustine returned to this point, time and again. Thus he begged the congregation to count their blessings. For God's promise of Christ, His crucifixion and resurrection had all been fulfilled. He sent His Gospel as He had promised, when He said: "How beautiful upon the mountains are the feet of him that bringeth good tidings, that publisheth peace, that bringeth good tidings of good"[18]. The Church had to suffer, because He promised us martyrs. It was written: "All kings shall fall down before Him"[19], and even those kings who at first persecuted the martyrs, came to worship Him in the end. 'Since He has given us all these great things, how, brothers, shall we not believe in Him?'[20]

[14] Ex sermonibus a Michaele Denis editis XXIV, 9, 10.
[15] Enarratio in Ps. 59, 8.
[16] 2 Tim. 2:12, 13.
[17] Enarratio in Ps. 23 II, 9.
[18] Is. 52:7.
[19] Ps. 72:11.
[20] Denis XXIV, 9.

In St. Augustine's day, there were many who mocked at God, particularly the Epicureans, who denied eternal life, and believed in only what they could see with their own eyes. St. Augustine warned his congregation seriously against this barren doctrine, saying: 'Certainly all those things which throughout the world now are seen, when God was working salvation in the midst of the earth, when those things were being spoken of, they were not then as yet: and behold at that time they were foretold, now they are shewn as fulfilled, and still the fool says in his heart, there is no God. Woe to the perverse hearts: for so will there come to pass the things which remain, as there have come to pass the things which at that time were not, and were being foretold as to come to pass. Has God indeed performed to us all the things He promised, and concerning the day of judgment alone has He deceived us? Christ was not on the earth; He promised, He has performed; no virgin had conceived; He promised, He has performed; the precious blood had not been shed whereby there should be effaced the handwriting of our death; He promised, He has performed; not yet has flesh risen again unto life eternal; He promised, He has performed; not yet had the Gentiles believed; He promised, He has performed; not yet heretics armed with the name of Christ, against Christ were warring; He foretold, He has performed; not yet the idols of the Gentiles from the earth had been effaced; He foretold, He has performed; when all these things He has foretold and performed, concerning the day of judgment alone has He lied? It will come by all means as these things came'[21].

In his sermon on Ps. 110, mentioned before, St. Augustine 'as the servant of God's Word and sacrament' preached that, through His prophets, God had made us rich promises, indeed. 'He promised everlasting salvation, and a life of bliss with the angels without end, a heritage that should never wither, everlasting glory, the sweetness of His countenance, the house of His sanctification in the heavens, from the resurrection from the dead no further fear of death. This is, as it were, His final promise, whither all our endeavours tend, which after we have reached, we shall seek nothing more, expect nothing more. Nor has He passed over in silence in what order that which shall happen at the end shall be reached, in His promises and prophecies. For He promised unto men the divine nature; to mortals,

[21] Enarratio in Ps. 73, 25.

immortality; to sinners, justification; to cast-aways, a state of glory. Whatever He promised, He promised to the unworthy so that not a reward was promised to works, but that grace was given by His name for nought. Nevertheless because what God promised seemed incredible to men, that men from this mortality, corruption, weak and abject state, this dust and ashes, shall become equal to the angels of God; He not only made a written covenant with men that they might believe, but also gave them a Mediator as a pledge of His promise; not any prince, or any angel, or archangel, but His only Son; so that the way, through which He was to lead us to that end which He promised, He might both shew, and give to us by the same, His own Son. For it was not enough for God to give us in His Son one who should shew us the path, He made Him Himself the way, that thou mightest go through Him ruling thee, as thou walkest through Himself'[22]. Thus all the paths of God lead to mercy and truth; mercy, because God does not pay us according to our deserts but according to His own lovingkindness, forgiving our sins and promising us eternal life; truth since He never deceives us in His promises[23]. He has fulfilled much already, much more than remains to be fulfilled. From what He has done, we must believe in what He will still do[24]. God's promises are always sincere, certain, firm, credible, and indubitable[25].

For that reason, the preaching of these promises can be based on firm conviction. 'God has promised this; He has said this; if this is not enough, He has sworn it. As then the promise is certain, not on account of our deservings, but of His pity, no one ought to be afraid in proclaiming that which he cannot doubt of. Let that strength then inspire our hearts, let us preach the truth of God, the utterance of God, His promises, His oath, and let us, strengthened on every side by these means, glorify God'[26]. But the congregation, too, must concentrate all its attention on these promises of God. 'For', as St. Augustine pointed out, 'no man in this world is strong, except in the hope of God's promises[27]. Here nowhere, in this life nowhere is security, except solely in the hope of the promise of

[22] Enarratio in Ps. 109, 1, 2.
[23] Enarratio in Ps. 61, 9; in Ps. 118 XXIX, 8.
[24] Sermo 130, 3.
[25] Enarratio in Ps. 74, 1.
[26] Enarratio in Ps. 88, 5.
[27] Enarratio in Ps. 88, 1.

God[28]. In the darkness of this world, in which we are pilgrims absent from the Lord, the Christian soul ought to feel itself desolate, and continue in prayer, and learn to fix the eye of faith on the word of the divine Scriptures as "on a light shining in a dark place, until the day dawn, and the daystar arise in our hearts"[29]. We are being held corrupted by the lusts of Babylon. In what manner in ourselves is formed again the love of our city Jerusalem, which by long sojourning we had forgotten? But our Father has sent from thence letters to us. God has supplied to us the Scriptures, by which letters there should be wrought in us a longing for return. And when we begin to be renewed, already with heart in Jerusalem we sing, with the apostle saying, Our conversation is in the Heavens. Already in longing we are there, already hope into that land, as it were an anchor we have sent before, lest in this sea being tossed we suffer shipwreck. In like manner therefore as of a ship which is at anchor, we rightly say that already she is come to land, for still she rolls, but to land in a manner she has been brought safe in the teeth of winds and in the teeth of storms; so against the temptations of this sojourning, our hope being grounded in that city Jerusalem causes us not to be carried away upon rocks[30]. To the last day of our life it will be needful for us to resort to the prayer which we can so truthfully utter, "Forgive us our tresspases", still trust that in Christ and in His promises we possess a true, certain, and unfailing hope[31]. See you now how much men suffer under the hands of physicians, when a man promises them an uncertain hope? You will be cured, says the physician: you will be cured, if I cut. It is a man who speaks, and to a man that he speaks; neither is he sure who speaks, nor he who hears, for who is speaking to the man has not made man, and knows not perfectly what is passing in man: yet as the words of a man who knows not what is passing in man, man sooner believes, submits his limbs, suffers himself to be bound, often without being bound is cut or burned; and receives perhaps health for a few days, even when just healed not knowing when he may die; perhaps, while being healed, dies; perhaps cannot be healed. But to whom has God promised anything, and deceived him?'[32]

[28] Enarratio in Ps. 99, 11; 69, 9.
[29] 2 Pet. 1:19; Epistula 130, 5.
[30] Enarratio in Ps. 64, 2, 3.
[31] De natura et gratia 70.
[32] Enarratio in Ps. 85, 9; see also En. in Ps. 102, 5.

For that very reason St. Augustine constantly besought his congregation to believe in God's Word. If it were their own, they would have every reason to tremble, but since it is God's they need not fear—He does not deceive[33]. For—and St. Augustine realised even this—it is precisely the characteristic of God's promises that they refer to His work and not to ours. That, after all, is the difference between a promise and a prediction, including prophecies of our sins. Promise is what God Himself will do. It was therefore that Isaac and the brethren in Christ were called the children of promise[34]. All God's children must hence rejoice in the knowledge that He who gave us the seal of His promise cannot deceive us[35]. 'Who would not rejoice, if suddenly while he was wandering abroad, ignorant of his descent, suffering want, and in a state of misery and toil, it were announced, You are the son of a senator; your father enjoys an ample patrimony on your family estate: I bid you return to your father: how would he rejoice, if this were said to him by someone whose promise he could trust? One whom we can trust, an apostle of Christ, has come and said to us, What is the reason that you despair of yourselves? Why do you afflict yourselves, and wear yourselves down with grief; why do you choose, following your own desires, to suffer grief in want of those other joys? You have a father, you have a country, you have an inheritance. Who is that father? Beloved, we are the sons of God[36]. Wherefore then see we not yet our Father? Because it has not yet appeared what we shall be. We are that now, but in hope: for what we shall be has not yet appeared. And what shall we be? We know, says he, that when He shall appear, we shall be like Him, for we shall see Him as He is[37]. Not any humble man may despair of the Lord. For the promise of God is ratified, sure, fixed, and unshaken, faithful, and devoid of all doubt, which does comfort the afflicted. Therefore the Psalmist says, Delight thyself in the Lord and He shall give thee the petitions of thy heart[38]. Whence do you delight in the Lord, except because you have a sure promiser, who has made Himself by promising a debtor? Fear not, therefore, lest any mighty man should corrupt the promises of God. He does

[33] Enarratio in Ps. 129, 6.
[34] Epistula 140, 48.
[35] Enarratio in Ps. 54, 3.
[36] 1 Joh. 3:2.
[37] Enarratio in Ps. 84, 9.
[38] Ps. 37:4.

not corrupt, because He is truthful; He has no one more mighty by whom His promise may be corrupted: let us then be sure concerning the promises of God[39]. Blessed is the nation whose God is the Lord. The Lord our God! Let Him be our inheritance, our possession. Do we haply speak rashly in making God our possession, when He is the Lord, the Creator? This is not rashness: it is the affection of desire, it is the sweetness of hope. Let the soul say, all secure let it say, Thou art my God, who sayest to my soul, I am thy salvation[40]. Let it so say, secure let it say, it will do no wrong, when so it says; nay it will do wrong, if it say not. Say then securely, This is thy possession. Scripture has said, has filled up your doubts with confidence: speak securely, love securely, hope securely. Thine also be those words in the Psalm, The Lord is the portion of mine inheritance'[41].

And if God's people can dwell in God's promise with joyous certainty, it is only because their joy is awakened by the Holy Spirit. Hence, St. Augustine could say in a sermon on Psalm 27: 'The Lord our God in addressing and consoling us vouchsafes to speak to us out of ourselves, to shew us that He is not only our Creator, but also our Indweller. These words of the psalm, which we have heard and partly sung, if we say that they are our own, we must be reverently careful, how we speak the truth; for they are rather the Words of God's Spirit than our own. Again, if we say that they are not ours, we do indeed lie. So each is true, both that the speech is ours, and that it is not ours; that it is the speech of the Spirit of God, in that but for His inspiration we should not speak thus; but it is not His, in that He is not miserable, but these words of distress are ours'[42]. St. Augustine then, as on many other occasions, referred his subsequent remarks to Christ entire, Head and Body[43]. The Psalmist's: "The Lord is my light and my salvation, whom shall I fear", became the occasion of the following explanation: 'The Lord enlightening, we enlightened; the Lord saving, we saved: if then He be the Enlightener and we the enlightened and He the Saviour, we the saved, without Him we are darkness and weakness. But having in Him a sure, and established, and true hope, whom shall we fear? He enlightens me, let darkness vanish: He saves me, let weakness

[39] Enarratio in Ps. 74, 1.
[40] Ps. 35:3.
[41] Enarratio in Ps. 32 II, 17.
[42] Enarratio in Ps. 26 II, 1.
[43] ib. 2.

vanish: walking in the light with firmness, whom shall I fear? For God gives not such salvation, as can be wrested by any one; nor is He such a light, as can be obscured by any one. Find one more powerful, and fear. I belong, in such wise, to the most powerful of all, to the All-powerful, that He both enlightens me and saves me; nor fear I any but Him'[44].

St. Augustine then stressed the fact that there is an insoluble bond between Christ and His people. And hence he exclaimed: 'What has been exhibited in the resurrection of my Head, may all the members hope for. Whom should my soul fear, which God inhabits? Whom should my flesh fear, when this corruptible shall have put on incorruption? How great confidence should there be in him, who could say, The Lord is my light and my salvation: whom shall I fear? The general is protected by guards, and fears not; a mortal is protected by mortals, and is secure: a mortal is protected by the Immortal, and should he be afraid and fear?[45] What can war do to me? Can it take away my hope from me? Can it take away what the Almighty gives? As He who gives is not conquered, so what He gives is not taken away[46]. For He has hidden me in His tabernacle in the day of my evils. My dwelling then shall be in His house all the days of my life to this end that I may contemplate the delights of the Lord. But whence my assurance of arriving thither? He who mercifully regarded me when far off, how shall He gladden me when brought near to Him? For which cause therefore I did not make that one petition (to contemplate in His temple) shamelessly; nor did my heart say to me, What are you asking, or from Whom are you asking? For dost thou dare, unrighteous sinner, to ask anything from God? Darest thou hope, infirm one, of heart impure, that thou shalt have any contemplation of God? I do, he answers, not of myself, but of His delight, not of self-reliance, but of His earnest. He Who has given such an earnest to the pilgrim, will He desert him on his arrival? For Christ died for the ungodly. Therefore let the soul of man dare to feel confidence, and make that one petition: it will have it in safety, it will possess it in safety. So greatly has she been loved in her deformity, how shall she shine in her beauty? For you are dead, says the apostle, and your life has been hid with

[44] ib. 3.
[45] ib. 4.
[46] ib. 5.

Christ in God[47]. And when Christ shall be manifested, who is our life, then you will be manifested also with Him in glory[48]. Christ our Head is already in heaven, our enemies can as yet rage against us; we are not yet exalted above them; but our Head is already there, whence He spake the words, Saul, Saul, why persecutest thou Me? He has said that He is in us here below: therefore we too are in Him above. See what an earnest we have, whereby we too are by faith, and hope, and charity, with our Head in heaven for ever; because the Head Himself, by divinity, goodness, unity, is with us on earth even unto the consummation of the world[49]. Therefore we sacrifice the victim of rejoicing, we sacrifice the victim of gladness, the victim of thankfulness, the victim of thanksgiving, which cannot be explained in words. But we sacrifice, where? In His very tabernacle, in the holy Church. What then do we sacrifice? Most abundant and inexpressible joy, with no words, with speech ineffable'[50].

Thus God's Word is the seal of His promises to successive generations, deliberately committed to writing so that we might read it. The children of the promise must study the Word, the better to appreciate with gratitude and awe what God has already fulfilled and what He will fulfil in the days to come. They have every reason to believe His Word even though He had fulfilled nothing, just as Abraham did. But living as they do in the age of fulfilment, which began with the birth of Christ and will end with the end of the world, they can see the wonderful fulfilment of God's promises all around them. They might even say that, since Christ became incarnate, suffered, died, rose up, and ascended to heaven, God has already given more than He has vouchsafed.

Reading of, and reflection on, the seal of God's promise, day and night, is therefore a blessed aid to salvation. Not only preachers, but also the congregation must, and can safely, base all their convictions and hopes upon it. Only then will life become full of gladness and joy, a hymn of praise and thanksgiving.

But this faith is at one and the same time a call to sanctity, to a life dedicated to God, our Father. God's people must not only base their faith and hope on God's Word, but must also live accordingly.

[47] Col. 3:3.
[48] ib. vs. 4; Enarratio in Ps. 26, 10.
[49] ib. 11.
[50] ib. 12; see also Romeis, op. cit. p. 6 ff.

God's rich promises must give us the strength to obey His commandments and to resist temptation.

St. Augustine stressed this fact especially in his meditations on Psalm 119, showing that submission to, and fulfilment of, God's commandment is always based on God's promises and God's grace. Like a refrain, he kept repeating the sentence: 'Your Word is your promise!' Thus whenever the quoted the Psalmist's: "That I may live and keep thy word", "Stablish thy word unto thy servant", or "Quicken me according to thy word", he always added 'Your word is your promise!' And, to St. Augustine, this promise was mainly of Christ, and of Christ's grace and spirit.

To the Psalmist's: 'Let thy mercies come also unto me, O Lord, even thy salvation, according to thy word"[51] St. Augustine rejoined: 'According to Thy Word, that is according to Thy promise. Whence the apostle desires us to be understood as the children of promise: that we may not imagine that what we are is our own work, but refer the whole to the grace of God. For Christ is of God made unto us wisdom, and righteousness, and sanctification, and redemption: that according as it is written, he that glories, let him glory in the Lord[52]. In the words then, Quicken me in Thy righteousness, he prays to be quickened in Christ, and this is the very loving mercy which he prays may come upon him. If therefore we ask what is that loving mercy, let us hear what follows: Thy salvation (that is, Christ Himself), according to Thy word. For this was promised by Him, Who calls those things which be not as if they were. For those unto whom the promises were made were not as yet in existence, that no man might glory in his deservings. And those unto whom it was promised, were themselves also promised; so that the whole Body of Christ may say, By the grace of God I am what I am. So they speak and do who trust in God's words, which means exactly, in God's promises'[53].

And this was St. Augustine's comment on the text: 'Reward thy servant that I may live and keep thy word':[54] if he had asked that good may be repaid him for good deeds, he had already kept God's Word. Why then say 'that I may keep thy word?' And what is this

[51] Ps. 119:41.
[52] 1 Cor. 1:30.
[53] Enarratio in Ps. 118 XIII, 1, 2.
[54] St. Augustine's reading of Ps. 119:17.

but to declare the dead incapable of keeping God's Word? No man without living faith can keep it. Hence he was asking for faith which through love, could alone give him the strength he needs. Thus he asked the Lord to repay his evil with good, to bestow His grace upon him[55].

For those who have been quickened, God's Word has become the path of righteousness, on which they walk through His grace alone. When the Psalmist asks "Wherewith shall a young man cleanse his way?" and answers "by taking heed thereto according to thy word", St. Augustine explained: 'But this younger people, the child of grace, the new man, who sings the new song, the heir of the new covenant, this younger people, not Cain, but Abel, not Ishmael but Isaac, not Esau but Israel, not Manasseh but Ephraim, not Eli but Samuel, not Saul but David, hear what is added, With my whole heart, he says, have I sought Thee: O repel me not from Thy commandments. What is to be repelled of God, save not to be aided? The Psalmist also sought the aid of God, lest the words of God might be hidden without fruit in his heart, unless works of righteousness followed[56]. He who hides in his heart the words of the Lord and tells with his lips all the judgments of His mouth, and in the way of His testimonies takes as much delights as in all manner of riches and talking or exercising himself in His commandments, has respect unto His ways and does meditate on His statutes, that he may not forget His words, yet prays and says, Blessed art Thou, O Lord: O teach me Thy statutes! Where he is understood to ask nothing else save the aid of grace, that he may learn in deeds what he already knows in words[57]. He justly says not, O quicken Thou me according to my merit, but according to Thy word: and what else is this, save according to Thy promise? He wishes to be the son of the promise, not the son of pride, so that the promises may be firm to all the seed of Isaac according to grace[58]. He asks, Set a law for me, O Lord, and I shall seek it always. He does not ask it as a son of the old covenant, but according to the new covenant, concerning the promise of Jer. 31, as a son of the free, that is, the heavenly Jerusalem, as a son of promise, a son of an everlasting heritage. He asks that by the Holy

[55] Enarratio in Ps. 118 VII, 1.
[56] ib. V, 3, 4.
[57] ib. VI, 5.
[58] ib. X, 3.

Spirit, as it were by the finger of God, the law of God may be written in the heart: not one which they may hold in remembrance, and neglect in life, but which they may know by understanding, perform by loving, in the breadth of love, not in the narrowness of fear[59]. Therefore he prays, O stablish Thy word in Thy servant, that I may fear Thee, that is, grant unto me that I may do according to what Thou sayest, not in the fear of bondage, but of love, that fear which fears to offend Him Whom it loves. Therefore the Psalmist prayed God: "Stablish Thy word unto Thy servant, who is devoted to Thy fear", that is, see that I do what you ask from the fear of offending Whom I love'[60].

But also in the strife and struggle, the hardship and sorrow of this world, God's Word is a constant source of solace to all pilgrims. God's promises support them, and help them to bear all afflictions. For, when the Psalmist said: "O remember Thy word to Thy servant, wherein Thou hast given me hope", St. Augustine asked: 'Is forgetfulness incident to God, as it is to man? Why then is it said to Him, O remember? The desire of him who prays is displayed because he asks for what was promised; God is not admonished, as if the promise had escaped from His mind. O remember, he says, Thy word unto Thy servant: that is fulfill Thy promise, wherein Thou hast given me hope: that is, in Thy word, since Thou hast promised, Thou hast caused me to hope. And so they have patience in their tribulations'[61]. Here, St. Augustine made a clear distinction between two kinds of hope: the hope which looks for eternal reward, and the hope which succours the downtrodden with God's sacred promise. It was this hope that St. Paul had in mind when he said: "God is faithful, who will not suffer you to be tempted above that you are able"[62]. Thus, though the children of promise, Abraham's seed, wander through alien lands, God's Words, i.e. God's promises, console them in all their tribulations[63]. God's Word, that is God's promise, serves them as a lamp unto their feet and as a light unto their path[64].

This, in brief, was how St. Augustine came to look upon Scripture

[59] ib. XI, 1.
[60] ib. XII, 3.
[61] ib. XV, 1.
[62] 1 Cor. 10:13; Enarratio in Ps. 118 XV, 1.
[63] ib. XIX, 2, 3.
[64] ib. XXIII, 3.

as the seal of God's promise, and upon God's Word as the light on His children's mortal path. In triumph as in trial, in happy as in gloomy days, in temptation and in strife, they must always live with, through, and by the Word of God. That Word must be the foundation of their pious hopes, the basis of all their prayers, the path in which they walk, and their inexhaustible source of solace and spiritual happiness.

Everyone knows, how the Reformers, after centuries of neglect, came once more to emphasise the importance of God's promises in the Scriptures, which were fulfilled in Christ. On them, they have built the aim and object of their faith, basing on God's promises in Christ, their firm conviction in salvation. Did St. Augustine share this certainty with them, finding it vouchsafed by God's promises, or were his true feelings rather expressed by the Council of Trent, which, under the influence of Seripando, the famous Augustinian leader of his day, spoke of the very firm conviction which must be placed in God's help together with fear and trembling and constant vigilance lest man fall?[65] We shall only be able to answer this question after we have discussed St. Augustine's views on predestination, sin, grace, justification, sanctification, faith, hope, and love. In this chapter we were merely concerned to show how great a stress St. Augustine placed on the role of the Holy Scripture as the Word of Christ and the seal of His promises in the spiritual life of the children of the promise.

[65] D. 806; see also Adolf Stakemeier, *Das Konzil von Trient über die Heilsgewissheit*, Heidelberg 1947.

CHAPTER VII

THE WORD OF GOD WITHOUT HOLY SCRIPTURE

There comes a time when Scripture as the Word of God has fulfilled its task. After all, the Bible was meant to kindle and support our longing for the fatherland, in which the Scriptures are fulfilled. According to St. Augustine, there are 'two states of life, preached and commended to the Church from heaven, whereof the one is in faith, the other in sight; one in the temporal sojourn in a foreign land, the other in the eternity of the (heavenly) abode; one in labour, the other in repose; one on the way, the other in the fatherland; one in active work, the other in the wages of contemplation; one declines from evil and makes for good, the other has no evil to decline from and has great good to enjoy; the one fights with a foe, the other reigns without a foe; the one is brave in the midst of adversities, the other has no experience of adversity; the one is bridling its carnal lusts, the other has full scope for spiritual delights; the one is anxious with the care of conquering, the other secure in the peace of victory; the one is helped in temptations, the other free from all temptations, rejoices in the Helper Himself; the one is occupied in relieving the indigent, the other is there, where no indigence is found; the one pardons the sins of others, that its own may be pardoned to itself, the other neither has anything to pardon nor does aught for which pardon has to be asked; the one is scourged with evils that it may not be elated with good things, the other is free from all evil by such a fulness of grace that, without any temptation to pride, it may cleave to that which is supremely good; the one discerns both good and evil, the other has only that which is good presented to view: therefore the one is good, but miserable as yet, the other better and blessed'[1].

Compared with life in the fatherland, in which everything is bliss

[1] Tractatus in Joannis evangelium 124, 5.

and eternal joy, life on earth is but one long struggle, filled with difficulty and sorrow. The older St. Augustine became, the darker and gloomier became the colours with which he painted the life of the pilgrim on earth, and the greater became his faith in the lamp that God has lit in life's dark corners. The Scriptures are full of His lamps which, in the midst of night, give witness of Christ, the light of the world[2].

Christ alone could say: "I am the way, the truth, and the life". 'When we shall see face to face', St. Augustine explained, 'we shall have the full fruition of the truth; for this also is promised to us. For who should dare hope for what God had not deigned either to promise or to give? We shall see face to face. The apostle says, "Now I know in part, now through a glass darkly; but then, face to face"[3]. And the apostle John says in his epistle, "Beloved, now are we the sons of God; and it has not yet appeared what we shall be: we know that, when He shall appear, we shall be like Him; for we shall see Him even as He is"[4]. This is a great promise; if thou lovest, follow[5]. I do love, you say, but by what way am I to follow? If the Lord thy God has said to thee "I am the truth and the life", in desiring truth and longing for life, thou mightest truly ask the way by which thou mightest come to these, and mightest say to thyself: A great thing is the truth, a great thing is the life, were there only the means whereby my soul might come thereto! Dost thou ask by what way? Hear Him say at the first, "I am the way". Before He said whither, He promised by that way: I am, He says, the way. The way whither? "And the truth and the life". First He told thee the way to come; then, whither to come. Remaining with the Father, the truth and life; putting on flesh, He became the way. It is not said to thee, Labour in finding a way to come to the truth and life; this is not said to thee. Sluggard, arise: the way itself has come to thee and roused thee from thy sleep; if, however, it has roused thee, up and walk. Perhaps you are trying to walk and you are not able, because your feet ache. But the Word of God has healed even the lame. Behold, you say, I have my feet sound, but the way itself I see not. He has also enlightened the blind[6]. All this by faith, so

[2] ib. 35, 6, 7.
[3] 1 Cor. 13:12.
[4] 1 Joh. 3:2.
[5] Allusion to Joh. 21:17, 22.
[6] Tractatus in Joannis evangelium 34, 9.

long as we are absent from the Lord, dwelling in the body; but when we shall have traversed the way, and have reached the home itself, what shall be more joyful than we?'[7]

Here, in the dead of night, we need the support of the prophetic Word—for we have neither seen the Lord Jesus nor heard the Father's voice upon the mountain. Hence did the apostle Peter enjoin us to heed it as a light that shineth in a dark place, until the day dawn and the day star arise in our hearts[8]. 'When our Lord Jesus Christ', St. Augustine remarked, 'shall come, and, as the apostle Paul also says, will bring to light the hidden things of darkness, and will make manifest the thoughts of the heart, that every man may have praise from God[9], then, in presence of such a day, lamps will not be needed: no prophet shall then be read to us, no book of an apostle shall then be opened; we shall not require the witness of John, we shall not need the Gospel itself. Accordingly all the Scriptures shall be taken out of the way—which in the night of this world were as lamps kindled for us that we might not remain in darkness—when all these are taken away, that they may not shine as if we needed them, and the men of God, by whom these were ministered to us, shall themselves, together with us, behold that true and clear light. Well, what shall we see after these aids have been removed? Wherewith shall our mind be fed? Wherewith shall our gaze be delighted? Whence shall arise that joy which neither eye has seen, nor ear heard, nor has gone up into the heart of man? What shall we see? I beseech you, love with me, by believing, run with me: let us long for our home above, let us pant for our home above, let us feel that we are strangers here. What shall we see then? Let the Gospel now tell us: "In the beginning was the Word and the Word was with God, and the Word was God". Thou shalt come to the fountain from which a little dew has already besprinkled thee: thou shalt see that very light from which a ray was sent aslant and through many windings into thy dark heart, in its purity, for the seeing and bearing of which thou art being purified.'[10]

We may find it strange that St. Augustine's answers the question 'What shall we find in the fatherland?' by quoting the beginning

[7] ib. 10.
[8] 2. Pet. 1:19; Tractatus in Joannis evangelium 35, 8.
[9] 1 Cor. 4:5.
[10] Tractatus in Joannis evangelium 35, 9.

of the Gospel according to St. John. But on reflection, we realise that this answer revealed his innermost feelings. We have seen that his thoughts underwent a clear change, and that he came to lay an ever greater stress on the spiritual aids needful on our pilgrimage, and also on the value of Christ's historic acts of salvation *qua* acts of salvation. Even so, all these things were not more than *means*, necessitated by man's sin and fall. Christ's incarnation, crucifixion, resurrection, and ascent were not ends in themselves, but merely showed us how we could recover what we have lost. The Scriptures, as the Word of Christ, show us what riches are in store for us, and the Word of God as proclamation effects communion with Christ and all His benefits. Hence they are indispensable on our pilgrimage. But once we have reached the fatherland, we are in direct, blessed, contact with the Word itself, that is with the truth, the light, the power and the wisdom of God, with the quintessence and manifestation of all God's goodness. Clearly, Neoplatonic ideas, no matter how transposed, continued to hold sway over St. Augustine's conception of final salvation in the beholding of the Word.

At first, this influence was very strong indeed, and the whole problem was thought to reflect the Neoplatonic antithesis of voice vs. word[11]. Traces of this appraisal can still be felt in a sermon delivered in 401 on John the Baptist's saying: "He must increase, but I must decrease"[12]. 'O, great and hidden mystery' St. Augustine exclaimed, 'verily, heed ye the person of the voice[13], which spoke with the mystery of all voices: "He must increase, but I must decrease". Observe, the apostle said: "For we know in part, and we prophesy in part. But when that which is perfect is come, then that which is in part shall be done away with"[14]. St. Augustine went on to ask what it is that is perfect, and answered with John 1:1—it is the Word. Perfect also is 'Who, being in the form of God thought it no robbery to be equal with God'[15]. It is He, Who is alike unto the Father and the Word that is in God, and by which all things are made, Whom we shall finally see as He is[16]. This we are promised, this we are taught, for this we cleanse our hearts.

[11] R. Kuypers, op. cit. Chapter V, *Vox und Verbum*, p. 59 ff.
[12] Joh. 3:30.
[13] Allusion to Luke 3:4.
[14] 1 Cor. 13:9, 10.
[15] Phil. 2:6.
[16] 1 Joh. 3:2.

'"Blessed are the pure in heart, for they shall see God"[17]. He has shown His flesh to slaves, in the form of a slave. As He gave us His voice, as one among many voices, so he also showed us His flesh. Philip has said that it sufficed him to see the Father. But should he not also have asked himself whether He Whom he heard sufficed equally? To Philip's request to see God, the Lord answered: "Have I been so long time with you, and yet hast thou not known me, Philip? He that hath seen me has seen the Father"'[18]. St. Augustine concluded that all voices must grow silent as we draw nearer to the sight of Christ. The further we advance in the sight of wisdom, the less we need the voice which was in the prophets, the apostles, the Psalms, and the Gospel. Once we see Him as He is, shall the Gospel still be read to us? Shall we then need to hear prophecies, and to read the Epistles? Once the Word increases, the voices grow silent. The Word by itself neither increases nor decreases. But of Him it is said, that He increases in us as we draw closer to Him, just as the light of the eye increases as we learn to see more, and decreases as our eyesight begins to fail. 'Thus the service of the voice decreases as the spirit draws nearer to the Word'[19]. The last sentence, in particular, is most characteristic.

Even on earth, we, the children of God, will have ever less need for the voices of the prophets and the apostles, or even of the Gospel, as we increase in wisdom. These voices become stilled as the Word grows stronger, that is as our understanding and grasp grow wider. At this stage of St. Augustine's development Neoplatonic intellectualism still ruled supreme[20].

Later, as St. Augustine's view of sin grew more profound, as he increasingly appreciated the full importance of grace, emphasised the redemptive work of Christ, and as he came to look upon Scripture as, above all, the Word of this Redeemer and as the seal of God's promises, such utterances became far rarer. Still, the final aim remained always the contemplation of the Word in which are found the deepest fulfilment and eternal life. To their death, all God's children need the Word of God as Holy Writ, but once in the fatherland, they will live eternally without this Word of God,

[17] Matth. 5:8.
[18] Joh. 14:8, 9.
[19] Sermo 288, 5.
[20] See Ljunggren, op. cit., p. 31 ff.

but with the Word of God that was in the beginning. St. Augustine based this opinion on three Biblical passages.

1. When Christ had been proclaimed by the voice from the cloud to be God's Son, the disciples fell to the ground. Christ stayed to touch them, saying 'Arise, and be not afraid'. Then they beheld Jesus alone. St. Augustine explained that whereas they had previously seen through a glass darkly, they afterwards saw the Lord face to face. When we shall do likewise, the tongues will cease, for 'What is perfect will have come'[21]. The disciples' falling to the ground and being raised up by the Lord was an allusion to the resurrection. After the resurrection, the Law and the Prophets have been fulfilled, and Moses and Elias no longer appear. All we are left with is: 'In the beginning was the Word and the Word was with God and the Word was God', so that God may be 'all in all'[22]. Moses will still be there, but not his Law. We shall also meet Elias there, but no longer as a prophet. The Law and the Prophets have been fulfilled by His suffering and resurrection[23], and it has come to pass that: 'He that loveth me shall be loved of my Father, and I will love him, and will manifest myself to him'[24]. 'How great a gift, how wonderful a promise! God has shown us, not one of his acts of lovingkindness, but Himself!'[25] And since this love for Christ can only be awakened and nourished by the preaching of God's Word, this exclamation is immediately followed by: "Come down, Peter, you who love to rest in the mountains, come down and preach the Word, be instant in season, out of season, reprove, rebuke, and exhort with all longsuffering and doctrine"[26]. 'Work, exert yourself suffer persecution so that you may wear the Lord's glittering garments, in love through the glory and beauty of righteous actions[27].

2. St. Augustine saw further evidence for his view in Psalm 104, 2, where we read that God stretcheth out the heavens like a curtain and in Isaiah 34, 4 where it is written that the heavens shall be rolled together as a scroll. Now according to St. Augustine the heavens were an allusion to the Holy Scriptures, and their stretching

[21] 1 Cor. 13:8, 9, 12.
[22] 1 Cor. 15:28.
[23] Luke 24:44–47.
[24] Joh. 14:21.
[25] Sermo 78, 5.
[26] 2 Tim. 4:2.
[27] Sermo 78, 6.

into a scroll to the book that is read. But, one day, the reading of the law will be put aside. 'For the law is read, because we have not as yet reached that wisdom which fills the hearts and minds of those who look upon it, and there will be no need for us to have anything read to us when there. For in what is read to us, syllables sound and pass away; that light of Truth passes not away, but remaining steadfast satisfies the hearts of those who witness it; as it is said, They shall be satisfied with the plenteousness of Thy house, and Thou shalt give them drink of Thy pleasures, as out of the river: for with Thee is the well of life. And behold the well itself: And in Thy light, shall we see light[28]. For reading is only necessary, as long as we know in part and prophesy in part, as the apostle says; but when that which is perfect is come, then that which is in part, shall be done away[29]. For is it not thus in that city of Jerusalem, where the angels dwell, apart from which we are now wandering? Is the Gospel, is the apostle read in that city where the angels are? They feed upon the Word of God: in order for which Word of God to sound forth unto us for a season, The Word was made flesh and dwelt among us. Nevertheless the written Law itself is our firmament: if our heart be there, it is not plucked up by the wickednesses of men. But when the season of need for the books passes away, it is written: The heavens shall be rolled together as a scroll. He therefore whose heart is on high, has a light in his own heart: he shines in heaven and is not overcome by the darkness. The heart is therefore in the book: if in the book, it is in the firmament of heaven. If the heart be there, let it shine thence, and it shall not be moved by the wickedness of the world beneath; not because it is there in heaven in the flesh, but our conversation is in heaven[30]. Thou canst not imagine that city, because thou seest it not as yet. Dost thou wish to imagine heaven? Think of the book of God. Hear the Psalm, And in His law will he exercise himself day and night[31]. And there he is called blessed'[32]. Once again, St. Augustine stressed our need of the Bible on our pilgrimage, and the blessing which it bestows on our hearts. Yet once we have reached the City in which God's Word as the

[28] Ps. 36:9, 10.
[29] 1 Cor. 13:9, 10.
[30] Phil. 3:20.
[31] Ps. 1:1, 2.
[32] Enarratio in Ps. 93, 6.

light of truth and wisdom, as the light of light, illumines and inspires our hearts directly, the Holy Scriptures have fulfilled their task and have become redundant[33].

3. The third allusion is found in Psalm 104:10–11: "He sendeth the springs into the valleys, which run among the hills, they give drink to every beast of the field". St. Augustine explained that the hills were the apostles, the founders of our faith. The springs, which run among the hills, are the preaching of the Word of Truth. Every twist, every deflection from apostolic preaching, is accursed. 'For then there will be no water to flow among the hills and to give drink to the beasts of the field'[34]. In a subsequent sermon he returned to the flowing of these springs: 'They are not staying, but passing: for all that teaching which in all this time is dispensed passes. Thence the apostle says, Both knowledge shall be done away, and prophecy shall be made void. Wherefore shall those things be made void? For we know in part, and we prophesy in part: but when that which is perfect is come, then that which is in part shall be made void. Unless perchance your Love thinketh that in that city to which it is said, Praise the Lord, O Jerusalem, praise thy God, O Zion: for He has made strong the bars of thy gates[35]—when the bars are now strengthened and the city closed, whence, as we said some time since, no friend goes out, no enemy enters—that there we shall have a book to read, or speech to be explained as it is now explained to you. Therefore it is now treated, that there it may be held fast: therefore it is now divided by syllables, that there it may be contemplated whole and entire. The Word of God will not be wanting there: but yet not by letters, not by sounds, not by books, not by a reader, not by an expositor. How then? As, in the beginning was the Word, was with God, and the Word was God. For He did not come to us as to depart from thence; because He was in this world, and the world was made by Him. Such a Word are we to contemplate. For the God of gods shall appear in Zion[36]. But this when? After our pilgrimage, when the journey is done: if however after our journey is done we be not delivered to the Judge, that the Judge may send us to prison. But if when our journey is ended, as we hope,

[33] See also Retract. I 16, 2.
[34] Enarratio in Ps. 103 II, 11.
[35] Ps. 147:12, 13.
[36] Ps. 84:7.

and wish, and endeavour, we shall have reached our Country, there shall we contemplate, what we shall ever praise; nor shall that fail which is present to us, nor we who enjoy. Great and wonderful shall be that contemplation, and who speaks worthily of it in this time, while the waters flow between the mountains? In the meantime therefore let the waters flow between the mountains, and pass: when the waters pass through, there is drink for us in our pilgrimage, lest for thirst on the way we faint'[37]. The springs will continue to flow among the hills, the preaching of God's Word according to the apostles and the prophets will continue until Christ's second coming, and His pilgrims will be quickened and refreshed by it.

But the pilgrimage must come to an end. The fatherland will be reached, the prophecy will be fulfilled, the tongues will cease, and the Holy Scriptures will have done their task. We ourselves shall then speak not with our tongues, but with our very hearts, saying Amen and Hallelujah—In truth we shall praise God. Once we see God face to face, we shall affirm the truth with an utterly different emotion, saying Amen with an insatiable satiety, satiety because we shall lack nothing, insatiable because our thirst for His blessings will never be quenched. And just as we are sated by the truth insatiably, so shall we say Amen through insatiable truth. Verily, who can utter what no eye has seen, what no ear has heard and to what no heart has risen up. But we shall see the truth plainly, without any blemish and with eternal joy. And set aglow by love for the truth, we shall cling to it with a sweet, and chaste, embrace, praising Him and saying with one voice, Hallelujah. All the inhabitants of the City will rise up in growing love for one another and, above all, in love for God, to give praise and to say Hallelujah because they have said Amen[38].

There will Christ, the Word of God, reveal Himself to us according to His promise and God will be all in all. And there the word will be fulfilled: "Blessed are they that dwell in thy house: they will still be praising thee"[39]. And ecstatically St. Augustine concluded his sermon with a rousing call: 'Let us, dwelling in the Lord, beseech Him for our sake and for the sake of all His people who share with us the forecourts of His house: May it please Him to save and to guard us through Jesus Christ His Son, Our Lord, who liveth and reigneth with Him in all eternity. Amen'[40].

[37] Enarratio in Ps. 103 III, 3.
[38] Sermo 362, 29.
[39] Ps. 84:4. Sermo 362, 31.
[40] ib.

INDEX